T0144920

Blank on the Map

Blank on the Map

Pioneering exploration in the Shaksgam valley and Karakoram mountains

ERIC SHIPTON

Vertebrate Publishing, Sheffield
www.v-publishing.co.uk

Blank on the Map

Eric Shipton

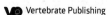 **Vertebrate Publishing**
Omega Court, 352 Cemetery Road, Sheffield S11 8FT, United Kingdom.
www.v-publishing.co.uk

First published by Hodder & Stoughton, London, 1938.
This edition first published in 2019 by Vertebrate Publishing.

Vertebrate Publishing
Omega Court, 352 Cemetery Road, Sheffield S11 8FT, UK

Copyright © Shipton Estate 2019

Eric Shipton has asserted his rights under the Copyright, Designs and Patents Act 1988 to be identified as the author of this work.

This book is a work of non-fiction based on the life, experiences and recollections of Eric Shipton. In some limited cases the names of people, places, dates and sequences or the detail of events have been changed solely to protect the privacy of others. The author has stated to the publishers that, except in such minor respects not affecting the substantial accuracy of the work, the contents of the book are true.

A CIP catalogue record for this book is available from the British Library.

ISBN 978-1-912560-07-3 (Paperback)
ISBN 978-1-910240-24-3 (Ebook)

All rights reserved. No part of this book covered by the copyright herein may be reproduced or used in any form or by any means – graphic, electronic, or mechanised, including photocopying, recording, taping or information storage and retrieval systems – without the written permission of the publisher.

Every effort has been made to obtain the necessary permissions with reference to copyright material, both illustrative and quoted. We apologise for any omissions in this respect and will be pleased to make the appropriate acknowledgements in any future edition.

Produced by Vertebrate Publishing.

Contents

Shipton's Legacy For Mountaineers by Hugh Ruttledge

When Mr Shipton honoured me by an invitation to write a foreword to his book, I accepted with a particular sense of both privilege and opportunity; of privilege because the book is an epic of mountaineering exploration, of opportunity because so little is yet known of three aspects of Himalayan travel: the comparatively easy and inexpensive access to some of the wildest regions, the almost unlimited scope for small but thoroughly competent parties, and the amazing strength and capacity of the Sherpa porter.

I had the good fortune to serve for nearly five years in the section of the Central Himalayan chain with which this book deals. I climbed there with Sherpa, Gurkha, Bhotia and Kumaoni – as well as British – companions; and we made four attempts to enter the great Nanda Devi Basin, as better mountaineers had done before us. It is therefore with some knowledge of the facts that I acclaim the success gained by Messrs Shipton and Tilman and their three Sherpa comrades as one of the greatest feats in mountaineering history. Not only that: it has proved beyond doubt that, in these regions at any rate, a small homogeneous party, self-contained, able to live off the country, with no weak links and ably led, can go further and do more than the elaborate expeditions which have been thought necessary for the Himalaya. What a field of adventure and enterprise this throws open to young mountaineers, now that most of the other great mountain ranges of the world are but too well known.

One word of warning is perhaps necessary: work of this kind should be undertaken only by those who have attained the highest degree of mountaineering skill, judgment and endurance. Those who read this book with understanding will realise the number of tight places this party got into, where nothing but the most brilliant technical competence could have got them out alive. It is not a game for the beginner, or for the lover of flesh-pots.

The greatest feat was the successful entry into, and departure from, the 'inner sanctuary' of the Nanda Devi Basin – a place only about seventy-five miles from Almora, yet hitherto more inaccessible than the North Pole. At last men have set foot upon the slopes of the greatest mountain in the British Empire; and to them will be extended the admiration of those who have struggled and fought for it – notably Dr T. G. Longstaff, who so nearly succeeded in 1907.

Less spectacular perhaps, but hardly less exacting, were the two great traverses of the Badrinath-Gangotri and the Badrinath-Kedarnath watershed, along lines famous in Hindu mythology. These were replete with all the misery that mountaineering in the monsoon season can entail, but the climbers have their reward in the completion of a task that was well worth accomplishment, and in the regard of good Hindus, in whose eyes this would be a pilgrimage of superabundant merit.

Mr Shipton has paid generous and well-deserved tribute to the three Sherpa porters who accompanied him. It is no exaggeration to say that, without men of this type, climbing the higher Himalaya would be impossible. On them are based our hopes of climbing Mount Everest, and for years to come there will be none among the Himalayan peoples to equal them as mountaineers, porters, and loyal, unselfish companions. They are well on their way to become a corps of guides as famous as the men of the Alps. In time there may be others as good – there is splendid material in Kumaon, in Hunza or in Baltistan, to name a few Himalayan regions; and the humble Nepalese Dotials who served Mr Shipton so faithfully in the Rishiganga are worth their salt. At present the Sherpa holds pride of place, and his morale and *esprit-de-corps* are tremendous assets. Given the right leaders – and they must be of the best – he is unbeatable. The description of him in this book is the most understanding and delightful that has ever been written.

The lists are now set for great deeds in the Himalayan snowfields. Messrs Shipton and Tilman have shown the way; let us hope that many will follow.

Hugh Ruttledge

Eric Shipton
by Jim Perrin

Early in 1930 a young planter in Kenya unexpectedly received a letter from an ex-soldier ten years his senior, who had settled in the colony after the Great War. The letter mentioned that its writer had done some climbing in the English Lake District on his last home leave, and asked advice about visiting the East African mountains. Its immediate results were a meeting between the two men, an initial jaunt up Kilimanjaro together, and the first ascent, later that year, of the West Ridge of Mount Kenya – one of the major pre-war achievements of British alpinism.

The two men were, of course, Eric Shipton and H. W. Tilman, and their chance meeting, out in the colonies at the very beginning of the decade, led to one of the most fruitful partnerships and entrancing sagas in the history of mountain exploration. Indeed, the centrality of their role in that history throughout one of its vital phases is unarguable. The chance of their acquaintance and the magnitude of their travels aside, there is another aspect of these two men which is perhaps even more remarkable. For they were both inveterate chroniclers of their climbs and journeys, and the quality of the writings so produced places them absolutely in the forefront of mountaineering and travel literature.

For the span of their contents alone, Shipton's books are noteworthy: *Nanda Devi* (1936), his first, deals with the 1934 penetration up the Rishi Gorge into the Nanda Devi sanctuary in company with Tilman, as well as the two traverses of the Badrinath-Kedamath and Badrinath-Gangotri watersheds. From the moment of its first publication, for reasons to be examined below, it was regarded as one of the revolutionary texts of mountain literature, and it remains an enthralling story of hazardous and uncertain journeying with minimal resources through unknown country. *Blank on the Map* (1938) describes the 1937 Shaksgam survey expedition undertaken with Michael Spender, John Auden, (brothers to the poets) and Tilman – an important venture into a little-known region of the Himalayas which provided a basis for much subsequent mountaineering activity in the Karakoram. (First editions of this very rare title now command fabulous prices amongst collectors.)

From 1940 to 1942 Shipton served as British Consul-General at Kashgar, in the Chinese Province of Sinkiang. During this period he completed a first volume of memoirs, entitled *Upon that Mountain*, published in 1943. This frank, vivid polemic set out his basic mountaineering creed, whilst also describing his early Alpine and Himalayan seasons, the series of climbs on Mount Kenya, and the four attempts on Everest and two survey-trips to the Karakoram in which he took part during the thirties. His next book was very different in tone. *Mountains of Tartary* (1950) is a series of light-hearted sketches of weeks or weekends seized from official consular work – in the main during his second spell of office in Kashgar – and spent on Bogdo Ola, Mustagh Ata, Chakragil (mountains which are again coming into vogue in the eighties since China's relaxation of restrictions on travel). *The Mount Everest Reconnaissance Expedition 1951* (1952) was basically a photographic volume, prefaced by a succinct and entertaining narrative about this vital piece of mountain exploration, which cleared the path for John Hunt's successful expedition to the mountain in 1953. The final book in this series, *Land of Tempest*, written in 1963, takes for theme the period of Shipton's life from 1958 to 1962 and includes accounts of three trips to Patagonia – on the last of which he made the first crossing of the main Patagonian ice cap – and one to Tierra del Fuego.

The above bald catalogue suggests the range, but captures little of the flavour, of this extraordinary man's life, the brief outline of which is as follows. He was born in Ceylon in 1907, his father a tea-planter who died before his son was three. Thereafter, Shipton, his sister and mother travelled extensively between Ceylon, India, France and England, before the family finally settled in the latter country for purposes of the children's schooling. Shipton's mountaineering career began in 1924 with holidays in Norway and Switzerland and was consolidated through four successive alpine seasons in 1925–1928. His first ascent of Nelion, the unclimbed twin summit of Mount Kenya, with Wyn Harris in 1929, and of the same mountain's West Ridge with Tilman the following year, brought him to the notice of the mountaineering establishment of the day and elicited an invitation to join the expedition led by Frank Smythe to Kamet, in the Garhwal region, in 1931. Shipton distinguished himself on this trip, being in the summit party on eleven of the twelve peaks climbed by the expedition, including that of Kamet itself, which at 25,447ft was the highest summit then attained. His performance in 1931 led to an invitation to join Ruttledge's 1933 Everest expedition. Thereafter the milestones slip by: Rishi Gorge 1934; Everest Reconnaissance 1935, which he led; Everest and Nanda Devi 1936; Shaksgam 1937; Everest 1938; Karakoram 1939 are the main ones amongst them, but virtually the whole decade was spent in Himalayan travel, and the extent of his exploratory achievement perhaps even now lacks full recognition.

He spent the Second World War in Government service in Sinkiang, Persia and Hungary, went back for a further spell in Kashgar from 1946 to 1948, accompanied by his wife Diana, and was Consul-General at Kunming, in Southern China, from 1949 to 1951. On his return to England he was asked to lead an expedition to reconnoitre the Southern approaches to Everest, in the course of which he and Ed Hillary first espied the eventual line of ascent up the Western Cwm to the South Col, from a vantage point on the slopes of Pumori. The following year he led a rather unsatisfactory training expedition to Cho Oyu. In the late summer of 1952, Shipton having been urged to lead a further expedition to Everest in 1953 and having accepted, the joint Himalayan Committee of the Alpine Club and the Royal Geographical Society performed an astonishing volte-face, appointing the competent and experienced but at that time virtually unknown Colonel John Hunt as leader, and accepting Shipton's consequent resignation.

This sorry episode effectively formed a watershed in Shipton's life. After the break-up of his marriage and loss of his post as Warden of the Outward Bound School at Eskdale, which occurred shortly after the events of 1952–53, he lived for a time in the rural seclusion of Shropshire, working as a forestry labourer. He was enticed back for a last trip to the Karakoram in 1957, and thereafter developed a new grand obsession with travel in the southernmost regions of South America, which absorbed most of the next decade in his life. Finally, in his sixties, he was a popular lecturer on cruises to such places as the Galapagos Islands, and leader of mild Himalayan treks. He died of liver cancer at the home of a friend in Wiltshire during the spring of 1977.

This, then, is the bare outline of an outstanding life. The man who lived it, through his involvement in the 1931 Kamet and 1933 Everest expeditions, had attained a considerable degree of national celebrity by the early thirties, yet at that time he was to all intents and purposes a professionless pauper and a kind of international tramp, whose possessions amounted to little more than the clothes in which he stood. There is an admirable passage in Upon That Mountain where Shipton recounts the dawning of a realisation that the way of life which most appealed to him perhaps presented a practical possibility. It happened on the way back to India from the North Side of Everest in 1933. In company with the geologist Lawrence Wager, he had made his way across a strip of unexplored country and over a new pass into Sikkim. Wager's influence shifted the emphasis of Shipton's interest away from the climbing of peaks to enthusiasm for a general mode of exploration – a fascination with geography itself. Twenty years later, this shift was to provide his detractors with an easy target. For the moment, his mind works over the ground thus:

> 'Why not spend the rest of my life doing this sort of thing?' There was no way of life that I liked more, the scope appeared to be unlimited, others had done it, vague plans had already begun to take shape, why not put some of them into practice? ... The most obvious snag, of course, was lack of private means; but surely such a mundane consideration could not be decisive. In

the first place I was convinced that expeditions could be run for a tithe of the cost generally considered necessary. Secondly if one could produce useful or interesting results one would surely find support …'

When he took into account his reactions to the milieu of the large expedition, ('The small town of tents that sprung up each evening, the noise and racket of each fresh start, the sight of a huge army invading the peaceful valleys, it was all so far removed from the light, free spirit with which we were wont to approach our peaks'), then the virtue to be made of necessity was obvious, and of it was born what came to be known as the 'Shipton/Tilman style of lightweight expedition'. I referred above to Shipton's Nanda Devi as a revolutionary text, and it was just that. I doubt if there has ever been a less formulaic account of an expedition. It has a magical, fresh quality, a get-through-by-the-skin-of-your-teeth spontaneity, a candour, a clear rationale, an excited commitment, an elation about the enterprise undertaken, which no previous mountaineering book had approached. From the outset the terms are made clear: five months in the Garhwal Himalaya to tackle some of its outstanding topographical problems, 'climbing peaks when opportunity occurred', on a budget of £150 each for himself and Tilman (some of Shipton's share of which is advanced by Tilman 'against uncertain security'). The scenes throughout, from the broken-toed, frock-coated setting-out from Ranikhet to the final descent from the Sunderdhunga Col to Maiktoli, are evoked in a clear and economical style. But it is the message – the simple moral that it is possible, and in terms of response to the landscape and its peoples even desirable, to travel cheap and light, to move fast and live off the land – which is the book's revolutionary charge, and which was to make Shipton and Tilman, in the words of the American writer David Roberts, 'retroactive heroes of the avant-garde'.

Two major characteristics distinguish *Nanda Devi* and were to become hallmarks of Shipton's writing. The first of these is an intense curiosity which remains with him, his conclusions growing more authoritative with increase of experience – about natural landforms, whether they be mountains, valleys, rivers, volcanoes or glaciers. This curiosity acts as a stimulus, a fund of energy, in his explorations, continually used as a basis, a point of reference: 'It was enthralling to disentangle the geography of the region … for me, the basic reason for mountaineering'.

Alongside this drive to understand the physical makeup of a landscape there operates a more reflective principle, very close to traditional nature-mysticism, which Shipton almost invariably carries off with great poise and delicacy, sure-footedly avoiding the obvious pitfalls of bathos or inflation.

> We settled down on a comfortable bed of sand, and watched the
> approach of night transform the wild desert mountains into
> phantoms of soft unreality. How satisfying it was to be travelling
> with such simplicity. I lay awaiting the approach of sleep, watch-
> ing the constellations swing across the sky. Did I sleep that night
> – or was I caught up for a moment into the ceaseless rhythm of
> space?
>
> *Blank on the Map*

A very satisfying irony lies in suggesting an affinity with mysticism of a man
who claimed throughout his adult life to be an agnostic, and who would probably, even if only for the sheer joy of argument, have vigorously rejected the
intimation. Perhaps his disclaimer of religious belief was like that of Simone
Weill, and masked a genuine sense of divine mystery within the universe.
Certainly much of the interest in Shipton's writings derives from a tension
between the very practical preoccupations with physical phenomena, and a
frequent lapsing into a more quietistic mode of thought. (To compound the
mischief, I have to say that *Nanda Devi* puts me in mind of no other text so
much as one of the late poems of that most ascetic of saints, St John of the
Cross, quoted here in the translation by Roy Campbell:

> The generous heart upon its quest
> Will never falter, nor go slow,
> But pushes on, and scorns to rest,
> Wherever it's most hard to go.
> It runs ahead and wearies not
> But upward hurls its fierce advance
> For it enjoys I know not what
> That is achieved by lucky chance.

Those who knew Shipton well sound a recurrent note in their reminiscences
which supports the contention that there was a mystical element to his character. It concerns a quality of detachment he possessed, and invariably fastens
on a specific physical detail. The following is typical:

> He had the most marvellous blue eyes, very kindly, very amused,
> and very wise. But there was always a sense, when you talked
> with him, that somehow he was not with you, was looking right
> through you, searching out farther and farther horizons.

In the course of researching Shipton's biography, it was remarkable and eventually almost comical how often that impression, almost word-for-word, was

repeated. Without the evidence of the text it could be taken as a mannerism, but in his books there recur time and again passages which define his response to landscape as one striving towards a mystical awareness.

In this he is very different to Tilman, his most frequent companion of the thirties, and it is interesting to compare the two men. The ten-year difference in age is for once significant, for Tilman's seniority ensured that he underwent the determining influence on his character of the First World War, and it affected him profoundly. It is what made him a master of that most serious of all forms of writing, comic irony, and it is what causes him to veer dangerously close at times to a distinct misanthropy. It explains the prelapsarian vitality with which he imbues his native characters, the neglectful portrayal of his compatriots, and the isolation which identifies his authorial persona. In his personal conduct, it provides the reason for his taciturnity, his phlegmatism and unemotional responses to situations. The vulnerability of youth, its lack of circumspection and eager commitment to affection or cause were in Tilman's case the victims of war, and the survivor, psychic and physical, of that particularly obscene war had need to be encased in adamantine.

Shipton's enthusiasms, on the other hand, operate under no such constraint. He can indulge his feelings as freely as he will, the zest and gaiety of the twenties glitters around his early activities. He commits himself freely, and as equally with a climb as a journey of exploration or to one of the many women who shared his life. A couple of comments upon him from 1931 by Frank Smythe capture the temperament of the man:

> No one who climbs with Shipton can remain pessimistic, for he imparts an imperturbability and confidence into a day's work which are in themselves a guarantee of success.

Or again, about his climbing:

> I saw Shipton's eye light up, and next instant he went at the slope with the energy of a boxer who, after months of training, sees his opponent before him.

The differences in their characters probably acted as a bond between Shipton and Tilman, and account for their sharing of some of the most ambitious undertakings of their lives. For Tilman, his own youth lost, Shipton's enthusiasm and boundless energy must have been inspiriting and invigorating, whilst the fatherless Shipton may well have found that Tilman's wry, benevolent maturity fulfilled a need in him at a certain stage of his life. In mountaineering terms, the roles were reversed, and the more experienced Shipton was the leader. One very telling indication of this occurs in Tilman's diary for 30 May

1934. After reconnoitring one of the crucial – and very tortuous – passages of the route up the Rishi Gorge, they have to hurry back to camp. The subsequent diary entry briefly states, 'Shipton's route-memory invaluable as usual, self hopeless.'

It has to be said, though, that a change occurs in Shipton's outlook, especially with regard to mountaineering, during the mid-thirties. It seems to me complex and cumulative rather than associated with specific circumstances. The influence of older companions such as Tilman and Wager would have played a part. So too, perhaps, did the relationship upon which he had embarked with Pamela Freston. But two related events could be seen as decisive in the transition from joyful mountaineering innocence to prudent experience. These were the two avalanches which Shipton witnessed on the slopes leading to the North Col of Everest during successive expeditions in 1935 and 1936. Of the first one, he had to say 'I am sure that no one could have escaped from an avalanche such as that which broke away below us while we were lying peacefully on the North Col'. The following year, as he and Wyn Harris were climbing up the same slope, this is what happened:

> We climbed quickly over a lovely hard surface in which one sharp kick produced a perfect foothold. About halfway up to the Col we started traversing to the left. Wyn anchored himself firmly on the lower lip of a crevasse while I led across the slope. I had almost reached the end of the rope and Wyn was starting to follow when there was a rending sound … a short way above me, and the whole surface of the slope I was standing on started to move slowly down towards the brink of an ice cliff a couple of hundred feet below …

Wyn Harris managed to jump back into the crevasse and re-establish the belay, the snow failed to gather momentum, and Shipton survived. It was the last attempt on the mountain that year. The point is, that Shipton's faith in the material he was climbing had been undermined – just as in personal relationships, when the trust has gone the commitment is withdrawn. Shipton's heyday as a climber is delimited by these events. Though there are inevitably some exciting and perilous escapades after 1936 – the climb on the Dent Blanche-like peak above the Bostan Terek valley is a striking example – henceforward, reading these books, we keep company with a much more circumspect mountaineer.

This line of reasoning inevitably leads us towards a consideration of what is generally and I think rightly regarded as one of the cruces of Shipton's life – the circumstances surrounding the choice of leadership for the 1953 expedition to Everest. It is very difficult to summarise in brief the main points of what is still a controversial topic. Even Walt Unsworth's *Everest* book, which comes nearest to being an authoritative history of the mountain, overlooked important material in its researches which throws a clearer light on some aspects of this vital area. What emerges, from close examination of relevant Himalayan Committee minutes and written submissions from its surviving members, is a bizarre tale of fudging and mudging, falsification of official minutes, unauthorized invitations, and opportunistic and desperate last minute seizures of initiative by a particular faction. It is a perfect illustration of the cock-up rather than the conspiracy theory of history, from which little credit redounds upon the British mountaineering establishment of the time. The saddest fact about the whole sorry tale is that it appeared to place in conflict two honourable and quite innocent men – Shipton and John Hunt.

There are two basic themes to be considered. The first of these is the general climate of feeling surrounding Shipton's attitude for, and interest in, the leadership of an expedition which, even in the early stages of its planning, was subject to a jingoistic insistence that Everest must be climbed by a British party. (That this was not to be achieved for a further 22 years scarcely mattered in the event, the national attachments of the first summiteers being clearly turned to the Commonwealth's greater glory.) This climate of feeling, accepting some of Shipton's own statements at face value, and drawing in other rather more questionable evidence, particularly that relating to the 1952 Cho Oyu expedition, where peculiar circumstances undoubtedly affected Shipton's leadership, had drifted towards the view that Shipton lacked the urgency, the thrust, the killer instinct which would be necessary to 'conquer' Everest.[1] It was immeasurably strengthened by Shipton's own submission to the Himalayan Committee meeting of 28 July, 1952, in which he expressed doubts about his suitability for the job on the following grounds: he had to consider his own career – with a wife and two young children to support, he was out of a job and needed to get one; he felt that new blood was needed to undertake the task; his strong preference was for smaller parties, lightly equipped.

At this juncture we need to pass over to a consideration of the second basic theme – the conduct of members of the Himalayan Committee over the matter of the leadership. The first point to be made is that the Committee was very weakly chaired. Because of this, the pro-Shipton faction carried the day at the meeting of 28 July and, chiefly through the efforts of Laurence Kirwan, Shipton was strongly prevailed upon to accept the leadership, the contention then resting with the matter of deputy leadership.

---

1 In *Upon That Mountain*, for example, he had written that 'there are some, even among those who have themselves attempted to reach the summit, who nurse a secret hope that Mount Everest will never be climbed. I must confess to such feelings myself'.

However, there also existed a pro-Hunt faction, headed by Basil Goodfellow and Colonel Tobin, who had both been absent from the 28 July meeting. These two men lobbied forcefully that the deputy – or assault – leadership should fall to Hunt, which would inevitably compromise Shipton, whose choice had been Charles Evans and to whom Hunt was therefore unacceptable in that role. The crucial committee meeting took place on 11 September. The pro-Hunt faction was present in force, determined to reverse the decision of the previous meeting. The more ardent Shiptonians – most notably Kirwan and Shipton's old friend Wager – were absent. Shipton was morally compelled to offer his resignation. The rest is history, apart from a few squalid diversions, such as the subsequent falsification of this meeting's minutes by Claude Elliott, the chairman – in the words of one contemporary observer, 'as bad a chairman of committees as one could find; he was hopelessly indecisive and hesitant and was too easily swayed by anyone (like Kirwan) who held firm opinions, however wrong these might be'.

What the effect would have been upon Shipton had he led the successful expedition to Everest is a matter for conjecture. John Hunt was patently well-equipped to cope with the ensuing celebrity, and used it tirelessly in the public good. It could perhaps be thought doubtful that Shipton would have enjoyed, and responded so positively, to the inevitably massive public acclaim.

After 1953, his life went through a difficult period, but it emerged into a golden late summer of exploration in an area completely fresh to him. His Patagonian journeys of the late fifties and sixties were a harking-back in many ways to his great Karakoram travels of the thirties. They would have been rendered immensely more public and difficult and perhaps thus less satisfying to him, by the burden of international fame. Instead, he was able to slip quietly away, pursue his own bent amongst the unknown mountains and glaciers of a new wilderness. It is a myth fulfilled, a proper consummation in the life of this explorer-mystic, whose outlook and progress resonate so closely with those of Tennyson's *Ulysses*, from which poem he took the motto for the first part of *Blank on the Map*, and the title for his magnificent second autobiography, *That Untravelled World*.

There is a phrase of Shipton's from this latter book which gives perfect expression to one of the great lives of our century – 'a random harvest of delight'. That is exactly what the books collected together between these covers are, in general terms. But they are also an opportunity for a new generation of readers to engage with one of the most attractive personalities the sport of mountaineering has ever produced, to keep company with his spare, lithe figure loping off into the ranges, seeking out the undiscovered country, his distant blue eyes lingering on the form of a particular peak, the passage over to an unexplored glacier. If curiosity, appreciation, aspiration and delight are a

Foreword
by T.G. Longstaff

Mountaineers usually seek the Himalaya in the hope of adding the ascent of some great peak to their experiences in the Alps or the Caucasus. But the exciting vastness and variety of the two-thousand-mile buttress of High Asia present conditions so different from anything which they have experienced in other ranges that their energies are often diverted from the climbing of peaks to the exploration of the unknown ridges and valleys which entice them on every hand. My own first climbing expedition to the Himalaya inevitably developed into a trek of nearly a thousand miles: I could not bring myself to waste time over second ascents on the same peak: there was too much to see and too many fascinating problems to be solved.

After notable ascents in Europe and Africa, the author of this book made four long journeys in the Himalaya. With his old companion Tilman he has again this year tackled Everest, on whose grim slopes he reached 28,000 feet in 1933. The first to unveil the Sanctuary of Nanda Devi, he has achieved some thirty new peaks and passes in the eastern and western Himalaya. Last year he turned far to the north-west, to the solitudes of the Karakorum, and in the present volume he appears essentially as an explorer, subordinating the climbing of peaks to his main objective of filling in a great blank on the map.

Nowadays would-be explorers are more and more forced to seek high latitudes or high altitudes. In these empty regions achievement is limited by the number of days' food the traveller can carry: success in both cases depends on a very special technique of travel. Today probably a majority of young explorers are dog-drivers or mountaineers. The days of the unveiling of continents are over: in almost all other regions of the world the tracks of an explorer will cross and recross those of former travellers.

But the mountaineer, whose training is so much longer than that required for any other form of travel, must further equip himself as a surveyor. For, as the actual area of the unknown shrinks, so rises the standard of accuracy and detail expected in his mapping. At once he is beset by new difficulties. His man-power must carry tentage, sleeping bags, food and fuel for a sufficiently long time to complete his survey work. Therefore his instrumental equipment must be of the lightest consonant with accuracy. It is equally essential that this method of survey be as rapid as possible, in order to lessen the food he must carry. For several years past, officials of the Royal Geographical Society, working with mountain surveyors and instrument makers, have been elaborating a very light theodolite combined with a small camera. An efficient instrument has now been evolved, and it has fallen to Spender, the leading surveyor of Shipton's party, to demonstrate its use by mountaineers in difficult country for filling gaps which could not be covered by his own more rigid survey. He worked out his results at Dehra Dun under the critical eye of Brigadier Clinton Lewis, the Surveyor-General of India, than whom there is no higher authority. One of the most inaccessible white patches on the map of the Karakoram is now filled in; the case for the new method is proven, but we badly need some generous benefactor who will give us a stereoplotter so that future photographic material can be quickly worked out in London.

It is to be feared that few readers of Shipton's modest account will quite realise all that is implied by the remarkable success of this expedition. The combined party has surveyed 1,800 square miles of one of the most difficult mountain fastnesses in the world, and Auden has revealed its geological structure. With a reversion to the practice of a generation ago, the venture was organised and financed with an avoidance of publicity and with an economy quite unusual today. Sums ten times as large have often been spent on expeditions which brought back one-tenth of the results obtained by Shipton and his companions. He knows the secret of counting men before means. Equipment you can buy. Individual qualifications you cannot buy. The personal attainments of the individual members of an exploring party are more important than the funds at their disposal: this is the heartening message of Shipton's book.

T.G.L.

The Athenaeum

1   How an Expedition Begins

' ... all experience is an arch where thro' Gleams that untravell'd world, whose margin fades Forever and forever when I move.'
Ulysses, Alfred Lord Tennyson

A fascinating way of spending a few hours of leisure is to sit down with a paper and pencil and work out in minute detail the preparations for an expedition into unexplored country. The fact that there is very little chance of carrying out the project matters little. These dream expeditions can be staged in any corner of the world. I have imagined them in the forbidding mountains of Nepal, and in the windswept ice peaks of Tierra del Fuego, and across the Antarctic continent.

On the 1936 Everest Expedition, during the tedious hours of a snowstorm on the East Rongbuk glacier, lying in my sleeping bag, I discussed a detailed scheme with Noel Humphreys for the exploration of the remote snow range above the dense, steamy forests in the centre of New Guinea. The plan was to charter a dhow from a Dutch port on the south coast and sail to the southern extremity of the island; then to land with sufficient food and equipment to last one and a half years, and to relay the loads for 300 miles, following a high ridge, above the fever swamps, that we hoped would lead to the snow range. We contemplated taking a dozen Sherpa porters with us to carry the loads inland and to help us live in the hostile country, and eventually to take part in the climbing. Lest the Sherpas be homesick so far from their country, for so long, we even considered allowing them to take their wives; and we discussed the possibility of planting crops in the foothills to help us live in the interior.

I often amuse myself by making a list of these imaginary expeditions in order of their attractiveness. Sometimes one heads the list, sometimes another. Always one plan is uppermost in my mind, until circumstances determine which shall be attempted.

Talking like this with John Morris, on the way down from Base Camp to Rongbuk, after the 1936 Everest expedition, he asked me if I had ever considered his pet plan of a journey from Hunza to Leh by way of the Shaksgam river. During the march back across Tibet there was plenty of time to discuss this project, and to weigh its possibilities. By the time we reached India it so far headed my list of plans as to exclude the thought of all others.

The Shaksgam river lies somewhere on the undemarcated frontiers of Chinese Turkestan, Hunza and Kashmir. It was necessary to obtain permission from the Government of India to take a party into that area. At the end of July I went to Simla to explain the project to the authorities. Some months later permission was granted. In August, while waiting for the start of a survey expedition to the Nanda Devi basin, I stayed with Bunty and Norman Odling in their lovely home in Kalimpong – a haven for so many travellers; during this pleasant interlude, with the aid of all the existing maps of the Karakoram, I made myself familiar with the geography of that range, studying the various routes, the costs involved, and the difficulties inherent in each plan of approach. Eventually I decided that instead of making the suggested journey it would be more valuable to establish a base in the middle of the Shaksgam area, with sufficient food to last three and a half months, and to make exploratory excursions from there in all directions.

At this stage my plans were necessarily vague, but I was fascinated by the idea of penetrating into the little-known region of the Karakoram. As I studied the maps, one thing about them captured my imagination. The ridges and valleys which led up from Baltistan became increasingly high and steep as they merged into the maze of peaks and glaciers of the Karakoram, and then suddenly ended in an empty blank space. Across this blank space was written one challenging word, 'unexplored'. The area is dominated by K2, the second highest mountain in the world, and is bounded on the south by the main Asiatic watershed.

The southern side of this range has been visited by many explorers and mountaineers who have partially surveyed its vast glaciers. But it is the northern side of this great watershed which has proved so difficult of access. The country is inhospitable and uninhabited, and no traveller can stay long in its remote valleys. These are deep and narrow with precipitous rocky sides. The unbridged rivers, fed by the huge glaciers, tend to flood to an enormous depth during the summer months when the ice is melting, and are then quite unfordable.

The first explorer of this part of the Karakoram was Sir Francis Younghusband, then a Lieutenant in the Dragoons. In 1887, at the end of his great journey across Asia, from Peking to India, he crossed the Aghil range, by what has since come to be known as the Aghil pass. This range lies to the north of the Karakoram. On the southern side of the pass he discovered a river which his men called the Shaksgam. From there he ascended the Sarpo Laggo glacier and crossed the main Karakoram range by way of the Mustagh pass. His account of this remarkable feat will be quoted later in this book.

Two years later he again crossed the Aghil pass to the Shaksgam river, which he followed upstream for a considerable distance. He then tried to enter the mountain country to the south-west; but failing to make his way up a great glacier, called by him the Crevasse glacier, he followed, in the late autumn, the lower reaches of the Shaksgam and so reached the Shimshal pass, which lies at the north-western extremity of this area.

Since then other travellers have visited various parts of this region. In 1926 Colonel Kenneth Mason led an expedition, financed by the Survey of India, to the Shaksgam. His object was to cross from the Karakoram pass, which lies at the eastern extremity of the Aghil range, to the head waters of the Shaksgam. From there he intended to work downstream so as to connect up with Younghusband's route, and to fix the geographical position of the Shaksgam river and of the Aghil pass. His way was barred by a great glacier, which, coming down from the northern slopes of the Teram Kangri range, dammed the Shaksgam river. The ice was so appallingly broken that it was quite impossible for the expedition to cross the glacier and to continue its progress down the river. Mason named the glacier the Kyagar. His party went up into the Aghil range and explored its eastern section. There they were faced by the great difficulties of travelling in an entirely uninhabited area. In August they found another great river, which at first they imagined to be the Shaksgam itself. They failed to follow it down-stream owing to the enormous volume of water which was racing through its gorges. But they went far enough upstream to realize that this river was not the Shaksgam. So Mason named it the Zug – or false – Shaksgam. The lateness of the season forced the party to leave the problem of its course unsolved.

In 1929 a party from HRH the Duke of Spoleto's expedition crossed the Mustagh pass into the Shaksgam valley, and followed it up to the Kyagar glacier. The work accomplished by this party will be mentioned in a later chapter.

In 1935 Dr and Mrs Visser, who have made three remarkable expeditions in the Karakoram, followed Mason's route and succeeded in crossing the Kyagar glacier and in mapping the great glaciers coming down from the Gasherbrum peaks on the main watershed. They were prevented from going farther down the river by the summer floods.

But to the west and north-west of the areas visited by these explorers there still remained vast regions of unknown country of absorbing interest to the mountaineer and to the geographer. It was the exploration of a portion of this area that was the main object of my expedition.

We had three principal interests. First, the section that lies between the Sarpo Laggo valley and the Shimshal pass, bounded on the north by the Shaksgam river, an area of about 1,000 square miles. Younghusband had touched the fringe of this country when he tried to ascend the Crevasse glacier. Second, the glacier system lying to the north and north-west of K2. Third, the portion of the Aghil range, west of that explored by Mason's expedition. The two outstanding problems of this last area were to find the lower reaches and outlet of the Zug Shaksgam river, and to fix the geographical position of the Aghil pass. As 1937 was the fiftieth anniversary of Sir Francis Younghusband's famous journey, we had an additional incentive to visit this pass. So far as we knew no European had been there since Younghusband's second crossing in 1889.

The first thing to be decided was how to tackle the problem of getting to the Shaksgam. Apart from attempting to reach it from China, three alternatives were open to us: first, to cross from the Karakoram pass to the head waters of the Shaksgam and make our way down over the difficult glacier trunks which had defeated Mason's party in 1926; second, to cross the Shimshal pass early in the spring, and force a route up the lower gorge of the Shaksgam before the river became too high; and third, to cross the main Karakoram range from the Baltoro glacier. The first two alternatives would probably have involved considerable difficulties with the river even early in the year, and would have rendered us liable to be cut off by the summer floods until late in the autumn. Besides this, the journey either to the Shimshal or to the Karakoram pass is very long and costly, particularly early in the year when the routes are not officially open. The difficulties involved by the third alternative, the crossing of the main Karakoram range, were of a purely mountaineering character, and though we were likely to have considerable trouble in getting several tons of stores and equipment over a difficult glacier pass early in the year, I chose this route.

Our rough plan of campaign then was this: to reach the Baltoro glacier by the end of May; to cross the watershed with sufficient food to last the party for one hundred days after reaching its base below the snout of the Sarpo Laggo glacier; leaving a dump there, to cross the Shaksgam and spend as much time in the Aghil range as possible without being cut off by the summer floods; to return to the Sarpo Laggo about the middle of July and to spend the remaining two months working on our other two objectives, the Crevasse glacier region and the area to the north of K2.

The chief difficulty which had to be faced in working out details of this plan was the fact that once across the main Karakoram range the party would have to be entirely self-supporting for the whole period of its stay there – nearly three and a half months. This, and the enormous expense of transporting each effective load across the watershed, necessitated the rigorous exclusion of every ounce of equipment which could possibly be dispensed with, and very careful rationing; and again, the exclusion of all delicacies which did not carry the maximum food value, or which interfered with a properly balanced diet.

The next matter that had to be decided was the all-important question of the composition of the party. I had originally asked H. W. Tilman to join me in the proposed journey from Hunza to Leh through the Shaksgam valley, and had intended that the party should consist of only the two of us, and four or five

Sherpa porters. Tilman and I hold the same views about expeditions. We have evolved a technique for light travel which has met with some success in the mountains of East and Central Africa, as well as in the Himalaya.

When, instead of making the journey, I decided to work from a base, it was obvious that by increasing the size of the party I could hope to bring back more valuable results. I therefore decided to take a surveyor to work near the base and form a nucleus of accurate mapping to which we could attach our long, less detailed exploration. It was likely to be a difficult task to begin such a survey.

Only one fixed point, the peak of K2, would be visible, and it might be necessary to determine the position of the map astronomically. Also a good deal of ingenuity would be required to cut down the loads of survey equipment to a practicable number. The man best suited to the job was Michael Spender, and I was lucky enough to enrol him as a member of the party. Spender had learnt his work in Switzerland and Germany. He had been the surveyor attached to the Barrier Reef expedition in 1928-29; he had taken part in two Danish expeditions to Greenland; and had been with me as surveyor on the 1935 Reconnaissance expedition to Mount Everest. He is a rapid and precise worker and has the ability to adjust his mind to unexpected circumstances. I also invited John Auden, of the Geological Survey of India, to join the party, to assist in the exploratory work and to carry out as much geological investigation as possible. Auden has done a good deal of climbing in Europe and had travelled widely in the Himalaya in the course of his work. In 1933 he had made an expedition to the Biafo glacier, beyond Askole, and his firsthand knowledge of the route and the people was a great assistance; he was a valuable asset to the party.

I decided to recruit seven Sherpa porters from Darjeeling. This was very expensive, for not only had we to pay their wages for the whole period of their absence from their homes, regardless of whether they were working or not, but also they had to be brought by rail right across India from Darjeeling to Srinagar. In fact, the expense of their inclusion in the party amounted to one-fifth of the entire cost of the expedition; but it was well worthwhile. They more than justified the expense and without their support we would have accomplished little. During the expedition I frequently regretted that I had not brought double the number of Sherpas.

There are good and bad among the Sherpas as among all other people, and not an unusually large proportion of good. It is necessary, therefore, to select the men who are to play so important a part in an expedition, with very great care, or one is liable to be badly let down. If one can find a Sherpa whose judgment can be relied upon absolutely, it is a good plan to entrust him with the task of choosing his own companions, for no one can know the Sherpas as well as they know themselves.

I was fortunate in having such a man in Angtharkay, who had previously been my companion on five Himalayan expeditions. As usual he thoroughly justified my trust in him, and brought with him a batch of men as tough and loyal, and as full of humour as himself. Owing to a generous contribution to the funds of the expedition we were able to engage four men from Baltistan for the whole journey. This brought our numbers up to fifteen: four Europeans, seven Sherpas and, later, four Baltis.

I estimated that the cost of the expedition, including three return passages to India (Auden joined from Calcutta) would amount to £855. With no private means it was necessary to rely on the support of scientific societies to raise this money. The Royal Geographical Society, the Survey of India and the Royal Society took an interest in the project and contributed generously towards the funds. In actual fact the whole cost of the expedition was less than my estimate by a few pounds.

2   Of the Real Value of Climbing

Those days in London, before we had even packed our rucksacks, were very strenuous. There were formal permissions to be set in order, supplies to be bought, passages to be booked, and a mass of detail to be attended to that seemed to have little relation to the life we would lead in the mountains. Was all this effort worthwhile? Why should we go to such lengths to plunge ourselves into a life of discomfort and privation? To me it is worthwhile because of what it leads to. Every time I start an expedition I feel that I am getting back to a way of living which is now lost.

With a wistfulness, perhaps a little tinged with sentimentality, I think of the leisurely days of a few hundred years ago, before life was so mad a rush, before the countryside was spoiled by droves of people, and beauty itself exploited as a commercial proposition.

It is true that the very act of looking back seems to touch the past with gold. Probably the 'good old days' were hard and uncomfortable, but they did foster individuality. Life had then an essential quality of reality which now we seem to have lost. We have become so accustomed to having everyday life made easy for us, that our energies are not absorbed in the art of living, but run riot in a craving for sensation. Individuality is swamped in the mass emotion of hurrying mobs of people whose thoughts are dragooned by the ready-made ideas of shallow press articles.

So many human activities have lost their power to refresh the spirit because people tend to do things for the wrong reasons – for publicity, for sensationalism, for money, or because it is the fashion to do them. A wrong attitude, based on an unreal sense of values, poisons our recreations no less than the more serious aspects of living. Reality should be the essential factor in sport as in life. Any other basic aim endangers the right attitude of mind without which there can be no real happiness nor the full enjoyment of any activity.

A man who is really keen about sailing is in the first place attracted by the sea with all its problems, hardships and beauties – by the very form of life which the sea offers. He sails because sailing teaches him the art of living in the environment which he loves. It gives him a larger, clearer view of the problems and difficulties of his craft; and so he comes to a realisation of the true aesthetic value of the sea.

In the same way the skier wishes to become part of the country of snow-laden firs and winter mountains which means so much to him. He finds in his sport a way of identifying himself with this enchanting world. He cannot easily achieve this in the competitive social atmosphere of a crowded winter sports resort. He must go to the higher mountains, or to the silent forests of Norway. So it is with the fisherman and his lakes and rivers; and with the big-game hunter and his jungles; and with the mountaineer and his peaks and glaciers.

But directly people allow the element of competition to rule their activities, and care more for trophies, or record-breaking, or acclamation, than for a real understanding of their craft, or even if they are content with short cuts to proficiency and superficial knowledge, they are in danger of losing the touchstone of genuine values which alone makes anything worthwhile.

The tendency nowadays to be artificial instead of genuine, and superficial instead of thorough, is caused partly by everyone being in such a hurry, and partly by things being made too easy for us. If a man has money to spend and feels that it would be exciting to go and shoot big game in East Africa, all he need do is to go to a travel agency and book his passage in a luxury liner. When he arrives, he engages the services of a 'white hunter', relies on that man's marksmanship and knowledge of the bush, and returns a few months later with a number of tall stories and several crates of trophies. But he has not lived the real life of a hunter; nor has he made the experience a part of his own life. He has taken an easy short cut to vicarious adventure. The mountaineer who goes to the Alps for a season's climbing, with a desire to climb more peaks than other men, and by more difficult routes, misses the real value of the experience – the love of mountains for their own sake. The real purpose of climbing, and of any other sport, should be to transmute it into a way of living, however temporary, in an environment which appeals to the individual.

Often when I have been climbing in the Alps I have thought how enthralling it must have been to see the Alps as De Saussure saw them, before they had been civilised out of their wild unspoiled beauty and tamed into a social asset. A hundred and fifty years ago men went to the Alps to investigate the phenomena of mountains. The result of their quest was the birth of the sciences of geology and glaciology, and the study of the rarefication of the atmosphere at high altitudes, together with its effect upon the human body and upon plants. But in addition to all these discoveries, De Saussure and his companions found in mountains not only the grim hostility which tradition had ascribed to them, but also infinite beauty, peace and solitude, and a recreation of spirit of which they had not dreamed. And just as hundreds of years before sailors had learned to love the sea though it confronted them with dangers and hardships, so these scientists and pioneer travellers came to love the mountains in spite of, or perhaps because of, their severity.

We, today, envy them the access they had to that unknown mountain world, and the unspoiled culture of its people. But even now the Alps themselves are potentially what they were, if only a man goes to them in the right spirit. Hilaire Belloc, in our own day, saw the Alps by the grace of his shaping imagination, as 'peak and field and needle of intense ice, remote, remote from the world'.

But it is useless to long for the past. We cannot put back the clock of time. We cannot set out with Columbus and experience the thrill of finding America, nor sail with Captain Cook in search of the mythical continent of the South Pacific. We cannot share the mounting excitement of the men who first crossed the high pass from Zermatt to Breuil and saw Italy below them, and above them the curving spire of the unclimbed Matterhorn. Now, whether we like it or not, the Matterhorn is surrounded by hotels, and if we climb it we have the help of fixed ropes and the security of other men's experience.

But the greater mountain ranges of the world are still surprisingly little known. We now have the opportunity to see the Himalaya as De Saussure saw the Alps a 150 years ago. Its peaks and valleys are unexplored. Its people are leading natural lives, instead of feverishly exploiting their country for profit of doubtful value. The Himalaya provides an even greater field of opportunity than the Alps gave to De Saussure. It is so vast a range that it embraces many countries and different types of people. The peaks and glaciers present such difficulties to the pioneer that exploring them calls for a higher standard of mountaineering skill than at present exists.

Let us approach this great heritage in the right spirit, not impelled by ambition. Let us study its people and their culture. Let us explore its vast tangle of mountains and glaciers, penetrating the deep sunless gorges to find the hidden beauty which lies beyond, crossing unknown passes which lead us from one region of mystery to another. Let us climb peaks by all means, because their beauty attracts us; not because others have failed, nor because the summits stand 28,000 feet above the sea, nor in patriotic fervour for the honour of the nation, nor for cheap publicity. Let us approach the peaks with humility; and, having found the way to them for ourselves, learn to solve their problems. Let us not attack them with an army, announcing on the wireless to a sensation-loving world the news of our departure and the progress of our subsequent advance.

But it is not yet time to climb these great mountains. With so much of the vast Himalaya still a blank on the map, our first privilege is to explore rather than to climb. In 200 years, when the Himalaya are known, then we may enjoy the range by climbing its peaks. In 2,000 years' time, when all the peaks are climbed, we shall look for more difficult routes by which to climb them, to recapture the feel of adventure, and perhaps to demonstrate our modern superiority!

It is unfortunately just as possible to go to the Himalaya, as to the Alps, with the wrong attitude of mind. Whether people realise that mountaineering is an inspiration, or condemn it as an insane risk of human life, it is obvious that its value lies in the motives of the climber. The ascent of Everest, like any other human endeavour, is only to be judged by the spirit in which it is attempted.

There is something fine in the desire to test human endurance against the deadening power of altitude, the difficulties of steep ice and rock, and the searching rigours of intense cold and wind; but the greatest value of the art of climbing, with its perfect co-ordination of mind and muscle, is that it teaches man a way of living in the beauty and solitude of high remote places.

And so – despite all the turmoil – the preparations of an expedition are for me so full of excitement that the irritation and delays only increase my longing to be off.

The voyage out to India was an interlude between a life and a life. We arrived at Bombay on 22 April.

3   Sherpas and Sahibs

Our first camp was on the railway platform at Rawalpindi. Tilman, Spender and I arrived there at 5 a.m. on the morning of 26 April. I was not very popular with my companions, as I had travelled from Karachi in complete luxury in a gleaming white-and-chromium special coach, whereas they had slept – or rather failed to sleep – on the dirty floor of a crowded second-class carriage. My exalted circumstances were due to 'friends at court'. On the strength of a slender introduction to Government House, I had been thrust into the luxurious comfort of a private saloon. My host welcomed me with the greatest kindness. The next morning, after a deliciously comfortable night in an air-conditioned bedroom, followed by a bath and a sumptuous breakfast, I emerged immaculate – having honoured the occasion with my best suit – and strolled along the platform of a wayside halt. I encountered two soot-blackened ruffians, their unshaven faces streaming with grimy sweat, their tired eyes regarding me with incredulous loathing. I could just recognize them as Tilman and Spender. I asked them how they had slept, and made some remark about it being surprisingly cool in the Sind desert for the time of year. Their effort at self-control would probably have broken down if the guard's whistle had not, at that moment, sent us hurrying back to our respective coaches. For the rest of the journey I kept a lofty distance.

We had arranged for our seven Sherpas to meet us at Rawalpindi. Auden was responsible for arranging to send them from Darjeeling and had told us when they would leave there. Timetables had led us to expect their arrival at 8 a.m. on the 26th. I have had a good deal of experience of sending Sherpas across India, and have come to realize that they do not always keep to the schedules laid down by the railway organizers for the convenience of ordinary mortals. So when the eight o'clock train had disgorged its noisy mob and we could see no sign of our men, I was not discouraged. We settled down to a routine of meeting each train that came into Rawalpindi from an easterly direction. The station authorities soon began to take friendly interest in our activities. They joined heartily in the spirit of the game and wired to their colleagues down the line instructing them to search all trains for pigtailed passengers.

When evening came and there was still no sign of the missing men, we became tired of the monotony of station platforms and began to suspect that something was wrong. At ten o'clock we abandoned our vigil and went to sleep. I was roused at 3 a.m. by the station-master, who was in a great state of excitement. The Sherpas had arrived suddenly out of the blue. Going along the platform I was met by a bellow of greeting from Angtharkay and his followers. I am not usually conscious at 3 a.m. of any emotion except intense irritation, but the sight of the little group of grinning faces and the sound of their excited chatter penetrated my jaundiced soul, and persuaded me that after all there are some things worth being woken for.

We had chartered a lorry for which we had been persuaded to pay far too much. At 5.30 a.m. we loaded it with our baggage, squashed in somehow ourselves, and started on the 200 mile drive to Srinagar. The Sherpas were in splendid spirits. They laughed and sang and fought with one another. It was difficult to believe that they had spent the last three nights and days on the wooden seats of a third-class carriage, chugging over the narrow-gauge lines of the cross-country route between Darjeeling and Rawalpindi, in the unaccustomed heat of the plains.

A long day in an Indian lorry is not a pleasant experience. In fact there are few hardships that I find more trying. We were delayed for several hours on the Kashmir frontier by the exasperating indecision of the customs officials; but by nightfall we reached Baramula, on the edge of the great plateau of Kashmir. We finished the journey to Srinagar on a brilliant frosty morning. The mists were rising from the green meadows; beyond them curved the placid hills, still white with winter snow. Lines of willows traced the course of lazy streams fringed with broad ribbons of mauve and white iris, a drift of colour above their stiff spear-shaped leaves. The cool air, bright with sunlight, welcomed us to the strange loveliness of this fabled land.

Srinagar was to be the starting point of the expedition, and we spent a busy week there completing our arrangements. The last few days before the actual start of an expedition are usually rushed, muddled and uncomfortable. Tempers are strained, and one eventually sets out with the frantic feeling that something vital has been forgotten. But our week in Srinagar was a welcome exception to this rule. We were the guests of Sir Peter and Lady Clutterbuck, who smoothed out all our difficulties. Large tents had been pitched on their lawn for us, and we had the secluded peace of their garden in which to make our preparations. Our host and hostess were endlessly kind to us, and their help was invaluable. Whenever there was a lull in our work we found that they had planned some pleasant distraction for us. The Sherpas, too, had the time of their lives. They looked so fat and happy that we began to have serious doubts whether we should ever induce them to leave such luxurious living.

But it is time I introduced the Sherpas. Angtharkay I have already mentioned. He is a man of rare qualities, which make him outstandingly the best of all the Sherpas I have known. He is a lovable person, modest and completely sincere, with an infectious gaiety of spirit. There were six others: Sonam

Tensing, known always as Sen Tensing, fat and jovial, with an engaging grin and a deep bass voice, with which he chanted religious incantations most of the day and night; Lobsang, serious, shy and slightly cynical, who regarded our activities with puzzled condescension; Ila, small, vivacious and shyly humorous; Lhakpa Tensing, wild and strong, who lived for laughter and nonsense and hard work; Angtensing, young in mind and behaviour; Nukku, slow in the uptake, but tough and strong as a mule. A fine band of men, both as friends and as servants.

Six expeditions to the Himalaya had convinced me of the tremendous advantage which a light mobile party has over the cumbersome organizations which have too frequently been employed for climbing and exploration in that part of the world. To my mind, the first essential of efficiency in planning and carrying out such an enterprise is to avoid taking any item of equipment not strictly necessary, and to see that every man in the party has his own particular job and that no one is redundant. In determining what clothes and equipment are necessary for the safeguard of health and efficiency and what items are superfluous one must rely on actual experience. One man, for instance, may find that he needs four sweaters to keep him warm at high altitudes; another may find that he is comfortable with two – should he take four, he is burdening the expedition unnecessarily. Some men can sleep without a pillow, others find this impossible. Some men wear out their socks more quickly than others do and must therefore take a larger supply. But in the case of equipment, one can generalize more freely. The most important items are sleeping bags, boots, tents and rope, and these must be the very best procurable. The most suitable sleeping bags are made of eiderdown, covered with silk fabric.

Here is a list of the personal kit allowance for each of the European members of the party, which we estimated as sufficient for a five month expedition:

2 pairs fingerless woollen gloves
1 Balaclava helmet
2 pairs snow glasses 1 pair
    ankle puttees
1 pair climbing boots
1 pair gym shoes
Camera and films
Ice axe
Tobacco
1 sleeping bag

1 rubber ground mat (2 feet × 3 feet)
1 windproof suit
2 pairs long woollen pants
3 sweaters
9 pairs socks
2 shirts (Tilman only took one)
1 pair shorts
1 pair pyjama trousers (these are used
    as a spare pair of trousers and to
    sleep in)

All these can be packed easily into one large rucksack, and the ice axe makes a good walking-stick for the march. Four or five aluminium cooking pots are needed for the whole party. For meals no one needs more than a tin mug, a tin plate, a spoon and a pen-knife. If a plate is lost, it is easy for two men to share. It is a mistake to add to the total weight by taking spare utensils.

It is far better to improvise than to take too much. For instance, when the remnants of my bootlaces were so knotted that they could no longer be used, I have often cut long strips of cloth from the ration bags, which have been just as effective. Should some of the spoons be lost, new ones can be fashioned out of bits of wood. Flat stones will serve for plates, and from the start a sharp twig makes an effective fork. If one's only pair of windproof trousers is wrecked on a jagged rock, and there is no more ration-bag cloth available as a patch, a piece of canvas out of the floor of a tent will serve to stop the draught. Every Sherpa can always produce a needle and cotton literally out of his hat.

I have found that such amenities as paraffin lamps are not necessary, for the party usually goes to bed with the sun. A glacier lantern, and a reasonable sup-ply of candles for it, must of course be taken for early morning starts, and in case of the party being benighted. Soap is a refinement that one soon forgets; like so many other essentials of the civilized world, it is not missed in a primitive life. A teapot is an entirely unnecessary gadget of civilization, for the best tea in the world is made by throwing a handful of tea-leaves into boiling water. For cook-ing above the altitude where wood-fuel is found, a Primus is the most efficient stove. The rationing and carrying of paraffin oil, for a long period, is a very diffi-cult problem: it is impossible to predict how long the party will remain above fuel-level, and containers are apt to leak when they have been roughly handled for several months. It is not advisable to risk running short of matches, for they are essential to the party's existence, and are light and easy to carry. Only expe-rience can teach one the rate at which such items as matches and oil will be used. It is important to make a note of this, at the time, for future reference.

When travelling through inhabited districts it is best to rely on food which the natives can supply. A healthy man can easily accustom himself to the native diet of any country. More care is needed in provisioning the party when living in uninhabited regions; but this, too, is easy enough when there is some means of communication with the outside world, as is generally the case when a party is attempting to climb one of the great peaks of the Himalaya. For this reason, little thought has been given by Himalayan travellers to the question of rationing as it is understood in the Arctic, where the uninhabited areas are so vast that an exploring party is often cut off from supplies for many months.

As I have explained in chapter one, we had planned to be beyond the reach of supplies for a period of about four months. It was therefore necessary to base our provisions on the various rations which Arctic explorers have so care-fully tabulated. It was, of course, advisable to make certain alterations to suit the different altitude conditions. I have found that fats are not easily digested at high altitudes; we therefore took a greater proportion of carbohydrates than is usually found in an Arctic diet, and in order to provide the same amount of calories we were obliged to take slightly greater bulk.

Our daily ration for each European member of the party was as follows:

Pemmican, 4 ounces.
Butter, 2 ounces.
Flour, rice and tsampa, 10 ounces.
Dried skimmed milk, 2 ounces.
Sugar, 8 ounces.
New Army Emergency Ration, 1 ounce.
Oats, 2 ounces.
Cheese, 3 ounces.
Total weight of food per man per day, 2 pounds.

Pemmican is a highly nutritious but dismally unpalatable meat extract in the form of paste. The new Army Emergency Ration looks rather like coarse chocolate, but I believe has some meat extract mixed with the chocolate.

Tsampa is roasted flour, a most convenient form of food used by the people of the Himalaya and throughout Central Asia. Skimmed milk was taken rather than full cream milk, because of its higher protein content. Vitamins A and D were provided for by Crook's Halibut Liver Oil, Vitamin C by Hoffman La Roche ascorbic acid tablets, and Vitamin B by dried yeast. We took a .375 rifle in the hope of supplementing this diet occasionally with fresh meat.

In accordance with their usual fare, the porters' rations were somewhat different from ours, and consisted of a much higher percentage of flour and tsampa. We also took with us tea, salt and curry powder, but these were not strictly rationed.

All the principal items of equipment had been brought from England, but we purchased cooking and eating utensils and minor domestic necessities in the bazaar in Srinagar. The Sherpas took a leading part in our shopping expeditions. They would not allow us to buy anything which they considered to be expensive. They know all the arts of bargaining, and regard it as a sacred duty. We spent hours in the bazaar comparing the relative weights of various makes of spoons, plates and mugs, and debating whether each member of the party should be allowed a knife, or whether one knife was enough for two of us. Tilman was strongly opposed to our taking plates, insisting that one could eat everything out of a mug. I maintained that if we happened to be eating curry and rice and drinking tea at the same time, it would be nicer to have them served in separate receptacles.

When we had decided exactly what was to be bought, the actual purchase of each article was left to the Sherpas, who played one shopkeeper against the next, in masterly style, until they had achieved rock-bottom prices.

We ordered, among other things, about a hundred canvas bags to hold the flour which was to be taken from the last villages which we should pass. It was essential that the flour should be kept dry, so we bought a tarpaulin to spread over the stores at night.

Our stuff had finally to be sorted out and made up into loads suitable for transport. To save weight, we packed everything in sacks, instead of wooden boxes. For the first few marches we were to use pack-ponies, and we interviewed a series of contractors, each desperately eager to secure our custom.

Meanwhile Spender was busy adjusting his survey instruments, and trying to reduce their weight to my rigid specifications. Auden arrived from Calcutta on 2 May already equipped with a full-grown beard, which he had acquired in his recent geological survey in the Garhwal Himalaya, and clung to through the social occasions of a three weeks' stay in Calcutta. He had brought business-like crates of equipment, which Tilman and I viewed with dismay and rejected without discussion, substituting instead one large rucksack, to which he resigned himself without much protest.

One of our chief difficulties was to forecast accurately the amount of money which would be required during the actual expedition. Most of the money had to be taken in silver, which weighs a surprising amount. We took 1,000 rupees with us from Srinagar and arranged to collect a further 3,000 from the Government Treasury at Skardu, which was a fortnight's march on our way.

All our arrangements were completed by 5 May, and at noon on that day we packed our loads and the Sherpas into a lorry and sent them off to Woyil Bridge, where the motor road ends. Sir Peter and Lady Clutterbuck, and my mother who had been staying with them, motored us there, and gave us a farewell picnic lunch, which we were often to remember in the lean days ahead.

4 Local Colour

The Vale of Kashmir is a wide plain, with many lakes, 5,000 feet above sea level. It is ringed by mountains rising to 15,000 and 17,000 feet. To the north and east the various passes across these mountains are closed to traffic in the winter months by heavy snow, and it is difficult to reach Ladakh, Baltistan and Gilgit. These passes are not usually declared open officially until June; but it is possible, by travelling at night, to cross them without much danger of avalanches earlier in the spring. Our way led from the Vale of Kashmir, up the Sind valley and over the Zoji La (11,500 feet) into Ladakh.

For the first two marches, 5 May and 6th, the valley was wide and well cultivated. The days were hot, and a gusty wind blew clouds of dust into our faces. We were not in a mood to enjoy life. We were out of training. We trudged petulantly along with parched throats, stiff muscles and blistered feet. The world seemed dry, harsh and unfriendly. But the marches were short and ended pleasantly in the comforts of a rest house and countless mugs of tea. It was chilly in the evenings, and we sat round splendid log fires, feasting on hot buttered toast. Lady Clutterbuck had given us a hamper filled with delicious fruit and English bread and cakes, luxuries from which we were soon to be parted. But the days of strict rationing were still far ahead, and every night Angtharkay fed us royally on soup, roast chicken, vegetables and potatoes. Spender had smuggled two pounds of coffee into his load. He had a real flair for coffee-making; I have never tasted better.

On the 7th we passed through a narrow gorge, choked with an immense quantity of avalanche debris – rocks, twisted tree trunks and cones of snow, a proof of the danger of these upper valleys in the winter months. This ravine led us into the open Alpine valley of Sonamarg. Drifts of snow still lay on its lower slopes, and where the grass showed it was sodden and dead. It was too early for the spring flowers. We spent a dismal rainy afternoon in the empty village. We paid for our ten pack-ponies and sent them back, as there was too much snow ahead for pony transport. Coolies had come up from below to take their place.

Our start the next morning was delayed by the usual pandemonium among the coolies, each man struggling to find the lightest load. But the upper valley was sunlit and peaceful. The morning light slanted across the pines, giving them a translucent silver sheen. The high, fantastic crags above them slept in frozen shadow.

Baltal, a typically Alpine village at the head of the valley, was set in deep woods of silver birch and tall firs. That evening we piled the fires with logs and branches, to make the most of our last chance of abundant fuel. Once across the Zoji La we knew that we should be in treeless country.

Tilman gloated over the opportunity of waking us early. At 2 a.m. I heard him clumping about self-righteously. There was no hope of sulkily defying his onslaught, for the coolies were equally eager to get across the pass while the snow was still frozen hard. They stood over us waiting to seize our bedding and pack up.

We had one glacier lantern between the thirty-eight of us, so I unselfishly volunteered to carry it! As Tilman had predicted, the thirty-eighth man (himself) did not derive much benefit from its faint light.

We climbed in single file up a narrow snow-filled valley, and, when daylight came, we emerged on to a desolate windswept snowfield. It was very difficult to recognise the actual crest of the pass, and long after we thought we had crossed it and were going down the other side, we came upon a stream flowing towards us. A bitterly cold wind numbed our faces and hands. Tilman had made a curious vow to march all the way to the Baltoro glacier in shorts. At this stage his bare legs were hideously purple.

Three miles farther on, the track crossed a steep snow slope above a river. A caravan of ponies was being driven up towards the pass. One pony had fallen down the slope and into the river. The owners were trying to pull it out without unfastening its load. Tilman jumped into the water and heaved the load off. He then succeeded in floating the animal into shallow water in midstream. But it could not be made to stand up. It had probably broken its back and was also paralysed with cold. The wretched creature eventually drowned. We advised the men not to take the rest of their ponies over the pass.

We soon reached the little grazing village of Machhoi. Here we met an astonishing party setting out to cross the pass. An elderly shopkeeper from Skardu, with his wife draped in a hooded purdah-cloak, which resembled the Ku-Klux-Klan disguise. They had with them a small baby and two other children, one with his arm in a splint. We persuaded them to postpone the crossing until the following morning. It was amazing that they should be attempting to cross the pass at this time of year, when a month later it would be an easy walk. The Zoji La is only 11,500 feet high, and to see it so deep in snow made us apprehensive about our plan to cross the main Karakoram range in less than three weeks' time.

We went on down a wide open valley, glissading comfortably down beds of hard snow. The country was dismally bleak and dull, and the bare rounded hills had little character. We reached Matayan that afternoon. It was remarkably like a Tibetan village with its low, square houses, and the same well-remembered smell. Here we met Captain and Mrs Wood on their way to

Leh, and enjoyed their company for the next three marches. But I am afraid our primitive ménage somewhat embarrassed them.

From Matayan we went on to Dras, the most important village in this part of the world. There we tried to buy eggs and a sheep, but Angtharkay said they were too expensive. He was adamant about this, so our fare was leaner than usual. Everyone in Dras who gave us the slightest assistance, or even spoke to us demanded 'baksheesh'. This is an unpleasant characteristic of the villages on any route by which Europeans journey. It is largely due to the thoughtlessness of travellers. It is so easy to be the 'pukka sahib' and to dole out money to all and sundry, but so degrading for everyone concerned.

Below Dras, we had a long march of twenty-two miles to Karbu. The country became more rugged and we entered a deep-cut valley. It was a hot, tiring day, and we were glad to reach the cool shade of the irrigated village.

The next day, 12 May, I started early and walked ahead of the others, thoroughly enjoying the cool morning air. After several miles, I halted on the sandy shore of the river. I was surrounded by steep cliffs, utterly barren, but across the river was a village in a mist of pink apricot blossom, its terraces of young corn climbing the hillside in steps of vivid green. It was like finding a corner of Kentish spring set in the midst of the arid crags of Aden. In this lovely place I waited for the rest of the party. We lazed in the sun and bathed, forgetting the time, and continued our march reluctantly in the heat of the day. In the middle of the afternoon we reached Kharal bridge, which spans the Dras river at its confluence with the Suru river, and marks the junction of the Leh and Skardu routes. There is no village at this point, but three miles away, along the Leh road, lies the important town of Kargil. We camped on a hot dusty shelf near the bridge. Angtharkay and Lhakpa Tensing went on to Kargil to see what they could buy. They returned in the evening with three chickens, two dozen eggs, two pounds of meat and a bottle of arak. They had drunk a whole bottle of this intoxicating brew, but, in spite of this, they did not think much of Kargil, though they were full of stories of the Coronation Day celebrations in this remote town. We drank to the occasion, and when the arak was finished our surroundings looked somehow less depressing.

From Kharal bridge we followed the course of the Suru river down through its barren rocky ravines. Every few miles we came to the startling contrast of irrigated villages, with their cascading terraces of young crops, shaded by spreading trees in new leaf, feathery against the light. The fruit-blossom here was over, but the tumbling streams were bordered with purple iris. This surprisingly swift change was due to the lower altitude, for only the previous day, at the first of these enchanting villages, the fruit trees had spread a cloak of blossom over the hillside. Between these villages, our path led down through a succession of ravines. It was sometimes carved out of the face of a vertical cliff, overhanging the Suru hundreds of feet below. The oily river slid silently through this strange country with sinister strength. From time to time it plunged over rapids, with a roar that echoed for miles up the valley.

We went on through increasing heat, glare and desolation. Every afternoon we camped in a pleasant oasis. It was good to wash away the dust of the march in clear streams, and to forget the day's heat, lounging in shady meadows. Stripping to bathe at Olthingthang I dropped my watch and broke the spring. My diary's comment reads: 'Bloody nuisance! But I suppose I shall get as used to being without it as I have got used to having no trousers to change into.' prophecy proved remarkably correct, and I spent the next five months without giving a thought to my loss.

We reached the Indus on 14 May, having followed a network of rivers from the tiny beginning of one of them in a mountain stream on the Zoji La, till we saw them pour finally into the Indus in a mighty force of water. To follow any river throughout its course is strangely fascinating to me.

For some curious reason, the Indus is destined from its very source to flow through desert for the whole of its journey to the Arabian sea. A few miles away from the Indus valley there is often fertile country, but the river itself seems to create arid desolation wherever it goes, except where human ingenuity has irrigated its banks into fertility.

It follows a peculiarly difficult route, and seems to delight in carving a way through the highest mountain barriers. It rises on the north side of the main Himalayan range, only a short way from the source of the Brahmaputra, and is at once attracted, as if by a magnet, to the great peaks of the Karakoram. When it approaches Nanga Parbat it alters its course towards it, and cuts its way through a maze of obstacles to reach the Sind desert.

Following the Indus downstream, we passed river terraces many hundreds of feet above us – indications of the river's course in former times, before it had cut down to its present level.

Tilman used to bathe several times a day, though the rest of us found the water too cold, and therefore maintained that it was a bad thing to do, though sometimes even I was tempted to have a dip. Once we passed a splendid waterfall plunging over a great overhanging cliff 200 feet high. It fell on to a circle of huge boulders, throwing up clouds of spray which watered a little green meadow below. Tilman and I stripped off our clothes, and climbed on to the boulders, while the spray beat up into our faces. It was very cold. The sun was diffused through a silver mist, and a brilliant rainbow formed round each of us, expanding and contracting in the drifting spray. It was a wonderful sight. After a pause to recover my breath and bask in the hot sun, I returned to explore the enchanting caves behind the waterfall. They were filled with moss and ferns, and beads of spray clustered everywhere like dew. Each drop reflected the colours of my personal rainbow as I moved.

We used to make a long halt each day, about noon, at one of the villages through which we passed. Those ahead would choose the halting-place. When the whole party had forgathered, we always lit a fire in the shade of the apricot trees and scrambled as many eggs as the village could provide. No one ever had the forethought to bring any utensils, so we always had to rely on the villagers for a cooking pot, and we ate out of this, to the vast amusement of the natives, with spoons made from bits of wood. In spite of these halts, or perhaps because of them, we never succeeded in accomplishing the daily march without a great deal of effort. We usually arrived at our destination thoroughly weary and footsore, complaining bitterly about the length of the march. Tilman declared dejectedly that we would certainly be turned out of any self-respecting hiking club in England. But I found solace in the fact that mountaineers are notoriously bad walkers. Frequently in the hot afternoons we suffered a good deal from thirst. This was particularly bad when we had succumbed to the temptation of drinking from a spring early in the day. During these thirsty hours, when we were marching over long waterless stretches, we would walk sullenly along, thinking of beer, and feeling that nothing else in the world mattered. But ten seconds after arriving at a spring, beer meant nothing, and we would not have gone a hundred yards to get it.

At every village and all along the route the natives were helpful and friendly, and one of my most pleasant memories of the journey was our daily contact with them. At Tolti, a large settlement with many square miles of terraced cultivation, we were honoured by a visit from the local Rajah. A sticky conversation was helped out by a few cigarettes that Spender had brought from Port Said, and ended by the Rajah's servant asking to see our rifle. We assembled it laboriously, but he insisted on seeing it shoot. We obliged, and blazed off into the air. But this did not satisfy him, and someone was sent to put up a bit of paper as a target, at about two hundred yards' range. Tilman was entrusted with the task of upholding our prestige. He had never fired the rifle before, and shot too high, completely missing the target. We were reluctant to waste more ammunition, but the Rajah's servant insisted on trying his skill. He had obviously never fired a rifle before, and he clutched it in a most haphazard manner, holding it loosely, with the butt in the middle of his chest. While he was aiming, we took the hurried precaution of making everyone stand well behind the firing line. He tugged at the trigger. The recoil nearly knocked him over, but the target was blown to bits! Inspired by this triumph, the Rajah then suggested that we should take on the local team at polo. But fearing further humiliation, we made specious excuses, and he departed with his retinue.

Polo is the national sport in this part of the world. All the larger villages have a polo ground, usually bounded by stone walls. A queer variety of the game is played, with no chukkers, and no change of ponies. The game does not end till one side or the other has scored nine goals – and not always then. It starts by the captain of one side galloping madly down the field and throwing the ball in where he feels inclined, usually just in time for him to hit a neat goal. If a Rajah is playing he is usually accompanied on to the field by the local band! Brighter polo perhaps, but I am not sorry that we decided to let discretion be the better part of valour.

The last march into Skardu, the capital of Baltistan, was twenty-one miles, mostly over sand flats, which made tiring going. We arrived there, after fourteen marches from Srinagar, on 18 May. Skardu is situated in a broad alluvial plain, at the junction of the Shigar river with the Indus. We had decided to halt for a day in Skardu, as we still had many things to settle. In the evening, we called on the Thasildar, the administrator in charge of the district. He was extremely helpful, and gave us much valuable information about transport and supplies. He advised us not to buy our flour in Skardu, but to rely on getting it in Askole, the last village through which we should pass, five stages farther on. He explained that as there had been a famine in Askole the people there would be only too willing to sell us all the flour we needed at very cheap rates. We did not quite follow this curious reasoning, and wondered whether he perhaps had a grudge against the local flour merchant! But as the plan would save us the enormous expense of transporting two tons of flour from Skardu to Askole, we decided to rely on his statement. He sent a chaprassi (orderly) ahead to see that the difficult route to Askole was open.

The next morning, we celebrated the rest day by lazing in bed till 7.30. But there was very little else in the day that was restful. Letters had to be written, for this was the last place from which we could post them, and our last purchases and final arrangements had to be planned. We bought 250 pounds of sugar, 500 pounds of tsampa, 280 pounds of rice, forty pounds of ghi (clarified butter used for cooking), forty pounds of salt, and twelve gallons of paraffin oil for the Primus stoves. We also bought several thousand coolie cigarettes for the porters. We went with the Thasildar to collect the 3,000 rupees which we had paid to the Kashmir Government in Srinagar, to be handed over to us in Skardu. The Treasury was heavily guarded, presumably from a mob of loafers who sat and chatted amicably with the guards, and who helped us to count the money and to detect bad rupees. We had tea with the Thasildar and discussed the administrative problems of the district. His secretary stood behind him swotting flies and joining enthusiastically in the conversation. The local doctor called on us in the evening. He said that he had recently vaccinated 30,000 people in the neighbourhood and wanted to add us to his victims.

The Thasildar had asked us to employ men from some villages near Skardu. They were a fine looking crowd and we agreed to sign on seventeen of them. Our transport column had now expanded to sixteen ponies. These and all the rest of our stuff had now to be transported across the Indus. The Thasildar accompanied us down to the shore, where we found the ferry arriving with a large cargo from Shigar. It was a big wooden barge of rough solid build, propelled and navigated by two huge oars astern, three crooked punt poles and half-dozen paddles. When it had disgorged its cargo, it had to be towed for several hundred yards upstream before we could embark. It would only hold eight ponies and half our kit, and we had to do the journey in two relays. The Sherpas were in a great state of excitement as we cast off, shouting wildly and bombarding those on shore with dried dung. They then seized the paddles and wielded them furiously in the wrong direction. However, as the craft relied for its progress mostly on the oars and the poles, their efforts did not hinder us much, and soon they abandoned paddling for the better sport of splashing each other with water. We were carried downstream by the current at an alarming rate, and seemed to make very little progress across the river. However, we eventually stuck in the mud on the opposite side and landed our belongings. Then the barge had to be dragged laboriously upstream through the shallow water before it was pushed out into the swirling river again. It took about three hours to get the whole party across.

In the afternoon we marched over hot sand flats to Shigar, bathing on the way. We camped on the dusty polo ground, and were so thirsty that we spent hours combing the bazaar for drink, but only succeeded in raising half a bottle of arak, which was deplorably inadequate.

Before leaving Shigar the next morning, we bought a large quantity of locally-woven blankets at five rupees each, for the coolies whom we were to take from Askole. It was another twenty-mile march to Yuno, the next halting-place, but the first half of it was very delightful, along a shady lane, the air fresh with the smell of green corn. We made a long halt at midday for a more than usually excellent lunch of scrambled eggs, dozens of them, and stewed apricots. The export of dried apricots is a considerable industry in Baltistan, and we were told that they send quantities to England. They are exceptionally sweet, and quite unlike the usual loofah-like atrocities in grocers' shops. The kernels, too, are delicious, with a delicate almond flavour.

As we went up the Shigar valley, we found that the people were a depressingly weedy crowd. We began to wonder if, at Askole, we would find men strong enough for the severe task of carrying loads over the main range. Most of the people we saw were afflicted with enormous goitres. The Skardu men, who by now had caught us up, looked magnificent in comparison. Some of the Skardu coolies were really fine creatures, tall, blue-eyed and well built.

At Yuno, we had to camp on a tiny, dusty terrace with no water near at hand. Angtensing and I went a long way up the hill to find an irrigation channel, and we opened a dam to let the water flow towards our camp. Before we had completed our task, we were attacked by an irate farmer, brandishing a spade and swearing unintelligible oaths. He drove us off, and rectified the damage we had done, so that we had to search elsewhere for water.

At the end of the next day's march to Dusso we had to cross the Shigar river, which was here a foaming torrent. The voyage had to be undertaken on rafts, each made of twenty sheepskin bladders lashed together, and strengthened by strips of wood. Four men paddled each raft with sticks that had no blade to them. It was a terrifying experience to entrust our lives and our belongings to such ridiculously frail craft, on a racing river with ugly rapids in sight ahead. The most alarming moment occurred when the crew downed sticks to blow up the leaking bladders! There were two rafts working, and they both had to make four complete journeys before all our stuff was across the river. It was an anxious time, and I felt very relieved when the last load arrived safely. We could not, of course, get the ponies on to the raft, and from here we had to rely entirely on coolie transport. We required forty-five men, and these had been collected by the Skardu Thasildar's chaprassi, who was waiting for us at Dusso. There was an aquamarine mine at this village, which Auden went to investigate.

The last two marches to Askole lead over very difficult country. The route has frequently to be altered according to the state of the river. Sometimes long detours are necessary to avoid an impassable gorge, and in places rickety ladders propped against the rock solve the problem of a vertical precipice. More alarming still are the rope bridges across the river. These are made of three strands of thick rope, constructed in the shape of a V, with one rope for one's feet, and the other two ropes as hand-rails. We managed to avoid these horrors by performing a delicate rock traverse across water-polished cliffs. The coolies negotiated the rocks with surprising skill, though they were each carrying sixty-pound loads.

Tilman, who returned by this route, was obliged to cross the rope bridges, as the river was flooded and he could not traverse the cliff. He gave me a vivid description of their perils, and said that Sen Tensing, who was with him, turned pale with fright.

As we went up the valley we noticed a greater number of cretins and deaf-mutes among the inhabitants, a state of affairs due, I suppose, to inter-breeding in this isolated district.

The last week had brought us rainy weather, which became worse as we approached the high mountains. With so much moisture it seemed strange that the country was so arid.

About four miles from Askole we came upon a sulphur spring. Tilman and I wallowed in its deep pools of hot water. It was rather like bathing in soda-water, for the sulphur bubbles hissed on the surface as we moved. Our ablutions were disturbed by the arrival of some Balti maidens, who giggled at our evident embarrassment.

A short way farther on we came to a village which was in a state of pandemonium. A battle was raging between the villagers and the Sherpas. It transpired that one of the Skardu men had damaged the tin of ghi that he was carrying. The Sherpas had remonstrated with him, and the argument had ended in a fight, in which the villagers had sided with the Skardu man. We managed to restore peace, but 200 yards beyond the village we found the blubbering figure of the culprit. He sobbed more violently as we approached, and displayed the wounds that he had received from one of the Sherpas. We pointed out that he was nearly twice the size of his assailant. We eventually managed to console him by promising to inquire into the whole affair when we reached Askole. He followed us, bursting into tears whenever we met anyone, or overtook one of the coolies. The matter was settled later by reprimanding the Sherpas, and compensating the injured man. But the incident did not improve our relations with the Balti villagers, whose goodwill was of such importance to us during the next few weeks.

5　The Passes of the Great Karakoram

We had now arrived at the most critical stage of the expedition. Everything depended on our being able to transport our equipment and about one and a half tons of food across the main Karakoram range into the Shaksgam valley. But besides this food, which was calculated to keep the party alive for three and a half months, we had to take with us food for the men who were carrying our stuff, and then food for those who had to carry that food. Not only had these men to be fed while they were with us, but they had also to be catered for on their return journey to Askole. It was the old problem which has to be faced whenever a journey is being planned through country where there are no supplies, and where everything has to be carried: a party cannot travel for many days without the carriers being burdened with so much of their own food that they cannot carry anything else. In this respect a man is a very inefficient beast of burden, for he eats more in proportion to his carrying-power than any of his four-legged rivals.

We estimated that the crossing from Askole to the Shaksgam could be made in eleven stages. Although the route had not been used by the people of Baltistan or Turkestan for a very long time, the Mustagh pass had been crossed twice by Europeans, whose accounts of their journeys we had to guide us in making our plans. This, of course, was a great assistance, and made our task comparatively straightforward.

In 1887, Younghusband, at the end of his famous Trans-Asiatic journey, crossed the Mustagh pass, from the Shaksgam river into Baltistan. Before leaving Yarkand, the last town through which he passed in Turkestan, he received a letter from Mr (now Sir Charles) Bell urging him to attempt the former direct route to Baltistan, over the main range of the Karakoram, by way of the Mustagh pass. This route had never been explored by Europeans, though its existence had been reported to the early explorers of the south side of the range. Younghusband found that a large number of Baltis – about two thousand – was settled in the Yarkand district. Several of these men were willing to accompany him. One of them, a native of Askole, whose name was Wali, said that he had come to Yarkand over the Mustagh pass many years before. He assured Younghusband that he had not forgotten the way, and undertook to guide the party.

They left Yarkand on 8 September 1887, and were obliged to take three weeks' supply of food with them, enough for the whole journey. They followed the course of the Yarkand river and reached the Shaksgam by way of the Aghil pass. The ascent of the Sarpo Laggo glacier and the actual crossing of the Mustagh Pass, was an astonishing climax at the end of Younghusband's great journey from Pekin to India. It is best described in his own words:

'When we ascended the valley of the Sarpo Laggo stream, towards the Mustagh pass, we came to a point where the valley was blocked by what appeared to be enormous heaps of broken stones and fragments of rock … On coming up to the heaps, I found that they were masses of solid ice, merely covered over on the surface with a thin layer of this rocky debris, which served to conceal the surface of the ice immediately beneath. And my dismay can be imagined when, on ascending one of the highest of the mounds, I found that they were but the end of a series which extended without interruption for many miles up the valley to the snows at the foot of the pass. We were, in fact, at the extremity of an immense glacier. This was the first time I had actually been on a glacier, and I had never realized till now how huge and continuous a mass of ice it is.'

The astonishing fact that Younghusband had at that time no mountaineering experience and had never been on a glacier, makes his achievement even more remarkable.

'To take a caravan of ponies up a glacier like this,' Younghusband goes on, 'seemed to me an utter impossibility. The guides thought so too, and I decided upon sending the ponies round by the Karakoram pass to Leh, and going on myself over the Mustagh pass with a couple of men. This would have been a risky proceeding, for if we did not find our way over the pass we should have scarcely enough provisions with us to last till we could return to an inhabited place again. Supplies altogether were running short, and the longer we took in reaching the pass, the harder we should fare if we did not succeed in getting over it. But while I was deciding upon sending the ponies back, the caravan men were gallantly leading them up the glacier. I rejoined the men, and we all helped the ponies along as well as we could; hauling at them in front, pushing behind, and sometimes unloading and carrying the loads up the stone-covered mounds of ice ourselves. But it was terribly hard and trying work for the animals … We had only advanced a few hundred yards, and there were from fifteen to twenty miles of glacier ahead. I therefore halted the ponies for the day, and went on with a couple of men to reconnoitre. We fortunately found, in between the glacier and the mountain-side, a narrow stretch of less impracticable ground, along which it would be possible to take the ponies. This we marked out, and returned to our bivouac after dark …'

'At daybreak on the following morning we started again, leading the ponies up the route we had marked out; but a mile from the point where our previous exploration had ended we were confronted by another great glacier flowing down from the left. We now had a glacier on one side of us, mountains on the other, and a second glacier right across our front. At this time my last remaining pair of boots were completely worn out, and my feet so sore from the bruises they received on the glacier I could scarcely bear to put them to the ground ...'

'We were in a sea of ice. There was now little of the rocky moraine stuff with which the ice of the glacier had been covered in its lower part, and we looked out on a vast river of pure white ice, broken up into myriads of sharp needle-like points. Snowy mountains rose above us on either hand ... and rising forbiddingly before us was the cold icy range we should have to cross ...'

'That night we held a council of war as to which of the two Mustagh passes we should attack. There are two passes, known as the Mustagh, which cross the range. One, to the east, that is to our left as we were ascending the glacier, is known as the Old Mustagh pass, and was in use in former days, till the advance of ice upon it made it so difficult that a new one was sought for, and what is known as the New Mustagh pass, some ten miles farther west along the range, had been discovered. It was over this latter pass that the guides hoped to conduct our party. They said that even ponies had been taken across it by means of ropes and by making rough bridges across the crevasses. No European had crossed either of them, but Colonel Godwin-Austen, in 1862, reached the southern foot of the new pass in the course of his survey of Baltistan. The New Mustagh pass seemed the more promising of the two, and I therefore decided upon sending two men on the following morning to reconnoitre it and report upon its practicability.'

'At the first streak of daylight the reconnoitres set out, and the remainder of us afterwards followed with the ponies along the route which we had explored on the previous day. We took the ponies up the glacier without any serious difficulty, and in the evening halted close up to the head of the glacier. At dusk the two men who had been sent out to reconnoitre the new pass returned, to say that the ice had so accumulated on it that it would be now quite impossible to take ponies over, and that it would be difficult even for men to cross it. The plan which they now suggested was to leave the ponies behind, and cross the range by the Old Mustagh pass, push on to Askole, the first village on the south side of the range, and from there send back men with supplies for the ponies and the men with them, sufficient to enable the caravan to reach Shahidula, on the usual trade route between Yarkand and Kashmir. This was evidently all we could do. We could not take the ponies any farther, and we could not send them back as they were, for we had nearly run out of supplies, and Shahidula, the nearest point at which fresh supplies could be obtained, was 180 miles distant. All now depended upon our being able to cross the pass. If we were not able to, we should have to march this 180 miles back through the mountains with only three or four days' supplies to support us. We might certainly have eaten the ponies, so would not actually have starved; but we should have had a hard struggle for it, and there would still have been the range to cross at another point.

'Matters were therefore approaching a very critical stage, and that was an anxious night for me. I often recall it, and think of our little bivouac in the snow at the foot of the range we had to overcome.'

This statement of Younghusband's problem clearly illustrates why it is that the pioneer in any mountaineering or exploring venture meets with difficulties enormously greater than any his successors have to face.

'Next morning,' the narrative continues, 'while it was yet dark, Wali, the guide, awoke us. We each had a drink of tea and some bread, and then we started off to attack the pass. The ponies, with nearly all the baggage, were left behind under the charge of Liu-san, the Chinaman, and some of the older men ... The ascent to the pass was easy but trying, for we were now not far from 19,000 feet above sea level, and at that height, walking uphill through deep snow, one quickly becomes exhausted. We could only take a dozen or twenty steps at a time, and we would then bend over on our sticks and pant as if we had been running hard uphill. We were tantalized, too, by the apparent nearness of the pass. Everything here was on a gigantic scale, and what seemed to be not more than an hour's walk from the camp was in fact a six-hours' climb. It was nearly midday when we reached the top of the pass ... There was nothing but a sheer precipice, and those first few moments on the summit of the Mustagh pass were full of intense anxiety to me. If we could but get over, the crowning success of my expedition would be gained. But the thing seemed to me simply an impossibility. I had had no experience of Alpine climbing, and I had no ice axes or other mountaineering appliances with me. I had not even any proper boots. All I had for foot-gear were some native boots of soft leather, without nails and without heels – mere leather stockings, in fact – which gave no sort of grip upon an icy surface. How, then, I should ever be able to get down the icy slopes and rocky precipices I now saw before me I could not think; and if it had rested with me alone, the probability is we never should have got over the pass at all.'

'What, however, saved our party was my holding my tongue. I kept quite silent as I looked over the pass, and waited to hear what the men had to say about it. They, meanwhile, were looking at me, and, imagining that an Englishman never went back from an enterprise he had once started on, took it as a matter of course that, as I gave no order to go back, I meant to go on. So they set about their preparations for the descent. We had brought an ordinary pick-axe with us, and Wali went on ahead with this, while the rest of us followed one by one behind him, each hanging on to a rope tied round Wali's waist to support him in case he slipped while hewing steps across the ice slope.

This slope was of hard ice, very steep, and, thirty yards or so below the line we took, ended in an icefall, which again terminated far beneath in the head of a glacier at the foot of the pass. Wali, with his pick-axe, hewed a way step by step across the ice slope, so as to reach the rocky cliff by which we should have to descend on to the glacier below. We slowly edged across the slope after him, but it was hard to keep cool and steady. From where we stood we could see nothing over the end of the slope but the glacier many hundreds of feet below us … We were standing on a slope as steep as the roof of a house. We had no ice axes with which to anchor ourselves or give us support; and though I tied handkerchiefs, and the men bits of leather and cloth, round the insteps of our smooth native boots to give us a little grip on the slippery ice, I could not help feeling that if any one of us had lost his foothold, the rest of us would never have been able to hold him up with the rope, and that in all likelihood the whole party would have been carried away and plunged into the abyss below. Outwardly I kept as cool and cheerful as I could, but inwardly I shuddered at each fresh step I took …

'At last we reached the far side of the slope, and found ourselves on a pro-jecting piece of rock protruding through the ice. Here we could rest, but only with the prospect of still further difficulties before us. We were at the head of the rocky precipice, the face of which we should have to descend to reach the ice slopes which extended to the glacier at the foot of the pass … The cliff we had now to descend was an almost sheer precipice: its only saving feature was that it was rough and rugged, and so afforded some little hold for our hands and feet. Yet even then we seldom got a hold for the whole hand or whole foot. All we generally found was a little ledge, upon which we could grip with the tips of the fingers or side of the foot … There was a constant dread, too, that fragments of these ledges might give way with the weight upon them; for the rock was very crumbly, as it generally is when exposed to severe frosts, and once I heard a shout from above, as a huge piece of rock which had been detached came crashing past me, and as nearly as possible hit two of the men who had already got halfway down.'

'We reached the bottom of the cliff without accident, and then found our-selves at the head of a long ice slope extending down to the glacier below. Protruding through the ice were three pieces of rock, which would serve us as successive halting-places, and we determined upon taking a line which led by them. We had brought with us every scrap of rope that could be spared from the ponies' gear, and we tied these and all the men's turbans and waist-cloths together into one long rope, by which we let a man down the ice slope on to the first projecting rock. As he went down he cut steps, and when he had reached the rock we tied the upper end of the rope firmly on to a rock above, and then one by one we came down the slope, hanging on to the rope and making use of the steps which had been cut. This was, therefore, a comparatively easy part of the descent, but one man was as nearly as possible lost. He slipped, fell over on his back, and came sliding down the slope at a frightful pace. Luckily, however, he still managed to keep hold of the rope with one hand, and so kept himself from dashing over the icefall at the side of the slope; but when he reached the rock his hand was almost bared of skin, and he was shivering with fright. Wali, however, gave him a sound rating for being so careless, and on the next stage made him do all the hardest part of the work ...'

'At last, just as the sun set, we reached the glacier at the foot of the pass. We were in safety once more. The tension was over, and the last and greatest obstacle in my journey had been surmounted. Those moments when I stood at the foot of the pass are long to be remembered by me – moments of intense relief, and of deep gratitude for the success that had been granted. Such feelings as mine were now cannot be described in words, but they are known to everyone who has had his heart set on one great object and has accomplished it. I took one last look at the pass, never before or since seen by a European, and then we started away down the glacier to find some bare spot on which to lay our rugs and rest.'

Not content with this staggering achievement, Younghusband set out two days after his arrival at Askole to investigate the problem of the New Mustagh pass.

'I would now willingly have had a rest,' he says, 'but ... I set out to try the other Mustagh pass – what is called the New Mustagh pass. It was depressing, just as I had reached the first village on the Indian side, to have to turn my back on India; but I did not like to leave this pass untried, and with a party of men from Askole we set out on the second day after our arrival to explore it ...'

'As I now had some new foot-gear, we were able to push along rapidly up the Punmah glacier. But on the third day from Askole ... we were brought to a standstill. At this point the glacier flowing down from the New Mustagh pass joins the Punmah glacier, and we were completely 'cornered' between the two glaciers. To reach the pass we should have had to cross the glacier flowing down from it; but this we found it impossible to do, for just at this point there had evidently been an immense ice-slip on to the glacier, and gigantic blocks of ice were tumbled about one on the top of the other, in a way which made it perfectly impossible to get any footing at all on the glacier. So we turned round and faced for Askole once more.'

Since Younghusband's journey the Mustagh pass has been crossed once by a European. This was in 1929 when the Italian expedition, led by HRH the Duke of Spoleto, working on the Baltoro glacier, sent a party, which included Professor Desio, across the pass to explore the upper reaches of the Shaksgam valley. Although they had their main base on the Baltoro glacier, and only required to take with them about a month's provisions, this strong party of mountaineers experienced considerable difficulty in getting their coolies over the pass.

On his return journey Desio went up to the head of the Sarpo Laggo glacier, where he reached a saddle from which he looked down into the Trango glacier, which is one of the lower tributaries of the Baltoro. Later he went up the Trango glacier from the south and reported that the saddle was practicable from that side as well.

This pass, discovered by Desio, seemed to us an attractive alternative to the Mustagh. But no pass can be considered proved until it has actually been crossed, and as so much depended on our being able to get over the range easily and quickly, we could not afford to run any avoidable risk. However, we deferred the important decision as to which of the two routes we should attempt until we reached the Baltoro glacier.

Before continuing with my narrative I should like to discuss briefly the causes of the abandonment of these ancient routes across the passes of the high Karakoram. In the passage quoted in this chapter from Sir Francis Younghusband's book, there are several allusions to this question. He also refers to it in the letter which he wrote to his father in 1887 describing his crossing of the Mustagh pass:

'On ascending towards the Mustagh pass my real difficulties began. Since my guides had crossed, an immense glacier had advanced, completely blocking up the valley with ice and immense boulders.'

In each case the suggestion is that the increase in the size of the glaciers is the principal reason for the disuse of the passes into Yarkand. This theory agrees with the view, stated many years before, of Godwin-Austen, who was the first man to do any detailed scientific work in the district. He states in his paper, 'On the Glaciers of the Mustakh Range' (Royal Geographical Society, 1864), that when he visited the district in 1861, the main Mustagh pass was already closed, 'owing to the great increase of snow and ice', and an alternative route had been found (the New Mustagh pass). He mentions that in his time ponies and yaks were frequently brought over the new pass from Yarkand. While he was camping on the Panmah glacier in August of 1861, four men came over the pass from Yarkand. They were Baltis who had emigrated to Turkestan some years before. They had experienced much difficulty on the actual pass.

In discussing the question in his paper, Godwin-Austen says:

'I have often been struck by the indications of considerable amounts of change of temperature within what we may call our own times … Many passes which were used even in the time of Rajah Ahmed, Shah of Skardo, are now closed. The road to Yarkund over the Baltoro glacier, which before his time was known as the Mustakh, has by the increase of the ice near the pass become quite impracticable. The men of the Braldoh valley were accordingly ordered to search for another route, which they found in the present pass, at the head of the Panmah glacier above Chiring. Again, the Jusserpo La can now be crossed only on foot whereas in former times ponies could be taken over it. The pass at the head of the Hoh Loombah is now never used, though there is a tradition that it was once a pass; no one, however, of the present generation that I could hear of had ever crossed it. Certain large glaciers have advanced, such as that at Arundu, of which the old men assured me that in their young days the terminal cliff was one and a half miles distant from the village. Mr Vigne says, 'It was a considerable distance'; it is now only about four hundred yards. A like increase has taken place at Panmah, where within the last six years the old road has been completely covered by the ice and moraine, and where Mahomed, my guide, told me the old camping ground was, now lies a quarter of a mile under the ice: the overthrown trees and bushes plainly testified to the recent advance which this mass had made; this evidence was equally well seen along the side of the Arundu glacier.'

In the same paper, however, Godwin-Austen mentions the decrease in the size of the main glaciers of the Karakoram. This apparent discrepancy is supported by present geological opinion, which holds that there are cycles in the increase and decrease of these glaciers, not necessarily simultaneous in the case of all glaciers of the district. John Auden, the geologist of our expedition, in his appendix to the paper I read to the Royal Geographical Society on 10 January 1938, says:

'All of us were impressed by the recent decrease in thickness of the Sarpo Laggo and Crevasse glaciers near their snouts. That these glaciers are subject to periodic changes is suggested by historical records, since at different times they have been easy and difficult of access. The Nobande Sobande branch of the Panmah was inaccessible to Younghusband in 1887 beyond Skinmang. It was so smooth and uncrevassed in 1929 that Desio was able to ski up to its head. In 1937 it was again highly broken up.'

In 1892, Conway, discussing the Nushik La, a pass lying between Skardu and the Hispar glacier, says: 'The pass was believed not to present any extraordinary difficulties, and even cattle were stated to have been taken over it. Of late years, however, the natives admit that they have rarely crossed it, if at all. They state that the road became buried in snow, and that it ceased to exist as a practicable route from their point of view.' The natives' explanation was corroborated by Godwin-Austen and subsequently by Major Cunningham, who both found this pass to be corniced with an overhanging wave of snow, leading to a difficult snow slope below. Neither of them crossed the pass, though Cunningham attempted it. Bruce and Eckenstein, members of Conway's party, experienced a good deal of difficulty in crossing this pass in 1892.

Colonel Schomberg in his book *Unknown Karakoram*, which describes his expedition to the Shimshal district in 1934, agrees with the theory that the ancient routes have become impracticable because of increased glaciation. He adds that in his opinion the change is exceptional and comparatively recent. He writes:

'From what I have seen of the glaciers of this region, and have gleaned from the large volume of tradition, I am certain that the extensive glaciation is recent, at a hazard not more than about one hundred years old. Before then, the accumulation of ice and snow did not prevent people from crossing to and fro from Baltistan to Hunza and Nagir, and certainly into several parts of the Mustagh valley ... I think, moreover, that the time is coming, but it will not be for some decades, when these routes will be again open, provided, of course, increased glaciation does not take place. There is no reason why it should, as judging from past history the great increase in the glaciers was definitely exceptional.'

But though Younghusband, Schomberg, and the other explorers all agree that the old passes have become impracticable because of the increased glaciation, it is probable, in my opinion, that this theory is incorrect, and that the present blocking of the passes is in most cases due to the disintegration of the glaciers: not to increased glaciation, but to the breaking up of the ice. In the earlier days there may have been easy snow-covered ice-slopes leading up to the passes, which in the gradual deterioration of the glaciers have become jagged, steep and impassable.

It should be remembered that the local reports on which the explorers have founded their theories, are those of untrained observers, who having encountered greater difficulty with the ice on the passes, assumed as a matter of course that there was more ice than before. Whereas, in my experience, glaciers which are in a rapid state of decay present many more obstacles than are met with on the smooth surfaces of actively growing glaciers. The decaying condition of the Sarpo Laggo glacier, which will be described later in my narrative, illustrates this theory. It was on the lower reaches of this glacier that the decay was most evident. And it was this condition that caused so much difficulty both to Younghusband in 1887 and to ourselves fifty years later.

In spite of this I do not question the fact that there has recently been an increase in some of the glaciers, and the passages quoted from Godwin-Austen's paper, read to the Royal Geographical Society in 1884, give definite proof of this. Later in the same paper he says, 'As we skirted the Kero Loombah glacier, evident signs that it was now on the increase were constantly to be seen in the masses of upturned and broken turf.'

Also, we ourselves found an astonishing increase in the side glacier which barred our way down to Mone Brangsa. This glacier had been reported by Desio, in 1929, to be an insignificant ice-stream, but by 1937 we found that it was a formidable obstacle.

With so much conflicting data it is extremely difficult to assert the correct solution of the problem. But personally, I do not think that the main reason for the closing of the passes is due to the increase of the ice. But whatever the reason, it is certain that these passes across the main range of the Karakoram were used extensively in former times by native travellers going from Baltistan into Yarkand, and are now completely impracticable for native transport. Of course the disuse may be due to other causes besides the difficulty of snow and ice conditions. Schomberg suggests that there is no incentive now for trade between Baltistan and Shimshal. For the Shimshalis can now get all they require from Hunza, owing to the development of the Hunza valley in the last century, without having to cross any difficult country to obtain supplies. This, however, does not explain the cessation of trade between Baltistan and Turkestan across the Mustagh pass, nor between Hunza and Baltistan across the Hispar pass.

Another theory is put forward by Godwin-Austen, who suggests that the old routes were abandoned because they were frequented by robbers. He says that the former route over the Hispar pass was given up because of the danger of these raids, and an alternative route was adopted, which seemed to be free from the menace of attack by bandits. This route must presumably have been up the Crevasse glacier which we explored. But in my opinion it is almost unbelievable that this route was ever used, for its length would have been enormous and its difficulties considerable.

But whatever the reason for the present disuse of the passes, it is a noteworthy fact that travellers nowadays not only find that the passes are closed, but they have great difficulty in getting any information about the former existence of the routes across them.

It would be valuable historically to send an expedition into this country to try and trace the remains of old routes and disused habitations, and to determine the migratory history of the primitive people of these remote districts.

6   Trouble with the 'Hungry Hundred'

When we arrived at Askole on 24 May, we sent for the Lambadar and the headmen of the neighbouring villages and opened negotiations with them for the recruiting of 100 men, and the collecting of 4,000 pounds flour. There seemed to be no difficulty about the latter; we were assured that almost any quantity was available. The Thasildar of Skardu had been right about this, though whether his reason was the correct one we did not discover. The question of porters was more delicate, and had to be handled with great care. At first it was assumed that we were simply going up the Baltoro glacier and coming down again, so for some time we talked at cross purposes. When at last it dawned on them that we intended to cross the range, their faces fell, and they told us that no one would consent to come with us. They said that it had only once been done, and then by a really well-equipped party; poverty-stricken novices like ourselves would certainly perish if we attempted anything so foolhardy. In any case, they said, it was far too early in the year, and it was impossible even to reach the higher pastures. At first this looked like a serious setback, but after some hours of diplomatic argument we managed to convince them that we were not so incompetent as we looked, and that we were willing to pay well for any help we received. They left us with a promise that they would collect the men and give the matter further consideration in the morning.

Early next day the male population turned up in force. This was a hopeful sign, but we soon found that everyone was strongly opposed to our project. We had to go through all the previous day's preamble again, with the added disadvantage that now we were trying to change the mind of a multitude, who all talked at once. Moreover, most of them could not understand what we said. The Thasildar's chaprassi worked hard on our side, hinting that if the headman did not help us too, their unfriendliness would be regarded with disfavour by the authorities in Skardu. The seventeen men we had brought from Skardu were also useful allies. They despised the Askole men and were glad of an opportunity to show their superiority. Besides, they realised that if the Askole men were not forthcoming, the expedition would have to be abandoned, and they would lose the chance of the well paid job for which they had come so far. The part played by the Sherpas in the dispute was of doubtful value to us, and I kept them as much as possible in the background. They believe in force rather than tact when dealing with a situation of this kind, though later, when the party was actually on the move, they displayed surprising skill in diplomacy.

Quite suddenly, after hours of apparently hopeless argument, we found that everyone was clamouring to come with us. Whether it was the blandishments of the chaprassi, or the scorn of the Skardu men, or our promise of very large bonuses which turned the scales in our favour, or perhaps the fear that, with such a large number of men they might find themselves left out of a good thing – I do not know. But the change was dramatic, and it was some little time before I realised what was happening. The men caused such an uproar in their eagerness to have their names written down that it was a long time before we could restore order. On the whole they were a poor looking lot and most of them had large goitres. Even with so many candidates to choose from, it was a difficult task to select enough who looked as if they were capable of carrying loads over a high pass. I had written down about fifty names when the head-men of some distant villages came and implored me to wait until the following morning when their men would come to offer their services.

We made a final effort to reduce the weight of our equipment loads. Every object came under dispute. Spender had to cling hard to the less vital items of his survey equipment, and Auden nearly lost his geological hammer. The rifle caused heated discussion; two of us were in favour of leaving it, the other two said that it should be taken. The disappointment of the Sherpas at the mere suggestion of leaving it decided the question. We imposed a limit of thirty-five pounds each on our personal equipment and bedding. This had to include sleeping bag, rubber ground sheet, books, tobacco, cameras and film, and all spare clothing. Spender cut his tobacco allowance down to one pipeful a day in order to take with him Tolstoy's *War and Peace* and Forster's *A Passage to India*. These were a great boon to us in our few bouts of bad weather, though Tilman and I felt ourselves morally obliged to pay with tobacco for the luxury of reading. The Sherpas have a remarkable way of adding to their personal belongings on their way through a country. Before leaving Srinagar we had issued them with a strict ration of kit and had seen to it that everything else was left behind. Now their bedding sacks weighed twice as much as they had weighed at the start. They were bursting with an amazing assortment of junk: wooden spoons, packets of snuff and spices, electric torches, nails, filthy rags, and other treasures which they were reluctant to leave behind.

Throughout the day the flour kept arriving in small consignments of a few pounds. This was packed in the green canvas bags which we had brought with us, and weighed up in sixty-pound loads. Every now and again a fierce shower of rain interrupted proceedings and everything had to be bundled under the tarpaulin or into the tents. Much time, too, was spent administering our usual remedies of Epsom salts and boracic lotion to the sick and ailing. The result of this was that we had a busy day doing very little. The last few loads of flour were packed and weighed after dark by the light of a candle, which was constantly extinguished by raindrops. Dinner that night was a memorable feast. Angtharkay excelled himself with a favourite Tibetan dish of mutton boiled with spaghetti. The spaghetti we had made ourselves with flour, eggs and milk according to a recipe which I had learnt from a friend's Italian cook.

Spender and Auden left fairly early on the morning of the 26 May. They were going ahead so as to have time to make a large-scale map of the snout of the Biafo glacier, which almost blocks the main valley about five miles beyond Askole. The Biafo glacier is one of the giant ice-streams of the Karakoram, and rises near the Hispar pass about thirty miles north of Askole. Very little scientific work has been done on these great glaciers, which present numberless geological problems. Auden had examined the Biafo in 1933 and was anxious to see what changes had taken place at the snout of the glacier since then.

Tilman and I spent a frenzied morning surrounded by heaving and shouting humanity. All the villages in the neighbourhood were now amply represented. The little field in which we were camped was as packed with people as a tube train in the rush hour, all clamouring for our attention. After an hour or so we succeeded in establishing some sort of order. We began by sorting out the men we had signed on the previous day. This was no easy task, for they only seemed to have about half a dozen names between them. These were served up to us in various combinations, so that a section of one of the lists we were making appeared something like this:

Ali Mohamad
Khan Mohamad
Ali
Ali Mohamad Khan
Mohamad Ali
Mohamad

Matters were made more difficult by the nepotism of the various headmen and those who had already been signed on. They pleaded with us to take their various sons, cousins, fathers and nephews. Also some of the suppliers of our flour threatened to take it back unless their families were chosen. During all these chaotic negotiations it drizzled steadily, wetting our clothes and our baggage, wrecking our tempers and soaking the scraps of paper on which we were trying to write the names of the coolies.

When at last we had extracted the hundred chosen men from the mob, we made up the loads and sent them off in batches of ten, writing opposite each name what the man was carrying. When they had all gone we found that there were four loads left over. The mob made a rush at these and we had some difficulty in rescuing our possessions from scores of tugging hands. But it was very gratifying to see such enthusiasm and we began to take a more optimistic view of the situation. We paid out large sums of money for the food we had received and the rent of the land on which we had camped, said goodbye to our friend the chaprassi and the headmen of the villages, and started on our way at 1.15 p.m. Among our caravan was a sheep which we had bought. We had put one of the Baltis in charge of it. It was very reluctant to walk, either because it had overeaten or was homesick; soon its stubbornness prevailed and the Balti carried it slung across his shoulders.

The rain had stopped by now, but great banks of grey mist hung low above our heads, and the valley, once we had left the irrigated fields behind, was depressingly barren and bleak. It was difficult to understand how the hillsides could remain so bare of vegetation when they were subject to such long periods of damp, cloudy weather. Presumably the reason is that the clouds deposit all their moisture on the high mountains, and that below a certain level there is very little precipitation. This also accounts for the enormous size of the glaciers. Before we reached the Biafo glacier, we saw on the opposite side of the valley an isolated patch of cultivation. A lonely clump of apricot trees reminded us that we had left behind the comfort and fecundity of the inhabited world. I wondered wistfully when we should see our next trees. Tilman replied dryly that it would probably be the same trees in a week's time!

Two hours of easy going took us to the side of the Biafo glacier. It thrusts its great boulder-strewn tongue down into the main valley, carrying with it the rubbish which falls from the great peaks standing above the upper reaches of the glacier. A dirty stream issuing from a black cavern in its side forced us to climb on to the ice and work our way over its dreary undulations, cutting up steep, muddy slopes and hopping from one unsteady boulder to another. We had left the Askole coolies a long way behind by now. The Skardu men, on the other hand, seemed to be determined to show their superiority by keeping ahead of us. They went really well on the glacier, moving with skill and agility. We came down off the ice on to some sand flats which lie between the snout of the glacier and the main river. It was a splendid place for a survey base and we expected to find Spender and Auden encamped there. But we did not see them and went on beyond the glacier to a shepherd's shelter, known as Korofon.

The rest of the coolies arrived at about a quarter to seven. The issuing of food took a very long time. Their ration was two pounds of ata per man, and they insisted on it being served out in small lots of four or eight pounds, instead of clubbing together and taking it away in sackfuls. It was weighed out in scarves, handkerchiefs, blankets, coat-sleeves and trouser-legs. Often the receptacle burst open and the contents were scattered on the ground. We had not eaten anything since our somewhat scanty breakfast and when our work was over we supped ravenously on the remainder of the spaghetti and some cheese-rind soup.

A coolie brought in a letter from Spender and Auden the next morning, reporting their progress, and I sent word back telling them to catch us up at Paiju, a couple of miles below the snout of the Baltoro glacier, by the evening of the 28th. We left Korofon at eight o'clock. A serious obstacle in the day's march was the river flowing down from the Panmah glacier system. It is bridged several miles upstream where its gorge is narrow. But the route to the bridge involves a big detour, and we hoped that, as it was early in the year, it might be possible to avoid this by fording the river lower down. Flowing over gravel flats in the main valley, the river was diverted into several channels, and with care in the choice of a route, it was not difficult to get across. But the water was terribly cold, and caused us agony each time we waded into it. The porters came across without much fuss. The Baltis are good at crossing rivers, far better than the Sherpas. Certainly they need to be, for the rivers of the Karakoram are the most dangerous and the most difficult to deal with that I have ever met. Sen Tensing, quite shamefacedly, bribed one of the Skardu men to carry him across, and came in for a good deal of jeering from the other Sherpas. Neither party divulged the extent of the bribe.

It was another dismal day. We got very cold waiting about at the river crossing. The rain held off until we had pitched camp at a place called Badumal, and then swept down on us in a steady drizzle. We were very depressed that evening. It looked as if an enormous quantity of fresh snow had fallen above 13,000 feet during the last week of bad weather. We knew that the spirit of the Baltis, already considerably chastened since the start, would not stand many camps in the snow. It would be impossible to take them far through deep snow, quite apart from the risk of avalanches; and in bad conditions there was no knowing how long it would take to reach either of the passes. If, on top of all this, we were to work in heavy mist and falling snow it was doubtful if we would be able to urge the men much beyond the snout of the Baltoro glacier. We had quite made up our minds that we should have to relay the loads across the pass ourselves, but the question was how far it would be necessary to induce the Baltis to come before it was worth even attempting to do this. We could not afford to send the men home to wait until later in the year. For one thing, it would have cost too much; and for another, we could not postpone our crossing of the Shaksgam river until much later than the middle of June. To cheer ourselves up we began to discuss many attractive plans. We contemplated an attempt to climb K2, or Masherbrum. Another tempting possibility was the exploration of the unmapped country to the south of the Baltoro glacier.

It rained most of the night, and was pouring down heavily when we finished our breakfast next morning. A slight clearing at nine o'clock induced us to start, but then the downpour came on more heavily than ever. I was very worried lest the flour should get wet. Some of it had to last us for nearly four months, and it would have entirely upset our calculations if it had gone bad. However, there was not much to be done, except to trust to the waterproof quality of the canvas bags, and to try and persuade the men to sacrifice their blankets to keep the flour dry. They did not much like the idea of going along one behind the other covered over with the tarpaulin, like a Roman Testudo. But soon the rain stopped, and the sun peered weakly through the clouds.

The first part of the march was over gravel flats. The coolies went maddeningly slowly over this easy ground, stopping to rest their loads on their sticks every fifty yards. Farther on, the river ran against the cliffs on our side of the valley, and forced us to climb a long way up the steep hillside. There were two really difficult places to negotiate, where only one man could move at a time. We reached Paiju at about four o'clock. Here we found wide stretches of meadow-land, wooded with willow thickets, beneath which there was a number of shepherd's huts and sheep-folds. It was an unexpectedly pleasant spot.

Tilman had complained of feeling shivery that morning, and when we got into camp he retired to bed with fairly high fever. Spender and Auden came in about five, and showed me a neatly drawn detailed map of the Biafo snout. They had met with difficulties crossing the Panmah stream that morning, and Spender had been completely submerged. After the usual brew of tea which always celebrates the arrival of a party in camp, Auden and I climbed a knoll in order to get a view of the Baltoro glacier that might help us to decide which of the two passes to attempt. We could see nothing that could influence that decision, but with the beginnings of the routes in front of us, we could visualise more clearly the scale of things we had seen on the map.

We identified Desio's Trango valley and were able to make a good guess at the position of the Mustagh glacier. It was a country of bold granite spires and huge rock precipices. Had we not known that the passes existed, nothing would have persuaded us to go up the Baltoro glacier in search of a way across the range. From the accounts of those who had visited the Mustagh pass, it was clear that it was not easy on the Baltoro side. With all this new snow about, it would probably be quite impossible to reach the pass so early in the year. On the other hand, the saddle which Professor Desio had reported as situated between the Trango and the Sarpo Laggo glaciers was described as being easy of access. Also the route across this part of the range appeared on the map to be a good deal shorter. But the fact that no one had ever crossed Desio's saddle had a bad moral effect on the Baltis. They knew that the Italian party had been up the Trango glacier, and they assumed that they had returned because they had failed to find a pass at its head. What worried them more, however, was the fear that if we managed to cross the pass, we should find ourselves in a country from which we could not return. They could not believe that we knew where we were going. At length after still further discussion, the fun of making a new way across the range weighted the evenly balanced scales in favour of the Trango route.

That night the meadows of Paiju looked enchanting in the flickering light of six huge camp fires which blazed beneath the willow branches. We sat by each fire in turn and chatted with the Baltis. The Skardu men sang with splendid strength and rhythm. We stayed in their circle for a long time to lend our feeble support. Later the party warmed up to some spirited dancing.

Tilman's temperature was still 102 degrees next morning, and Sen Tensing, too, was down with a similar fever. We were faced with rather a difficult problem. Obviously they could not start marching up the Baltoro glacier immediately. But we could not afford to wait with this huge party of porters. Apart from the money it was costing to employ them, we were consuming over 200 pounds of food a day. It was too early yet to make any sort of diagnosis of the fevers. They might subside in twenty-four hours, but they were more likely to go on for two or three days at least, and a decision had to be made at once. Auden most unselfishly volunteered to wait at Paiju with Tilman and Sen Tensing. It was decided that Spender and I should go on with the main party and attempt to get the loads across the pass. If we failed, it would take us several weeks to relay the stuff over ourselves, and Auden would easily be able to get in touch with us on the Trango glacier. If we managed to get the porters across, Spender could begin his survey on the other side of the range, and, if necessary, I could come back to deal with any situation which might have arisen. Meanwhile, two Baltis were to wait with Auden. If the sick men recovered within the next three or four days the party was to follow us up. If they were delayed more than four days Auden was to send word up to us. If the fever developed into anything serious, which necessitated sending the patients down, or sending to Skardu for help, no word was to be sent up to us. It was agreed that if we received no news within nine days of leaving Paiju I was to start back. It was an unsatisfactory arrangement, but probably the best we could make.

All this took some time to arrange, and it was late before we got our army on the move. It took us an hour to reach the glacier. We mounted on to it by way of a steep gully between the ice and the rock wall at the side of the glacier. A fierce wind was blowing down the valley. This dislodged stones from the crags above our heads, which made the ascent of the gully rather dangerous. Angtharkay said he saw some ibex joining in the fun of bombarding us; but this may have been imagination. Half a mile farther on we came to the first tributary glacier – the Uli Biaho – coming from the north. It is almost entirely free from moraine deposit, and appears to mount on to the Baltoro. The clean ice was very broken, and though it was easy enough for us to cross, we had to cut a tremendous number of steps for the Baltis, who were wearing skin boots which slipped on the ice. Beyond this point, we climbed up to a remarkable corridor, running between the ice and the great overhanging granite cliffs which tower above the glacier. Though the corridor was, in places, so narrow that it was difficult for a man to squeeze himself through, its floor was flat, and provided us with wonderful going. It had obviously been formed by a glacial stream which had found itself a new course.

The corridor opened out into a large triangular courtyard which was roofed by a slanting buttress. A number of juniper trees grew on the rocky walls, their great gnarled roots wedged in the fissures. A trickle of clear water ran over the sandy floor. Here was the ideal site for a camp, offering shelter, abundant fuel, and good water. The altitude of this place was 12,600 feet. Though it was only the middle of the afternoon we decided to stop for the night. The longer we were able to keep the Baltis really comfortable and warm, the longer their spirit would hold, and the farther they would come with us. A large quantity of wood was collected. This was to be carried up with us for use in the higher camps. Some wood had already been brought from Paiju, as we had not expected to find any juniper on the northern side of the Baltoro. Ten loads of ata had already been consumed and some food had been left at Paiju, so that at least a dozen men were now available for carrying wood. The Baltis spent a long evening baking sufficient bread to last them for the next few days, so that they should have less cooking to do at the higher camps. They have a very simple and efficient method of bread-making. The flour is kneaded into a stiff dough, which is rolled into fat round loaves, about seven inches across and one inch deep, and then baked in the red-hot ashes of the fire. The result, when treated by Balti hands is excellent, and later nearly all our bread was made in this way. But the Sherpas could never master the art to our satisfaction.

At sunset, I walked out on to the Baltoro glacier. It was a beautiful evening. Only small wisps of cloud remained, interlaced among the innumerable rock spires. There was a promise of better weather. I sat for a while on a mound of moraine debris, 200 feet high and tried to grasp the scale of my surroundings. The enormous size of these glaciers, compared with those on Mount Everest and in Sikkim and Garhwal, made me feel as bewildered as when I first went to the Himalaya after being used to Alpine mountains.

We made the most of our last unrestricted camp fires. Half a dozen furnaces blazed with such fury that it was impossible to go anywhere near them. The Baltis were in high spirits, and each group vied in song with the next. The Sherpas, too, added to the tumult with their tuneless dirges. The crags above echoed this boisterous medley of sound. The Baltis enthusiastically promised to go as fast and as far as they could on the following day, though we realised that the promise would lack determination when morning came. We hoped that day to reach a point on the Trango glacier from which we could see the route to the pass, for we did not want to waste any time in reconnoitring.

There was a heavy frost that night, and a consequent reluctance to start early on the following day. But we got the party moving by seven, and by eight we were complaining of the heat of the morning sun. We soon realised our mistake in succumbing to the temptation of the 'ideal camp site'. We could have gone at least two hours farther on the previous day and would still have found plenty of juniper fuel. Moreover, the Baltis were marching with their usual slow reluctance, and it was obvious that we were not going as far, that day, as we had hoped. After a mile or so of excellent going we turned a corner into the Trango valley. We kept to the true right bank of the glacier until we were forced by a difficult icefall on to the glacier itself. At noon we halted for a meal. We had intended to give the men an hour's rest. But it was very nearly an hour after we had stopped that the last stragglers of the party, pursued by torrents of abuse from Lobsang and Angtharkay, arrived at the halting-place. These men also required an hour's rest. In the meantime, a sudden storm had blotted out the sun, and it was snowing. A freezing wind swept down the glacier. The Baltis huddled together in little groups under their blankets, and looked as if they had no wish but to die where they sat. At length we persuaded the Skardu men to start, but as we remained behind to try and urge the others forward, the Skardu contingent sat down again fifty yards away. The only thing we could do was to go ahead and leave the Sherpas to deal with the stragglers. It was a long anxious business coaxing our 'Hungry Hundred' over the desolate intricacies of the glacier. The ice was very broken, and it was not easy in such weather to find a way through. Often we had to retrace our steps, which did not increase the confidence of the coolies.

We did not succeed in reaching the point from which Professor Desio had seen the pass. We were far from certain up which of the side valleys it lay. But we found a good place for a camp. It was a little grassy plain formed by the corner of a steep side glacier flowing into the main ice-stream, at an altitude of about 14,000 feet. It was a pleasant surprise to find that, in spite of the recent weeks of bad weather, most of the winter snow had already gone from the level glacier at this altitude.

Shortly after we had decided to camp, it started to snow, and soon our tents, loads and bundles of firewood looked like a picture on a Christmas card. It was unusually cold for snow to be falling so heavily. This gave us a faint hope that the bad weather would not last much longer. Otherwise the outlook seemed pretty hopeless. Spender amused himself by describing in detail what 30 May should look like in England. I had not seen it for nearly ten years. But as he talked I remembered beech leaves, in the late spring, frail, almost transparent against the light; and in the woods, the pale green fronds of young bracken uncurling; everywhere flowers opening and sap rising towards the full life of summer. In actual fact, it would probably have resembled more closely the dreary scene outside!

7 Mutiny on the Hanging Glacier

The bad weather brought out the worst trait of the Baltis. When conditions were bad they seemed entirely incapable of looking after themselves. They crumpled up where they stood and refused to do anything towards making themselves comfortable or protecting themselves from the weather. It was surprising to find this failing in people whose livelihood depended so much on their ability to use difficult country to the best advantage, and whose forefathers were in the habit if making arduous journeys across these glaciers. Much of their lives must have been spent in the open, herding their flocks in high mountain pastures, and yet they seemed to be ignorant of the simplest notions of outdoor comfort: camping in the most protected places, building walls for shelter, crowding together for mutual protection and making use of rock overhangs. But I must admit they were tough, and put up with more cold and discomfort than I had expected they would endure. We spent a busy and exasperating evening trying to make them work in order to improve their unpleasant circumstances. The trouble was that they were thoroughly dispirited by the weather and our evident ignorance of the country through which we were leading them. We made a dump of six loads of ata for the Baltis' return journey, and two loads of wood were burnt. So we discharged eight of the weakest men. Thirty asked to be included in this discarded party!

It was clear that if the bad weather lasted into the next day, or we had any difficulty finding the way, there would be a wholesale desertion.

At sunset on 30 May the weather cleared and it began to freeze very hard. We dined off boiled rice, washed down with mugs of excellent mutton broth. Unfortunately, Angtharkay had seasoned the soup with curry according to his own taste, This caused us acute agony, and our faces poured with sweat.

I woke the next morning to find the mouth of my sleeping bag crusted with the usual coating of ice, caused by the freezing of moisture from my breath. The first task of the day was to bring back life to the apparently frozen bodies of the Baltis. This done, we drank a cup of tea with tsampa, and then supervised the packing of the loads. There was a good deal of fuss, because someone had stolen some of the firewood for the higher camps. Of course no one would confess to the crime; not that it would have helped much if they had.

Our luck was in, for the day was brilliantly fine. Down the valley, across the Baltoro glacier, rose the mighty ice spire of Masherbrum, framed by the clear-cut walls of the Trango. On the opposite side of the glacier, towering six or eight thousand feet above our heads, were immense columns of granite supporting graceful summits, so remotely inaccessible that they seemed hardly to be part of the same colossal structure. The flanks of these peaks were frosted over with ice and powder snow sparkling like a million diamonds in the morning sunlight.

After two hours of easy going up the Trango glacier we reached the first large tributary coming down from the main watershed. We supposed that it was at the head of this that we should find the pass. But we were by no means certain, and, with the porters on the verge of mutiny, we could not risk taking them up the wrong glacier. So, leaving the party below the junction, Spender and I went ahead to reconnoitre. Soon we were up to our knees in soft snow. When we had turned the corner into the side valley, we found that it curved to the left. We could not see round this bend. As far as we could see, a rock precipice, crowned by a hanging glacier, walled in the upper part of the valley. But, in order to get a clear view of the head of the glacier, where we hoped the pass lay, we had either to go to the bend, which would involve several miles of trudging through soft snow, or to climb a steep ridge immediately above us, till we were high enough to see round the bend. We decided to climb the ridge. The snow was soft and very deep. We flogged our way up for many hours, without seeing the view we wanted. It was exhausting work floundering up to our hips in soft snow, while the sun, reflected from the surface with redoubled strength, scorched our faces and parched our tongues. We poured with sweat as we toiled upwards. It seemed crazy to think that a few hours ago our feet and hands had been numb with cold. But I have been hotter on the ice slopes of the North Col on Everest, at an altitude of 22,000 feet, in glaring sun, than ever in the plains of India in May.

At about 17,000 feet the ridge that we were climbing became difficult and dangerous. The higher we got, and the more our view extended, the less likely it seemed that there would be a route from the head of the glacier. I went ahead, in a despairing effort to make certain of this. But soon I reached a steep rock buttress which I could not negotiate with reasonable safety, owing to the deep snow on its ledges. I sat at the foot of this, feeling crushed by a sense of futility and frustration. When we had left the coolies that morning, we had no idea that we should have to spend the entire day in reconnoitring the valley. We had imagined that within half an hour of leaving them, we should know definitely whether or not the pass was at the head of the first glacier. Now, not only had the day been wasted, but we were still uncertain where the pass lay. If it were not at the top of this glacier, the chances of our getting the coolies to the next glacier, in such bad snow, seemed hopeless. Their morale, already so nearly broken, would not stand much more hardship, and their supply of fuel would soon be finished. Unless we could find the pass quickly, and get to it easily, we were beaten.

From where I sat, though I could see enough to be almost certain that there was no feasible pass at the head of the glacier we were reconnoitring, yet there was still some of it that I could not see. In my despairing mood I was tempted to put all my faith in the slender possibility that the unseen part hid the pass, and I contemplated taking the whole party up there on this frail chance.

Still undecided, I began to descend. A small avalanche slid away below me, and I was able to glissade down its track to rejoin Spender, whom I found also dejectedly contemplating the problem of our next move. We climbed down from the ridge together and trudged wearily back to the place where we had left the coolies. We arrived at halfpast four, exhausted and thoroughly depressed. The coolies sensed our mood and realized that we had met with a reverse.

After a short rest, we roused ourselves to deal with our various tasks. A further batch of men had to be discharged, boots, snow-glasses and rations had to be distributed. Such incredible confusion ensued that all our other problems were dwarfed into insignificance. Everyone shouted at once. No one listened to what was said. Occasionally blows were exchanged between the coolies themselves. A hundred angry men surrounded us, all yelling and cursing and getting in each other's way. The Sherpas struggled nobly to help us to deal with this ugly crisis. Large numbers of the Baltis again demanded to be discharged. It was a long time before the matter could be settled. When all the items of equipment had been amply distributed, there was a clamour of protest. Some had no glasses; some no warm clothes; some no gloves; some no boots; some no blankets; some had sore eyes; some had boils; and everyone had too much to say. No one thought of making himself as comfortable as possible for the night. When darkness fell the mob was still arguing and had made no attempt to dig out platforms of rock from under the snow on which to sleep. The Sherpas had to show them how to do this. At last, with the stars, came peace and soup and rice, and sufficient quiet to discuss again the tangle of bleak plans.

The next morning, 1 June, the weather was still fine and clear. We started very early, so as to cover as much ground as possible while the snow was frozen hard. We were pleasantly surprised to find perfect snow conditions. The going was so good that we decided to take the party up the main glacier to the next side valley, instead of attempting to find a way up the first valley which we had unsuccessfully reconnoitred the previous day. The hard snow and clear frosty air seemed to improve the temper of the Baltis. I went ahead very fast, with the Skardu men not far behind.

We had now reached a point where the moraine-covered surface of the glacier gave place to clear ice. As the glacier was very broad and open to long periods of daily sun, most of the winter snow had already left the surface of the ice. We made astonishingly swift progress and reached the next side glacier in a few hours. We cut steps up a steep icefall at the bottom of this side glacier, which led to a rock shelf. Ahead of us was a glacier descending in a precipitously steep icefall. At first we thought that we were again faced by an impasse, but when we reached the rock shelf we found that another glacier, farther to the right, led up to an easy col. It was still only 9.30. We debated whether we should make straight for the col; but although the Skardu men had already arrived, some of the other Baltis lagged a long way behind, and by the time they reached us the hot sun was rapidly melting the deep snow ahead. If we took the coolies on through this, and failed to reach the col, we should lose our present advantageous position. It would be impossible to camp with the Baltis anywhere above the shelf. It seemed more prudent to stop where we were, and not to attempt to reach the col till the following morning.

Tantalizing though it was to waste the whole of the rest of the day when we appeared to be within easy reach of the col, we made the decision to camp on the shelf at 17,000 feet. It was a bleak and exposed place, and when the Askole men realized that they were expected to spend the night on it, a mob of them bombarded us with clamorous demands to be sent down at once. Eventually we discharged eight men who departed promptly, strung together with a rope made of yak hair.

We wrestled with the usual jobs in the fierce noonday sun; we dug through the snow to the rock to make platforms for the men to sleep on; we even had to take off their boots ourselves, and put them in the sun to dry. Some of the men to whom we had issued snow-glasses on the previous day offered to sell us the spare pairs which they had scrounged, to issue to those who had none. At three o'clock ominous clouds and a biting wind blew up, and it was soon bitterly cold. We feared a change in the weather and began to regret our decision to wait here until the following day. Bad weather at this stage would have been disastrous.

That evening we broached our supply of Danish pemmican. We finished a whole tin between the two of us, with the result that I felt horribly sick all night, for it is most indigestible, and it is necessary to accustom oneself to it gradually. At midnight the wind increased and the cold became more intense. I was very worried about the Baltis who were not really equipped for such severe conditions. But they did not seem any the worse for it, and made a surprisingly early start in the morning. To our relief, the fine weather still held.

For the first 700 feet the snow was as hard as iron, then suddenly the conditions changed and we sank into deep powder snow which was covered over with a vicious crust that broke at every step. The very hard work of stamping a track was shared by the Sherpas, and we reached the col (about 18,000 feet) before 9 a.m. To our dismay we found that the col was not the crest of the pass we were seeking. Beyond, more than a mile away, across a curving basin of snow, we could see another col a few hundred feet higher. This was a devastating discovery. In order to encourage the Baltis, we had assured them that the first col was our objective. Before they arrived we plunged down in the basin and waded through the soft snow until we were halfway across. The basin proved to be the top of the hanging glacier terrace which we had seen at the head of the first side glacier on the previous day. The Skardu men followed without any protests, and we hoped that the others would come at least as far as this, if only to get their pay. Angtensing and Ila went on to stamp a trail up to the higher col. We sat in the snow for a long time, waiting for the rest of the coolies to appear over the crest of the first col. When at last they got there, they sat down in the snow. It looked as if nothing would ever move them. We yelled at them till we were hoarse trying to make them come over to us. But nothing happened. At last we sent Angtharkay back to try and induce them to follow. Eventually most of them came on.

By the time they joined us it was midday, and it was quite evident that, with the exception of the Skardu men and two of the others, they were determined not to go a step farther. Many of them complained of mountain sickness; and some of these lay in the snow, holding their heads and groaning. Of the whole number, only seventeen were fit and willing to go on. The rest had to be paid off at once and sent back. So, on top of a hanging glacier terrace, in the torrid heat of the afternoon, we solemnly sat down and counted out great piles of rupees. The usual uproar, despite the mountain sickness, was as vehement as ever.

We watched the retreating army safely over the col. When they had gone we made a huge stack of most of their deserted loads, and staggered along with as much as we could possibly carry. Although a track had been stamped through the deep snow, it was gruelling work, and we were thankful when, after two hours of it, we reached the second col, and stood at last on the Central Asiatic divide.

It was a thrilling moment; and all the exasperation and worry of the last few days slid away from our minds. To the north, the Sarpo Laggo glacier curved down towards the desolate rust-coloured ranges of Chinese Turkestan. This was our first view into the country which we had come so far to see. There is something fascinating about these great continental watersheds, which divide the rivers of two such vast areas, so entirely different in character. Our contemplation of the momentous significance of the pass was cut short by the usual afternoon flurry of bad weather. The icy wind made us glad of the shelter of some rocks which jutted out of the snow.

We had intended to camp on the crest of the pass and to spend the next day bringing up all the loads. But there was not room to camp, as the ridge was too sharp. The first rocks at the side of the Sarpo Laggo glacier did not look so very far away, and we expected to have ample time to reach them before dark. The descent on the northern side of the pass was very steep. We lowered the loads by the simple method of rolling them down the snow slope: finding that the powdery snow was inclined to avalanche, we fixed some ropes, down which the party slid in safety.

When we reached the level glacier, we were disappointed to find that the snow conditions were even worse than they had been on the other side of the range. By this time we were all very tired. The Baltis wanted to sleep where they were. Spender and I were inclined to agree with them. But the Sherpas urged us to push on until we found rock to lie on and water to drink. We plodded wearily along through the soft snow, sinking up to our knees at every step. The straps of our heavy loads bit painfully into our shoulders, and the rocks we had noticed never seemed to get any nearer. When at last we reached them they were inadequate and comfortless – a most unsuitable site for what was to be a lengthy stay. But at least there was plenty of water, and we were too tired to bother about anything else. It had been a long and strenuous day, and we had eaten very little food. Sleep tempted us more than supper; we were too weary to eat. We crawled into our sleeping bags, contented that at least some of the party were on the right side of the pass.

8   Loads across the Watershed

The next day Spender and I stayed in camp to make preparations for the start of the survey. The Sherpas and the seventeen remaining Baltis went back to the dump in the snow basin and brought another batch of loads across the pass into camp. Early on the morning of 4 June, soon after Spender had left camp to climb to his first survey station, Auden arrived with his two Baltis. They brought the welcome news that Tilman and Sen Tensing were somewhat better and were following slowly. I sent a Sherpa and two Baltis back to help them. Auden had come through from Paiju at a tremendous pace, and was very tired.

Although a great number of loads were still on the other side of the pass, I decided to take a relay from our present camp down the glacier, so that the less rigorous conditions of lower altitudes would give the men I took with me a welcome rest. They were cheered by the prospect of an off-day when we got down there. Leaving Auden in camp, I set off down the glacier with the Baltis and three Sherpas. We took with us as much as we could carry. Below the camp, snow conditions improved and in just over an hour we reached a grassy glade by the side of the glacier, known as Changtok. Here we found traces of Professor Desio's camp; possibly some of these were the remains of Younghusband's halt at this place, for it is indeed the only suitable base on the north side of the Mustagh pass.

We also found relics of much earlier date, which indicated that Changtok was an important halting-place on that remarkable ancient route which connected Baltistan and Yarkand. It was difficult to visualise the significance of this place in those days. We could not tell whether the stone circles and the remains of stone buildings marked the site of a permanent caravanserai, or a grazing ground, or whether it had only been used by occasional parties of local adventurers. It is difficult to imagine that they could ever have used the route for regular trading. In any case, the pass we had just crossed for the first time, now to be called the Sarpo Laggo pass, would have been a much easier route than the Mustagh pass with its difficult precipice, though the latter is supposed to have been used by these ancient travellers.

On the grassy slopes we found the whitened bones of large animals. These were probably the skeletons of wild asses, though it is said that ponies were taken over these passes in olden days. This I find very hard to believe, and Younghusband's experiences in failing to get ponies across the Mustagh pass supports my doubts. Scattered about we saw a number of bharal horns (a bharal is a mountain sheep), and the droppings of some very large birds, which we afterwards found to be a kind of snow-cock.

Changtok was a lovely place, surrounded by vast, curving, open glaciers. It was sheer delight to see grass again, and though it was too early for the spring flowers, the grass had the scent and feel of life. A few small birds were already here; their gay singing made the place an island of spring set in a waste of snow and ice. Clear streams lingered in limpid pools which mirrored the surrounding snow peaks. But we could not stay. I was anxious to reach Mone Brangsa, which was several miles farther down the glacier. There I hoped we should find some scrub which could be used for fuel. We had Desio's compass sketch map to guide us, and we knew that his party had camped at Mone Brangsa.

It was easy walking at the side of the glacier, with only a few difficult stretches to check our progress. Halfway down we came to a clear blue lake. From its shores we could see, far away to the south-east, the famous peak which the early explorers of the Baltoro glacier had named the Mustagh Tower. Beyond the lake, half a mile before we reached the place marked on Desio's map as Mone Brangsa, we were surprised to find that a large side glacier barred our way. Desio, when he had sketched this map in 1929, showed this glacier as ending a long way above the floor of the main valley. Since then it had evidently made an astonishingly rapid advance, and was now a considerable tributary of the Sarpo Laggo glacier, joining it in a tangled confusion of ice pinnacles. Desio's photograph of the place confirmed the fact of this remarkable change.

It was a formidable obstacle. We could not cross it, for its sides were vertical, and we were obliged to make a big detour on to the main glacier. This took many hours, and it was nearly dark before the whole party reached Mone Brangsa. It was a disappointing camping-place: a stony trough, bare and ugly, shut in by untidy scree slopes and piles of moraine rubbish. No distant peaks could be seen. Nothing relieved the dreary monotony. There was no grass. The only vegetation was a bare wiry plant, like dead heather, which clung to the barren rocks. This provided us with firewood of a sort, but in order to keep it burning, the fire had to be blown continuously. A Sherpa's lungs are better than any bellows, but even so it was a difficult job to coax a blaze out of the stubborn fuel.

The next morning we slept late, until the sun poured into the deep valley. After breakfast we lazed in its warmth. My morning peace was shattered by the arrival of two snow-cock, which perched screeching near the camp, and strutted about protesting indignantly against our intrusion. The Sherpas were wildly excited, exclaiming that the gods had sent us the best meat in the world. They insisted that I should shoot our visitors. There was a wild rush for the rifle, which was packed in its case. By the time our fumbling, eager fingers had put it together, the birds had begun to suspect us of evil intentions. Before we were ready to launch the attack, they had flown away and perched somewhere in the crags above us, squawking their provocative taunts out of sight. This challenge was too much for Angtharkay, who insisted that he and I should stalk them. I felt forced to go, though I fully realised the stupidity of pursuing two birds in a maze of precipitous crags, with a .375 rifle which I had never tested and which would probably blow them to pieces if by any remote chance I managed to hit them. We sweated a long way up a scree slope, scarcely daring to breathe as we approached the crags in which we thought the birds were hidden. An occasional gobbling sound led us on from crag to crag, while we performed terrifying feats of rock gymnastics which we would not have dared to contemplate in cold blood. Eventually, as we paused on a dizzy ledge, we heard the birds' mocking challenge floating across from the far side of a wide ravine. Angtharkay saluted their cunning with a farewell grin, which broadened into a bellow of laughter as he caught sight of me, clinging precariously to the sheer face of the crag, with unlaced boots over which bulged the torn remnants of my pyjama trousers, the tail of my shirt flapping in the breeze.

Auden arrived in the late afternoon, having had some difficulty in finding the camp. After our early evening meal, the birds were located again by a party collecting fuel. In spite of my protests Angtharkay induced me to renew the chase. He led me up a steep, scree slope at a terrific pace, which gave me outrageous indigestion after my huge meal of rice. I remembered repentantly that I had been one of those who voted against leaving the rifle at Askole. This time we actually succeeded in getting within twenty-five yards of one of the birds. I was panting heavily with the exertion of the climb. This, coupled with the unfortunate fact that I used the three hundred yards' sight, caused me to miss badly. We returned to camp empty-handed to face the jibes of the disappointed party. Next morning I restored my self-esteem with a little range practice, which proved, to my satisfaction at least, that the rifle was throwing high and to the right.

We all returned to Changtok on 6 June where we found Spender encamped. He had made a good beginning in his survey work during the last three days of fine weather. From the upper part of the glacier the great peak of K2 was clearly visible. It was the only fixed point which could be seen from anywhere in the district, and the whole of the survey had to be based on it. Using a Wild theodolite, subtense-bar, and plane-table, he had laid out a base and fixed the relative positions of a large number of prominent peaks in the district, which formed a network of fixed points for a plane-table survey. This process was repeated at intervals throughout the season, in order to keep a check on the plane-table work, and to renew the circle of distant fixed points. Azimuth determinations fixed the map with relation to K2. (An Azimuth is an exact bearing to a point, and is generally determined astronomically.) Spender also made observations for latitude from time to time.

Leaving Spender to continue his work at Changtok, we went on the same afternoon to the upper camp, where we spent an uncomfortable night in that inhospitable spot. Early the following morning we set out to fetch the last remaining loads from the dump on the other side of the pass. By this time there was a well-trodden track over the upper part of the glacier, and after two and a half hours of steady going we reached the top of the pass. On the other side we saw Tilman and his two Sherpas toiling up the steep slope which led from the snow basin. It was a great relief to see them, though we noticed that Tilman was moving with evident difficulty.

While our porters went down to the dump to collect the loads, Auden and I climbed a prominent rock spur above the pass to observe a round of angles with the theodolite. The climb proved to be much more difficult than we had expected, and a biting wind whipped the snow into our faces as we struggled with the survey work on the summit. [1]When we got back to the pass again, Tilman had arrived. He told us that at his last camp he had been ill again with another attack of fever which had not yet left him. We escorted him slowly down to the camp. He was very weak and was obliged to halt every few yards to rest.

The porters arrived at about five o'clock, staggering under the weight of enormous loads. After vehement persuasion, I managed to induce the Baltis to proceed as far as Changtok that evening. I was anxious to do this so that the whole party and all the loads could reach Changtok the following day. The porters had already done a strenuous day's work, and the seventeen Baltis were reluctant to do any more. But as an inducement I offered them treble pay for the day and the prospect of a pleasant camp site. The Sherpas, of course, came with me cheerfully, without any of these bribes. In fact they took a prominent part in urging the unwilling Baltis along. Tilman was too ill to go any farther that day, so he remained in the upper camp with Auden and Sen Tensing.

The bad weather of the day had quietened into a tranquil evening. The last of the daylight lingered in the sky and touched the ice with delicate opal colours. Dusk was falling as we reached the first glades of Changtok. We lay down there to sleep on soft cushions of grass; the hollow where we camped was brimmed with peace.

This place was more than a mile above Spender's camp, and the next morning, while the rest of the party fetched the remaining loads from the upper camp, Angtharkay, Nukku and I relayed the loads from the hollow to the place from which Spender was working. Auden and Tilman joined us later in the day. Tilman was still very ill, but fortunately he had time to recuperate in this delightful spot, while we were relaying all the loads down to Mone Brangsa.

---

1 The height of this point is 5,748 metres.

This relay work was tedious. We had hoped that, having left the hardships of the high glacier camps, the Baltis would be more contented and would work more willingly. But two days later our strength was further reduced by the departure of five more Baltis, who suddenly refused to work any more. We paid them in full and sent them away without our blessing. This desertion lengthened the time necessary for transporting our loads to Suget Jangal, which lies about six miles below the snout of the Sarpo Laggo glacier. It was the place we had selected for our main base.

It was now nearly the middle of June, and before long the summer melting of the glaciers would make the Shaksgam river unfordable. If we were to attempt our proposed expedition to the Aghil range, which lies to the north of the Shaksgam river, it was imperative to get there quickly. We therefore decided to leave a big dump of loads at Mone Brangsa, and to take with us only the equipment and food which we would require for three weeks' exploration in the Aghil range. Even so, two relays were still necessary, as our party had to be fed during the next week while we approached the Shaksgam river. But this slow progress gave Spender time to complete his survey of the ranges surrounding the Sarpo Laggo glacier.

By 10 June all the loads were at Mone Brangsa. On the 11th we took as much as we could carry farther down the glacier. As we descended, the valley became more dreary and desolate. There was no life. It seemed as if nothing living had ever moved there. Mysterious hollow sounds rumbled from the glacier, and the melancholy clatter of falling stones echoed weirdly from the bleak crags. Though the cliffs were steep and menacing, there was nothing grand or shapely in the muddle of the graceless flanks – only crumbling decay. It was hard to get along, as the walls of the valley rose abruptly above the glacier, and we were obliged to work our way laboriously over the torn debris-covered surface of the ice.

As we went farther down the glacier our admiration for Younghusband's achievement increased. To have attempted such a difficult route at the end of his tremendous journey, having already travelled for many days through uninhabited country, nearly at the end of his resources, must have called for rare courage.

We only covered three miles before camping again in this dismal valley. On the next day the second relay of loads was brought down to this dump. On the thirteenth we had a long day. Though we started early, it was 2.30 before we reached the snout of the glacier. It was a relief to be able to walk freely again after days of scrambling over boulders, leaping across chasms, fording rivers, and chipping steps up ice slopes, always uncertain of finding a way through. We had hoped to reach Suget Jangal that day, but after marching rapidly for two hours over the river flats below the glacier, we decided to camp, still about three miles from our objective. In this place we found plenty of fuel and water. The position of the camp was strategically suitable as a main base. For although it was a full day's march away from the junction of the Sarpo Laggo river and the Shaksgam, it had the advantage of being within carrying distance of Mone Brangsa. Also the site commanded a fine view of the Crevasse glacier, and into the vast area of unexplored country beyond, which was our main objective.

Our immediate objective, however, was the usual brew of tea; and as we swallowed great mug-fulls of it, we discussed the unnamed peaks which we saw at the head of the Crevasse glacier. The most distant of these formed a circle of snow domes. It was intriguing to speculate how far off they were. None of us could agree. Tilman's estimate was fifteen miles, but Auden was convinced that they were quite forty miles away. We had one of our usual bets on this question. The stake for all our bets was a meal at Simpson's. Though since our return none of us seems to have had enough spare cash to honour his debts. Auden's estimate was the more accurate, for Spender measured the distance the next day, and found that the peaks were quite thirty miles from our base camp.

In the evening Spender and I wandered down the valley to see if we could find the extensive oasis which Younghusband's men had called Suget Jangal. It was too far away to reach it before dark, but from some rising ground we saw the place in the distance, a dark patch of trees which stretched like a shadow across the bleached gravel flats of the valley. As we turned to go back to camp we looked again up the Crevasse glacier and saw, in the far distance, a superb mountain, shaped like a trident, piercing the sunset sky. I felt stirred by a compelling impatience to find out how high it was, and where it stood. I longed to set out at once into such enticing country. At that moment it seemed exasperating to think that six weeks must pass before we could start the journey up the Crevasse glacier. The once fascinating problem of the Aghil range seemed to fade into insignificance before the urge of this immediate desire. Also I dreaded the possibility of floods in the Shaksgam river cutting us off from the chance of carrying out this plan. We returned to camp and ate our supper by the faint light of a young moon.

That evening was for me one of the greatest moments of the expedition. Warmed by the unaccustomed luxury of a blazing fire, its leaping flames fed with unstinted wood, I felt that after long days of toil and disappointment we had at last arrived. East and west of us stretched an unexplored section, eighty miles long, of the greatest watershed in the world. To the north, close at hand, across the Shaksgam river, was the Aghil range, with its romantic associations and unknown peaks and valleys. To share all this, I had with me three companions as keen as myself, supported by seven of the most stout-hearted retainers in the world. We had food enough to keep us alive for three months in this place of my dreams, and the health and experience to meet the opportunity. I wanted nothing more.

9   Finding the Aghil Pass

On 14 June the Baltis and four of the Sherpas started at dawn and spent a long day bringing the rest of the loads down from the lower Sarpo Laggo glacier camp. Spender laid out a survey base on the gravel flats which stretched for miles around our camp, and fixed the position of all the distant peaks in view; Auden was busy with his geological work. Tilman, Angtharkay, Lhakpa Tensing and I set off down the valley taking the rifle with us. After an hour's quick walking we reached the long stretch of meadow-land and willow groves referred to by Younghusband as Suget Jangal. It was a delightful place of clear springs, shade and soft green turf. It was deserted except for a few hares playing on the grass, which scuttled under cover as we approached, and some small birds singing in the willows. Everywhere there were tracks of wild asses (kyang), and a great number of bharal horns littered the ground.

We lay for a while on the grass and then climbed up the hillside for about 1,500 feet, until we stood on the crest of a ridge which divides the Sarpo Laggo valley from another big valley which descends from the north face of K2. Far away to the south-east we could see some of the great ice peaks of the main water-shed which cluster round the head of the Baltoro glacier. K2 itself was hidden by a corner of the valley. For want of a better name this valley had been called the K2 nullah[1]. Our position on the ridge commanded a fine view down the Shaksgam river and far up into the unknown ranges of the Crevasse glacier. We quite forgot to hunt for game and discussed excitedly the various aspects of the view. Suddenly a herd of about a dozen bharal ran out from a hollow below us, not fifty yards away. They hesitated for a moment, then plunged over a shoulder into the K2 nullah. Angtharkay and I followed, climbing gingerly over each section of rising ground and peering into the gully beyond. We stalked for nearly two hours before we found the animals again grazing peacefully on the hillside at a hundred yards' range. It seemed criminal to kill them, and when it came to the point I felt very reluctant to shoot. But the chance of adding to our scanty rations outweighed my scruples and I shot two of the creatures. The Sherpas were in a great state of excitement. They

---

1   'Nullah' is the English spelling of the Hindustani word 'nala' meaning valley or stream bed.

shouldered the dead animals and trotted back along the steep hillside under the great weight of meat, laughing and shouting as they went.

While I was walking back across the flats, I saw something standing alone by the river. It was some way off, and the shimmer caused by the hot afternoon sun on the gravel made it difficult to distinguish what it was. I thought it must be Spender working with his plane-table. Then I saw that it was coming towards me. When it drew nearer, I realised that it was a wild ass. It came up to within fifteen yards of me and stood switching its tail about and staring at me. When I turned round to go on it followed me, stopping when I stopped and walking when I walked, rather like an obedient dog. However, it lagged behind as I approached the camp and kept a respectful distance away.

That night we had a feast of rice and meat, and then sat round the fire feeling bloatedly contented. The Baltis were Mohammedans, and would not join in the meal as their religion forbade them to eat meat that had been killed by someone of another faith. It was a beautiful starry night, and Spender made some astronomical observations to determine our latitude and the exact bearing to the peaks that he had fixed.

As I have explained in an earlier chapter, we had brought enough food down from Mone Brangsa to enable us to carry out our projects across the Shaksgam river, in the Aghil range. We had not allowed more than three weeks' supplies, firstly, because we could not carry more without the tedious business of relaying, and secondly, because 10 July was the latest date on which we could be reasonably certain of being able to cross back over the Shaksgam before the summer floods, which are caused by the intensive melting of the glaciers. Even so, we would be running some risk of being cut off, and in order to save time, we had planned to take all seventeen Baltis up the Shaksgam as far as the foot of the Aghil pass, to avoid any relaying of loads.

While Spender and Auden were continuing their scientific work, Tilman and I spent a busy morning weighing and checking the food, and making detailed plans for our movements during the next three weeks. We had promised to give the men a day's rest, and the Baltis slept peacefully during the morning. But, in the afternoon, they announced with determination that they did not propose to accompany us any farther. We argued with them, pleaded and bribed, pointing out that we were only asking them to come on for another two days over flat, easy country, But nothing would shake their determination to go back straight away. So we paid them their money, and they departed that evening. We sent Angtharkay and Nukku to escort them for part of their journey. Only four Baltis remained with us; these were the four who had undertaken, from the beginning, to stay with us as long as we required them. They were: Mancho, tall and gaunt, with a huge beak-like nose; Mahamad Hussain, elderly and philosophical, an amazingly daring climber on rotten rock, known always to us as Buddha; and Mahadi and Hussain, inseparable friends, who had followed us from Parkutta, a village in the Indus valley. These men greatly increased our carrying strength, and they served us well, particularly in the valley below the snow line. While we were travelling over glaciers or crossing high passes, however, they became very depressed, and caused us a great deal of trouble.

The departure of the rest of the Baltis and the temporary absence of two of the Sherpas weakened our position considerably. We cut down the weight of our equipment loads still farther, and also left some of the survey instruments and all the money at our base. Even so, and with all the men carrying seventy or eighty pounds each, we could not move everything that was necessary. On 16 June, Tilman and Auden went to the junction, with the four Sherpas and the four Baltis, carrying as much as they could manage. Spender, Angtensing and I spent the day relaying to Suget Jangal all the loads that were left. The other four Sherpas returned there from the junction in the evening. Sen Tensing was very ill with a recurrence of his fever, and the next day we had to leave him behind in this delightful spot to recover, and to await the return of Angtharkay and Nukku. We left a small dump of food for him, and while the others were carrying the rest of the loads to the junction, Spender and I spent the day doing a series of high survey stations on the ridge above the entrance of the K2 nullah. It was fascinating work getting to know the features of the country and speculating how the individual pieces would fit into the whole intriguing puzzle which new country always presents. We crossed the mouth of the K2 nullah and marched to the junction in the late afternoon. We found Tilman in his tent, down with fever. He had been ill since the previous evening. Auden had taken the Baltis with a relay of loads seven miles up the Shaksgam. He had sent the men back, and was camping there alone, in order to have a clear day for his geological work. Near our camp, at the junction of the two rivers, there was a number of old huts and some oval-shaped rings which looked like graves. These puzzling relics of former habitation seemed to accentuate the isolation of the country.

The next morning Tilman's temperature was down, and though he felt very shaky, he was able to come with us. The Shaksgam valley was a weird place, shut in on both sides by gaunt limestone cliffs, slashed across with twisted streaks of yellow, red and black strata, which gave them the strange, bizarre appearance of a camouflaged ship. The bottom of the valley was composed of sand and gravel flats, often half a mile wide. Over these the river flowed; sometimes concentrated into one great body of water as it swirled round a bend in the valley; sometimes split up into a dozen streams which sprawled their independent courses across the flats, for ever changing their pattern. As long as it was possible to keep to the valley floor our progress was easy and quick. But every now and again the river hurled itself against the cliffs on our side of the valley, and forced us, either to attempt a fording, which would have been very difficult in most places, or to look for a route along the face of the crags. Spread out at long intervals along the valley we found curious clumps of tall vegetation which grew, for no apparent reason, out of the sand. The main river was turbid, but at each side of it clear streams flowed through a chain of deep green and blue pools, close under the crags. Steep glacier-filled corries split the sides of the valley, and we looked up them to a profusion of Dolomite spires.

Angtharkay and Nukku caught us up on the evening of the 18th. They had come all the way from the Sarpo Laggo glacier, and had brought with them Sen Tensing, who had now recovered

Beyond our camp of 18-19 June, the river flowed for a long way against the cliffs. A narrow ledge, a few feet above the water, helped us to overcome this obstacle, though in places its continuity was interrupted, and we had to negotiate some awkward steps. After this, for the next few miles, we were able to walk along the gravel flats.

Our problem now was how to find the valley which led to the Aghil pass. We had Younghusband's description of it to guide us, but as there were a great many narrow side valleys, all with much the same characteristics, it was not an easy task to choose the right one. The only important tributary coming down from the Aghil range was wide and open, and we could see up it for many miles. It seemed to be the obvious valley to choose as an approach to the interior of the range, and Desio had shown it on his map as descending from the Aghil pass, but it did not resemble in any way the one described by Younghusband. The difficulties of the cliffs on the southern side of the main valley prevented us from climbing high enough to get a view that was of any use to us.

Farther up, the valley became more open, and the river, spread over the whole of its width, offered a good fording-place. Angtensing and I led the way across the stream, holding on to each other for mutual support. We very nearly came to grief. Angtensing was swept off his feet, and I had great difficulty in holding him up until he had recovered enough to struggle ashore. He and his load of survey instruments escaped with nothing more serious than a wetting. After this we humbly followed the lead of the Baltis, who knew far more about this hazardous business than any of us, and faced the torrents with surprising nonchalance. But the experience was quite unpleasant enough to serve as a warning to us to keep a very close watch on the increase of the rivers of the Aghil range, and not to prolong our stay on the northern side of the Shaksgam until it became quite unfordable.

A remarkable feature of the country through which we were travelling was the ancient river terraces that lined the sides of the valleys. These terraces were roughly level on top and cut vertically at their outer edges as if by a sharp knife. Sometimes the cliff so formed was only twenty feet high, sometimes it stood as much as 1,000 feet above the present level of the river. In some places the terraces were no more than inconspicuous fringes clinging to the sides of a valley; in others they covered almost its entire floor, leaving only a narrow canyon for the river. They were composed of a mass of boulders and pebbles in a matrix of sand, and, being uncemented, were very friable – a structure known to geologists as conglomerate, it is difficult to visualise the conditions in which these deposits were laid down, and to understand the extraordinary changes that must have taken place to produce the present phenomenon. A rejuvenation of the whole mountain mass seems to be the only way to account for the rivers having suddenly cut into the wide beds of gravel which they have built for themselves.

The river terraces and their conglomerate cliffs play a most important part in travel through this country. The cliffs are absolutely perpendicular, and it is impossible to climb them if they are high. It is possible to go for many miles along a valley without finding a place where one can climb out. Similarly, though a terrace will make an excellent highway, comfortably remote from interference from the river, it is often difficult to descend from it. Often, too, terraces are slashed across by ravines, cut by side streams to such a depth that they are quite impassable. When an unfordable river runs through a narrow canyon of high conglomerate cliffs it is generally an insuperable obstacle. Although the tops of these terraces occasionally provide a path, their cliffs confront the traveller with difficulties second only to the problem of crossing the swift, quickly-flooding rivers.

Soon after we had crossed the Shaksgam to its northern side, we were stopped by the river running against a conglomerate cliff, 300 feet high. In order to avoid recrossing the river we climbed a steep gully. We had a good deal of difficulty, and it took us nearly two hours to get the party on to the terrace. We soon regretted this move, for the terrace was cut by a number of ravines, and progress was slow. We could not get down to the valley floor again, and when at last we reached the valley, which we had chosen to ascend in our search for the Aghil pass, we found ourselves stopped by a chasm cut by the very stream that we wanted to reach. Tilman and I tried to get round the end of the cut-off by climbing along the cliffs above the terrace. We got on to an old glacial till, in which we chipped steps, but became involved in horrible difficulties, and had to give up our attempt. We then joined the Sherpas, who were engaged in trying an even more desperate-looking manoeuvre. Eventually we succeeded in lowering our loads into the ravine and climbing down ourselves, on rounded boulders jutting out of the face of the cliff. Several great chunks of the wall fell away as we were doing this and crashed with an alarming roar. We climbed up the bottom of the ravine for a few hundred yards, and emerged on to a terrace at the mouth of our valley. Here we pitched camp. All this trouble had been caused by our choosing the wrong place to cross the Shaksgam.

Near the camp we found some more remains of stone buildings, which gave us a comforting clue that we were still on the ancient route, and that we had been lucky in our somewhat blind choice of the valley. Even with this evidence we were far from sure of the way to the pass, and debated whether we should send parties to reconnoitre some of the other valleys as well. But as we had such a very short time at our disposal for our various jobs, we decided to put all our eggs into one basket and rely on our first choice being the right one. Our plan was to find the pass and, using it as a central dump and meeting-place, to disperse the party in various directions with all the food that was available. The view from our camp was very fine. We were on the northern side of a sweeping curve of the Shaksgam river. To the south-west we looked down the desolate gorge up which we had come. To the south-south-east, upstream, we could see twenty miles of the river's course, interrupted here and there by the mighty, pinnacled glaciers coming down from the Teram Kangri and Gasherbrum ranges. Farther to the east was a range of magnificent peaks, which, we supposed, lay between us and Mason's Zug Shaksgam. Opposite us, to the south, towering Dolomite peaks formed a barrier to the unexplored northern glaciers of K2.

We started on the morning of 20 June in a great state of excitement. So much depended on whether we would find the pass at the head of the inconspicuous valley on which we were pinning our faith. We had left dumps of food along our route for the return journey, so we were no longer so heavily laden. We passed through a narrow defile into an open rocky basin. Beyond, the valley divided; the eastern section seemed to be surrounded by great granite precipices; the western branch, descending from the north, held out promise of better things and we started up it, encouraged by the discovery of more traces of human occupation; we even found a nail. The going was very easy, and, a great deal sooner than we expected, we stepped on to the crest of the divide. It was, unquestionably, the Aghil pass. To the north the ground fell away in a gentle slope to a placid tarn. Beyond, across a deep valley, was a range of gently rounded, snow-capped peaks, so typical of the mountains of Central Asia. This was the valley of the Surukwat river, by which Younghusband had approached the pass, and the peaks were those of the northern part of the Aghil range. West of us were the limestone peaks of the Shaksgam, standing like sentinels above this remarkable pass. A keen wind blew from the north, driving sleet into our faces, and snow was falling on the neighbouring peaks. It was too cold to sit for long on the pass, but neither the wind nor the bleakness of the scene could spoil our first experience of the view which Young husband had seen with the same excitement fifty years before.

10 Finding the Zug Shaksgam River

We camped above the lake and took stock of our food supplies. We found that we had enough to last us for fifteen days. As we had left dumps for the return journey to the Sarpo Laggo, all the supplies that we had with us could be used in the Aghil range. It was decided that Spender should work in the vicinity of the pass. Having fixed its position in latitude, and in relation to K2, he was to make a detailed survey of as wide an area as possible. He was allotted four Sherpas and one Balti to help him with his work. Auden, with Lhakpa Tensing and Mahadi, was to traverse the range to the Yarkand river, continuing his geological studies. Afterwards he was to explore towards the west and attempt to force a new route across the range to the Shaksgam. Tilman and I were to work over to the east to try and find the Zug Shaksgam river.

We were surprised to find that the ground was littered with a great quantity of yak dung. Evidently the pastures round our camp were used extensively as grazing grounds, presumably by the people living on the banks of the Yarkand river. Yak dung makes excellent fuel and it was a great relief to find it, for there was no wood of any sort in the vicinity, and, although we had brought with us a certain amount of paraffin, the problem of fuel had been worrying us.

That evening, Angtharkay and I walked down the valley in search of game. The gentle grass slopes above the lake were covered with mauve primulas, a lovely splash of colour in the evening light. At first we could see no sign of life. I was searching the valley through binoculars when suddenly Angtharkay clutched my arm excitedly and pointed to an apparently barren hillside. I could see nothing but boulders. Then it seemed to me that the whole hillside was moving slowly upwards, and I realised that I was looking at an enormous herd of bharal. We went on down the valley until we were out of sight and then climbed up and made a big detour, using what cover we could find. The stalk was very successful and we got close to the herd, but in the fading light I missed every shot and we returned empty-handed to camp, after dark.

The weather had improved and the next morning was fine. The Aghil pass had a quite different appearance in the warm sunlight which danced on the rippled surface of the lake. We said goodbye to Auden, who was leaving us for twelve days, and he went off down the valley with his two men. Spender was busy with the preparations for his survey. Tilman and I had decided to climb a peak to the east of the pass in the hope of seeing into the country towards the

Zug Shaksgam river to get a better idea of our problem. The peak looked so easy that we stupidly decided not to take a rope. For the first 3,000 feet we climbed at a steady pace, first over boulders, then over easy rock, and then kicking steps in the firm snow. Gradually the ground became more complicated, and soon we were climbing along a sharp arête of really awkward rock. An enormous load of winter snow, which had not yet melted and so had created the illusion of simplicity from below, made climbing exceedingly difficult. Each hold had first to be cleared of snow before it could be used, and we had to chip the ice out of the vertical cracks before it was possible to wedge arms and legs securely. Our fingers became numbed by continual contact with the snow, so that when a hold had been made it was difficult to grip it. We climbed close together, one man supporting the other with his ice axe while the snow was flogged away from the rock. As the pitches succeeded one another with increasing difficulty, we cursed our folly at not having brought a rope. As usual in such circumstances, we overcame several obstacles before we realised what was happening, and our subsequent reluctance to turn back was due more to a dislike of going over this dangerous ground again than to a desire to reach the top. After an exciting climb, we emerged on to a plateau covered with soft snow, in which we sank up to our hips. It took us another two hours of hard work to climb to a snow dome which was the summit of the mountain. There was a violent wind blowing, and on the way up Tilman had lost his hat, which floated down to one of the glaciers to the east. It was 4.30 when we reached the top. We estimated its altitude to be about 20,200 feet.

The view was magnificent, but we had not time to contemplate it, and the wind had robbed us of the inclination to do so. Earlier in the day, while we were on the easy lower slopes, we had watched the great peaks of the Karakoram mount above their lower satellites as we climbed, and had marvelled at the beautiful symmetry of K2 soaring above the rest. Now our view was too vast to comprehend, in the uncomfortable ten minutes that we spent on the summit. I tried to memorise the form of the country to the east, which we had come to see, but it was far too complicated, and I could not disentangle its intricacies. All we could gather was that a wide system of glaciers flowed towards the east into a deep river basin, and that a high ridge of peaks separated it from the valley of the Surukwat. We took a complete round of photographs and started to descend. We followed a snow gully down from the summit. It became very steep and icy lower down, but was a good deal easier than the rock ridge that we had been on earlier in the day. We finished the descent with some swift glissades which brought us back to camp before dark.

Spender left the camp soon after five the next morning to do a high survey station above the pass. Tilman and I lazed in bed until the sun reached the valley and warmed the tent. After our reconnaissance of the day before we had decided to follow down the Surukwat river to the north, to go up the first big side valley coming from the east, and to look for a pass at its head to the glacier system that we had seen. We hoped that in this way we would be able to reach the Zug Shaksgam river.

Tilman, Angtharkay, Lobsang, Mancho, Buddha and I started at nine o'clock. We took with us a light photo-theodolite, the rifle and enough food to last us for twelve days. We marched rapidly over the grassy meadows below the lake. Three miles down we came to a recently used shepherd's encampment, consisting of three strongly built pens and a curious erection of long willow poles. We found a well-constructed fireplace and a complicated wooden implement, the use of which we could not understand. It was a pity that the place was not occupied, for if it had been we should have learnt something about the present inhabitants of the range. We were most anxious, too, to find out if any of the ancient routes across the ranges were known to the people of the Yarkand at the present day, and if so, what possible significance they could have.

The Sherpas were very excited at our discovery, and evidently felt themselves to be approaching the luxury of a civilised metropolis. They said that, even if we did not find a village a few miles farther down, this place was sure to be occupied when we returned. I am afraid that they were destined to be disappointed. I do not know when these mountain pastures are used, but from what we learned later in Shimshal, I suspect that it is during some months of the winter. The Baltis were not enthusiastic at the idea of meeting anyone. They said that the people on this side of the range were a race of giants and were not friendly towards intruders. This was probably a legend from the days of banditry in these parts.

Two miles farther on, we came to the junction of three streams which formed the Surukwat river. The other two came from the mountains to the west, which made a barrier of vertical precipices in that direction. We lunched by a spring, resting on a green bed of chives, which made a savoury addition to our bread and cheese. Below this point, the valley became dreary and unattractive. The river ran steeply down through a narrow canyon and we were forced to climb high up on the side of the valley. Rounding a corner, we looked down on a series of immense river terraces through which the stream had cut a gorge 300 feet deep. It was easy walking along the flat top of one of these terraces and we soon came to the first big tributary valley on the east. We were fortunate enough to find a narrow gully by which we could climb down from the terrace, and we camped by a clump of wild rose bushes at the foot of the side valley. We found some rhubarb growing there, so we called the valley Kharkul Lungpa (Balti for Rhubarb Valley). The rhubarb stewed was excellent, but it required more than our ration of sugar to make it sweet.

By timing ourselves over each section of the march and taking a compass reading whenever we changed direction, we were able to plot, with reasonable precision, our position relative to the Aghil pass.

The weather was set fine and we did not bother to pitch tents. My night, which started with that delicious sensation of dozing in the moonlight, was disturbed by lice. We had found some of these creatures in our clothes a few days before, and though we adopted drastic measures to get rid of them, alternately boiling and freezing our shirts, we could not check the increase of their numbers. It is the first time that I have ever been troubled with lice in the Himalaya. Presumably we caught them from the Baltis, though they never seemed to be bothered by them. But I found that one soon became almost immune to their irritation; weeks later I used to take as many as a hundred at a time out of my shirt without having been worried unduly. In the end, garments were de-loused simply as a means of passing the time during bad weather!

We started up the Kharkul Lungpa at eight o'clock next morning. It took us in a direction about ten degrees south of east. We halted at the end of each hour for a short rest. At about half-past ten, Tilman went down with yet another bout of fever. It seems probable from the symptoms that these recurrent attacks were caused by an infection of malaria which he may have picked up during our march up the Indus valley. After some discussion, it was decided that I should leave him behind with one of the Baltis, provided with a tent and food enough for four days and the rifle, while I went on with the rest of the party to explore the head of the valley.

Farther up I found that the valley divided into two branches, one containing a fair-sized glacier coming down from some high peaks on the right, and a narrow nullah filled with shale on the left. It was difficult to know which to choose, as one seemed to lead too far to the south of our general line, and the other too far to the north. I chose the left hand, or northern branch, as it appeared to be the easier of the two. We toiled for many hours up slate scree, with our heavy loads and reached a col, about 18,000 feet high, at the head of the nullah. I was disappointed to find that it led into another big tributary of the Surukwat. It was possible to descend into this valley, at the head of which there seemed to be another col which would take us farther to the east; but I decided to go back and try my luck with the southern branch of the Kharkul Lungpa. I set up the theodolite, and took a round of photographs and angles of all the conspicuous points I could see. In this way, when Spender had fixed some of the points which I observed to the west, the position of my station could also be plotted, and the country drawn in from the photographs. I got a fine view northwards across the Yarkand river to the mountains of the Kuen Lun range in Sinkiang. We ran down the shale nullah at a tremendous speed, and reached the main Kharkul Lungpa at about half-past eight. It had been a disappointing day, but a very interesting one. The country was exceedingly complicated and I realised the truth of what Mason had told me: that the Aghil range followed none of the normal rules of mountain topography.

I sent Mancho down with a note to Tilman next morning, and Angtharkay and I started very early to reconnoitre the southern branch of the valley. We climbed on to the glacier, which proved to be a great deal longer than we had expected. Higher up the snow was soft and progress was slow and laborious. The glacier had its origin in a complicated mass of peaks to the south. At its head there was a col leading over to the south-west, while to the east, in the direction we had planned to take, there was a steep and broken icefall. The prospects looked so unpromising that I nearly gave it up, but I thought that I might as well climb to a high point to get a clearer idea of the country. A rock rib, covered in deep powder snow, led us up by the side of the icefall, and at one o'clock we reached the crest of a ridge about 19,000 feet high. On the other side I was delighted to see a glacier flowing gently down towards the east. It was tantalising to have to wait for another day before we could cross this exciting pass, and to be obliged to toil all the way up to it again. But it was a great relief to have found it, and I returned to camp thoroughly pleased with the day's work.

When we got back we found that Tilman had arrived. His fever had not lasted twenty-four hours, and it proved to be the last attack of the series.

Angtharkay and I had eaten nothing since our breakfast tea and tsampa, so we were ravenously hungry, and spent the rest of the evening eating, and drinking mug after mug of tea.

We were away by seven o'clock on 25 June. The Baltis went extra-ordinarily well considering how much they disliked the idea of crossing a high glacier pass. When we got on to the snow, it transpired that they had left their snow-glasses behind at the dump in the Sarpo Laggo valley. I made substitutes with little discs of cardboard with a tiny slit in each. They could not see much, and later suffered a certain amount of eye-strain, but it prevented them from getting snow-blindness. Our tracks of the previous day made things a great deal easier than they had been before. Also the sky was overcast during the morning and we did not suffer much from the oppressive lassitude which is so great a trial on Himalayan glaciers. Tilman was, of course, still feeling weak, but this hardly seemed to affect his pace.

We reached the pass at 1.15 and sent the porters on down the glacier to the east, while Tilman and I did a survey station on a rocky point above the pass. The weather had cleared and we got a good round of angles and photographs. We also had time to study the country to the east. We gave temporary names to some of the peaks and made sketches of them to help us to identify them later. The whole job took about two hours and when it was finished we packed up the instruments and followed in the tracks of the porters. We ran easily down the smooth surface of the glacier for two miles, when broken ice forced us to climb on to steep rocks on the left bank. Farther on, after we had overtaken the porters, we climbed on to the glacier again and worked our way over the ice, until we reached a place where the glacier plunged down in a precipitous icefall for a thousand feet. To the left of this we found a scree-filled gully, which we ran down in a few minutes to a wide, grassy trough, or ablation valley, formed between the high lateral moraine of the glacier and the flanks of the main valley. We were following a large ice-stream which would have been regarded as a major glacier in the Eastern or Central Himalaya, though of course it did not compare with the main glaciers of the Karakoram range. It was joined by several big tributaries from the south. We had not expected to find such extensive glaciation in the Aghil range.

The trough offered us easy walking and we followed it at a good pace until darkness forced us to camp. Some dried moss growing on the rocks provided us with scanty fuel, but we supplemented it with our Primus, and used some of our precious store of paraffin to cook our meal of tea and pemmican and tsampa. We estimated our height to be about 16,000 feet.

The ablation valley was a godsend, and on 26 June we hurried swiftly down it, past some very complicated sections of the glacier, where forests of ice pinnacles would have delayed us for many hours.

When we reached the end of the glacier our difficulties began. The river entered a narrow conglomerate gorge, and ran from one side of it to the other with such merciless frequency that we were never able to follow one bank for more than a few hundred yards at a time. Fortunately, as it was still fairly early in the day, the river was not flooded, and though crossing it was an unpleasant business it was not really dangerous. By wading through the stream from side to side, we were able to keep to the floor of the gorge. This was fortunate as I do not think that it would have been possible to climb along its precipitous sides. I had a severe headache all day, due, no doubt, to a touch of sunstroke.

As we were most anxious to reach the end of the valley that day, we could not afford to stop for a rest, because the afternoon floods might at any moment prevent us from continuing. We had seen from the glacier that the gorge joined a big valley running roughly from south-east to north-west. It took far longer than we had expected to reach this valley, and when we were still a mile away from it we realised that the river had become too dangerous to ford again. But by then our gorge had widened slightly and we were able, with a good deal of difficulty, to climb for another half-mile, high up along its right flank. Then we dropped down to the river again, and camped in a little jungle of birch and wild roses. It was wonderful to have ample fuel again and we brewed many pints of tea. The late afternoon sun beat down on us, and the heat in the narrow airless gorge was terrific. The sand on the shore of the river was so scorched that we could not sit on it with comfort. I spread a sleeping bag over some rose bushes, crept under it for shade, took a large dose of aspirin, and slept.

Tilman went on down the valley to reconnoitre, and, by the time I woke, he had returned. He had reached the big valley after some difficult rock climbing.

He found that it contained a large river, fully as big as the Shaksgam. This was good news, for it seemed likely that this really was the Zug Shaksgam, for which we were searching. To his surprise, on a well-wooded spit of land at the junction of the two rivers, he had found a collection of stone huts. There was no possibility of grazing in the vicinity and the huts must have marked a regular halting-place on some route. But where the route could lead and from whence it came we could not imagine. It was an intriguing problem that we wished we had enough time to solve. A thorough investigation of the question would be an interesting piece of work, but it would take many months to accomplish.

Early next morning, we went down to the junction. The stream in our gorge was quite low, but in spite of that we were forced to do an unpleasant piece of rock climbing to get down. We cooked breakfast at the huts and discussed our next move. Below the junction, the river entered a gorge which looked quite impassable, but the huts suggested that a route through it must exist. We assumed from the direction in which it was flowing that the river, whatever it was, must flow either into the Surukwat or direct into the Yarkand. We decided to try and follow it down and to make our way back to the Aghil pass from its junction with either of these rivers. But we had enough food to last us for seven more days and we were anxious to prove whether this river really was Mason's Zug Shaksgam; so we decided to spend two days exploring upstream in the hope of reaching a point from which we could see into Mason's country. We sent Angtharkay and Mancho to look for a route through the gorge while the rest of us started upstream. Each party took food enough for one night and we agreed to return to the huts on the following evening. We dumped all our spare food and equipment there; as we did not require tents or stores or warm clothing we had very little to carry and were able to travel at a great speed.

We fancied that we had found a track leading up the valley from the dump, but it did not take us far, and before long we were obliged to do a very hazardous climb up a conglomerate cliff. I thought the risk was quite unjustifiable at the time, for I could see nothing to prevent the whole face of the cliff tumbling down on top of us. It seemed that if one stone were dislodged the whole structure must collapse. Buddha was a tower of strength; he led up these places with absolute confidence, climbing like a young chamois, and pulling us up after him. It occurred to me afterwards that his serenity was in reality his Mohammedan fatalism. If one relied completely on divine providence to hold the rocks in place, the climbing was not unduly difficult! And Buddha was in all things a philosopher. However, I am glad that I did not analyse his daring at the time or I should have been even more frightened on those conglomerate cliffs than I actually was during the climb. After we had reached the top in safety, we walked for two miles along a river terrace and came to an oasis watered by a spring. At first it looked like a village of fertile orchards and fields, but when we reached it we found that the vegetation, though varied and very dense, was wild, and there was no sign of former cultivation. There was, however, a number of old stone huts with skilfully built, dome-shaped roofs. It was obvious that with a little irrigation these river terraces could be made fertile; but we could not see any trace of an attempt to do this, and the purpose of the huts remains a mystery.

A short way beyond this place, we came to another large tributary coming from the west. We supposed that it drained the glacier system that we had looked down upon from the peak above the Aghil pass on 21 June. From the size of the stream it looked as if these glaciers were even larger than those which we had recently descended. It was still early and we crossed without difficulty. Several more ravines cutting across the terrace by side streams caused us some trouble. After that, the valley opened out surprisingly, its sheer sides became gentle slopes and the terraces diminished to a manageable size. By evening, we had come a long way, and the character of the country suggested that we were approaching the most westerly point reached by Mason in 1926. We camped by a spring of clear water which rippled away in a tiny stream, edged with emerald banks of grass and chives, patterned with flowers. For wood we found an ample supply of the same aromatic plant that we had found in the Sarpo Laggo. After a supper of pemmican and boiled chives, we settled down on a comfortable bed of sand, and watched the approach of night transform the wild desert mountains into phantoms of soft unreality. How satisfying it was to be travelling with such simplicity. I lay watching the constellations swing across the sky. Did I sleep that night – or was I caught up for a moment into the ceaseless rhythm of space?

11 In Unexplored Zug Shaksgam

Tilman roused us at 2.45 a.m. for we had a long day before us. We breakfasted off salted tea and bread which Buddha had baked for us on the previous evening. We started marching up the valley again, with Lobsang carrying the survey equipment. Buddha was left behind to resume his interrupted sleep. A waning moon floated in the cloudless sky and lit our way across rough ground, scored by countless stream furrows. We were making for a high spur which stood above the inside of a sweeping bend in the valley. As soon as we started climbing, we became involved in a maze of steep, conglomerate gullies, a strange and lovely setting for that enchanting moment when moonlight merges into early dawn.

With the full light of day, we stood high above another big tributary flowing south-west from a group of tapering ice peaks. These resembled the peaks that we had seen from the southern side of the Aghil pass, and were probably in the same group. We were strongly tempted to change our plans and to explore this valley for a pass which would take us back into the Shaksgam. But the solution of the problem of the Zug Shaksgam was more important. We had to descend a long way to cross the side valley and to climb up the other side to the spur we were making for. We reached its summit at half-past six. The view from the top proved quite definitely that we were in the valley of the Zug Shaksgam. We were only five miles below Mason's farthest camp in this direction, and the features on the limits of his map were easily recognisable. We set up the theodolite and took a round of angles and photographs. Then, sending Lobsang straight back with the survey load, Tilman and I ran down about 3,000 feet to the river. We walked two miles farther up the valley to get a clearer view of its upper reaches, where it flows due north. The river itself at this point flowed over a broad bed. It was split up into many streams and might have been fordable.

We did not get back to camp until noon. Our little spring had dried up during the morning, which was disappointing as we had been looking forward to a long drink of its clear water. We ate the last of the food, which consisted of one round of bread each, and then started off down the valley. We went as hard as we could, for we were all anxious to reach the dump that night and did not like the prospect of spending a hungry night. Having been over the ground before made a great deal of difference, as we knew just where to find a way across the difficult ravines. We might easily have arrived at the dump before dark, but at four-thirty, when we reached the big tributary that we had crossed the day before, we found that the river was so swollen that there was not the slightest chance of crossing it. We had rather expected this disaster, but we did not meet it quite so philosophically as Buddha, who simply curled up on the bank and went to sleep. The situation seemed to appeal to a perverted Sherpa sense of humour, for Lobsang made a lump of mud to look like a loaf of Balti bread and solemnly handed it to me. There was no difficulty in getting the party away early next morning, and crossing the river with ease, we reached the dump by half-past seven. We ate last night's dinner and this morning's breakfast in one, and had started on lunch before our hunger was satisfied.

Angtharkay and Mancho had returned from their reconnaissance. They reported that the gorge was quite impossible from the very start. They seemed to have had a hair-raising time trying line after line before they gave it up. Certainly that report corresponded with what we had seen of the gorge from above and we should probably never have thought of attempting to find a way through it had it not been for the huts. Angtharkay and Mancho had climbed a very long way up the side of the valley and Angtharkay said that he thought it would be possible to get over into another valley which might take us back into the Zug Shaksgam below the gorge. Mancho, however, did not think much of the idea, and strongly advised us to recross the pass by which we had come while there was food enough to do so. We decided to pin our faith on Angtharkay's judgment. We packed up the loads, and at eleven o'clock, guided by Angtharkay, started climbing the precipitous side of the nullah. It was very hard work, as our loads were still fairly heavy. We climbed about 4,000 feet on to a sharp ridge which commanded a superb view of the Zug Shaksgam valley. Here we halted long enough to do a survey station, and then traversed across to another ridge, from which we looked down a steep nullah into the side valley that Angtharkay had mentioned. We slid down the nullah on frozen scree until we came to a trickle of water. There we camped on little platforms dug out of the slope. I was very tired and fell asleep at once.

The next morning Tilman, Angtharkay and I climbed a rocky peak to the north, while the others went on down the nullah, with instructions to wait for us when they reached the valley below. There was a thick haze over everything and we had to wait for a long time for it to clear sufficiently before we could observe to the more distant points or take any photographs. We did not finish the work until eleven. Then, in order to save time, we started climbing down a steep gully to the north, which descended directly to the valley that we hoped to reach. At first it was easy, but lower down we became involved in very delicate work on rotten rock before we reached the valley nearly 5,000 feet below. The theodolite nearly came to grief. It was dropped ten feet on to a ledge while the load of survey equipment was being lowered over a difficult place. Tilman, who was not very fond of the theodolite, and was standing where it landed, showed great self-restraint in not encouraging it to fall the rest of the way.

When we reached the valley we walked up it for half a mile and found the other three waiting for us in a grove of bushes at the foot of their nullah. At half past three, after a meal, we started down towards the Zug Shaksgam. Soon we came to a place where an overhanging wall of rock forced us to cross to the other side. Although the stream was muddy and swollen, it did not appear to be a serious obstacle. But we under-estimated both its volume and the angle at which it was flowing. Tilman started across and very soon got into difficulties. When he had nearly reached the far side he was swept off his feet, and was carried, load and all, about ten yards down before he could haul himself on to the bank. His leg was bleeding freely and he had lost his ice axe. But in spite of this I did not take the river very seriously and thought that with reasonable precautions it was perfectly safe. I threw a rope across to Tilman, and together we held it taut across the torrent. Lobsang and Angtharkay waded out into the stream, hanging on to the rope. In a moment Angtharkay was knocked over. Lobsang made a desperate effort to hold on to him, but Angtharkay was wrenched from his grasp by the force of water, and was carried down, battered against the rocks in midstream as he went. Twice he managed to stop himself, but was dragged on by the pressure of water on his sodden load. We could do nothing, for if we had let go of the rope, Lobsang, who was hanging on to it for all he was worth, would have been swept away too. It was horrible to stand there watching Angtharkay being pounded to death without being able to do anything to help him. Each time he was flung against a rock I thought he would be stunned, and every moment I expected to see his head disappear for the last time. He was approaching a steeper drop in the river bed, when, by an amazing chance, he was caught up on a large rock sticking out of the water. Lobsang had got across to the other side by now, and I was able to run down the bank and help the Baltis to get hold of Angtharkay and haul him ashore. His load was so heavy from the weight of the water in it that it took two of us to lift it on to the bank. Happily Angtharkay was not seriously hurt. His body was very bruised and he was completely exhausted. It was some time before he could move, but when we had taken off all his clothes and wrapped him in a sleeping bag by a fire, he soon recovered. I was acutely aware that my own stupidity had very nearly caused his death.

Of course we made no attempt to join Tilman and Lobsang, nor to get them back to our side of the stream. We corresponded by throwing notes, packed in a snow-glass case, across to each other, for we could not make ourselves heard above the roar of the torrent. Having exchanged cooking utensils and food by hauling them over the river on the rope, each party settled down for the night. After all the fine weather we had been having, we did not think of sending tents across to the others. Nor did we pitch them ourselves, and went to sleep, as usual, in the open. At about ten o'clock it started to rain heavily. With a good deal of trouble we managed to erect a tent in the dark, though it was impossible to get one across to the others. I spent a sleepless night wondering if, in this bad weather, the river would subside sufficiently for us to get across. The rain soon turned to snow, which was still falling when the dawn broke.

As soon as it was light enough to see, we started packing up our stuff. In the excitement of the previous evening we had left everything strewn round our makeshift camp. Now it was all buried in snow and we had great difficulty in collecting our possessions. My boots were on the wrong side of the river, as I had thrown them across before our troubles had begun. It was very painful walking about in the snow in bare feet. To my great relief the river was no longer dangerous. The raging torrent of muddy water had subsided into a clear stream, so shallow that the water hardly reached our knees. Tilman and Lobsang had spent a miserable night, without a tent, in the snow; they were wet through. We found Angtharkay's ice axe stuck in a crevice in the river bed, but we did not recover Tilman's axe, though we searched for a long time.

While we were sorting ourselves out and re-distributing the loads, we heard a series of sharp reports among the crags above, followed by an ominous whirring sound. A cannonade of boulders, that had been loosened from the cliffs, crashed into the valley a short way below the place where Tilman had been sleeping. This was a prelude to a continuous bombardment all the way down the valley. I have never before seen such a number of rock-falls. We had continually to be on the look-out, ready to take cover when we saw them coming, for, owing to the noise of the stream in the narrow gorge, we could not always hear them. Both sides of the valley were extremely steep, and we had to cross the river repeatedly from side to side. But it was now so small that it caused us no trouble. It was hard to realise that it was this same stream which had nearly caused a tragic disaster on the previous day.

We reached the Zug Shaksgam at about nine o'clock, after we had been going for two and a half hours. We lit three enormous fires in a clump of birch trees near the junction to dry our waterlogged kit and to cook our breakfast. While this was being done, Tilman and I went on to reconnoitre the ground. We found that we had rejoined the Zug Shaksgam valley just below the point where the river emerged from a narrow gorge; probably the same one that Angtharkay had reconnoitred on 27 June. From here it flowed over wide sand flats and was split up into a number of streams. But the cliffs on either side were very steep, and, as the river ran from side to side of the valley, it was not likely that we would have an easy journey down it. We went up to the mouth of the gorge. It was a most impressive chasm, with precipices of clear-cut rock rising perpendicularly from the floor of the valley for thousands of feet. When we returned to the porters we found a splendid breakfast of tea, cheese and hot bread ready for us. Our kit, too, was dry, and after we had fed and smoked a pipe we started down the valley feeling greatly refreshed.

All went well for about a mile. Then, as we had expected, the river flowed up against the cliffs on our side of the valley for about a hundred yards. The Baltis were determined to get round the obstacle, and performed some appallingly hazardous feats of climbing on the conglomerate cliffs overhanging the river. We did not follow them, and they soon abandoned what was obviously a completely futile attempt. Re-tracing our steps for a few hundred yards, we started up a steep gully of congealed mud. We climbed fast for four hours without a halt, chipping steps in the mud and soft rock as we went; it was very steep and smooth and it would have been difficult to check a serious slip.

When we had climbed about 4,000 feet the slope eased off and we crossed to a sharp ridge which bounded the gully on our right. From there we started a gradually descending traverse over steep slopes of scree. This took us for several miles at a fine speed and landed us on a wide river terrace which stood high above the river. By this manoeuvre we had rounded a big bend in the Zug Shaksgam valley which was now running due west, and we were delighted to see that it joined a valley six miles away which was obviously the Surukwat. But our difficulties were by no means over. The terrace that we were on was cleft by a ravine fully 500 feet deep. There was no chance of climbing down to the floor of the main valley to avoid it. When we had succeeded in getting across this obstacle we were confronted with more steep mud slopes in which we had occasionally to cut steps. Tilman had damaged his heel in his struggle with the river the day before, and found this traversing painful, particularly as he had no ice axe to assist his balance.

Two more difficult ravines were crossed before we reached a continuation of the terrace along which we could walk freely. It was already six o'clock and we began to think about camping. But since leaving the river that morning we had found no water. We hunted for a way down from the terrace, but everywhere conglomerate cliffs, hundreds of feet high, prevented us from descending to the floor of the valley, and we were forced to continue along this high-level route. A storm was brewing down the valley, and a violent, gusty wind swept against us. We came to another deep rift into which we descended, laboriously hewing steps in the soft, crumbling rocks, while the wind did its best to tear us from the cliffs. More perpendicular conglomerates faced us on the other side. But we were dealing with these villainous-looking cliffs with more confidence now. This was due probably to the reckless energy that so often comes to a party at the end of a long and exhausting day. But whatever the origin of this spurt, we were for once climbing with more dash than the Baltis, and even old Buddha was glad of a pull on the rope.

On reaching the terrace once more, we had a discussion as to whether to go on or to resign ourselves to a waterless, and consequently foodless, night. Our strenuous efforts during the last nine hours had made us very parched and the prospect of a night without water was not attractive, but, on the other hand, it was already eight o'clock and would soon be getting dark. Most of us were in favour of stopping, but Angtharkay's indignation at the idea seemed to outweigh the fact that he was in the minority, and we went on. Several small ravines split the terrace that we were on, but none of these caused us much trouble. Angtharkay followed one of these gullies in the hope of finding a way down to the river, but it ended abruptly, high up on the wall of the terrace. We raced on over rough ground in the gathering dusk. Half an hour later, as the Baltis were some way behind, I tried another of these ravines. I left Tilman and Angtharkay with my load at the top, and plunged down into the gully on scree. The ravine narrowed until the walls met over my head. I passed through a dark tunnel into a cavern lit from above by a ghostly green light. Beyond this the passage was so narrow that it was quite difficult to squeeze through. The corridor seemed to go on for ever, and I thought I should never reach the end of it, but eventually I emerged on to the wide sand flats of the river. I ran back as fast as I could for it was becoming almost too dark to see. Soon I came to a place where the passage divided, and I could not remember which of the two branches I had come down. So I waited there and shouted. It was a long time before I heard any reply, and when it came the voice sounded far away but directly above my head. Tilman had walked along the top of the ravine and was shouting down to me. I could not make out what he said, nor whether he understood what I was trying to tell him. There was a long, perplexing silence before I heard the clink of ice axes coming down the ravine.

By the time we reached the sand flats it was quite dark. We felt our way along, spread out in order to find a pool of water. Frequently we stumbled over bits of driftwood, which we collected for fuel. Presently Angtharkay, who was on the extreme left of our line, found water immediately under the cliffs of the terrace. We closed in on him and pitched camp. The storm had spent its energy elsewhere, and we were left in peace to eat and drink and fall asleep beside a blazing fire.

Our task was now completed. We still had two days' food in hand, and all we had to do was to make our way up the Surukwat river to the Aghil pass. Half a mile beyond our camp there was an extensive jungle of tall bushes and grassy meadows which stretched as far as the junction of the Surukwat and the Zug Shaksgam. From there, only two miles to the north, we could see the place where these rivers joined the Yarkand. We marched up the Surukwat in drizzling rain, sometimes walking on the sand flats of the river, sometimes along low terraces. At frequent intervals we came upon traces of habitation. Some of these remains were on the very brink of conglomerate cliffs, and were occasionally cut in half by the edge. They could not originally have been built in such a position, and though the denudation of these terraces is comparatively rapid, the remains were certainly very old.

As a result of the last few days of strenuous activity, we were all feeling rather lethargic, now that the excitement of finding our way through difficult country was over. But we covered the ground quickly, as it was easy and straightforward. The river was an insignificant stream and could be crossed and recrossed at will. Farther up the valley we noticed a number of recent footprints in the sand, and were not surprised, when we reached the Kharkul Lungpa that evening, to find Spender's party encamped there. We had intended to spend the night there ourselves, but we had seen a herd of bharal on the hillside beyond, and in stalking the animals we had passed right under their camp without seeing it. We were creeping cautiously along when we were startled by a shout from behind, which sent the bharal galloping out of sight. Tilman and Angtharkay went on in pursuit, while the rest of us returned to Spender's camp.

The reunion was a great event; the Sherpas and Baltis enjoyed it as much as we did. It was exciting to hear the other party's news and to compare notes. Spender had made full use of the ten days of fine weather which had followed our arrival at the Aghil pass. He had accomplished an astonishing amount of work. Having completed the important task of fixing the geographical position of the pass, he had extended his survey to the north, and had mapped, in great detail, an area of about 250 square miles, as well as fixing the position of many of the more distant peaks of the range. Besides the value of his map, this survey made a splendid base on which to attach our rough theodolite survey and Auden's compass work. It was a great pity that we had so short a time to work in this enthralling range; but it had been a memorable fortnight of rare freedom and interest. We had all thoroughly enjoyed ourselves and were reluctant to abandon this country for the more cramped and complicated life of high glacier exploration.

It started to rain very heavily soon after we arrived. Tilman and Angtharkay returned, soaked to the skin, without having seen the bharal again. It rained hard all night, but the morning of 3 July was fine, and Spender did a high survey station before breakfast, while the others carried the loads on up the Surukwat to the shepherd's encampment that we had found three miles below the pass. Angtharkay and I set out in search of game. We had a long day's stalking, and managed to secure two bharal, to the delight of all, except the Baltis. When the others had arrived at the shepherd's huts, they had found a note from Auden, that had been sent up the day before from the Shaksgam valley, where he was engaged in some geological work. It was good to hear from him, though he did not tell us much of what he had been doing. He was very concerned about the state of the river which, he said, was covering almost the entire floor of the valley. This was most disturbing news.

I had promised to take one of the Baltis shooting in the morning, for they said that as long as an animal's throat was cut by one of them immediately it had been shot, they would be able to eat it without breaking their religious laws. Buddha and I set out soon after dawn. He was not much help, and, when eventually we spotted a herd, he got so excited that I had to hold on to him to prevent him from dashing up the hill after them. He became almost uncontrollable during the stalk, but, in spite of his antics, we succeeded in getting within reasonable distance of the herd without their seeing us. I missed my first shot; Buddha dashed wildly out in front of me, and I had to fire over his head. Eventually, I got three of the unfortunate creatures, and the Baltis were thoroughly satisfied. But all this extra meat, though it kept the men in good heart, and provided us with a welcome change, did not seem to make very much difference to the length of time that our rations lasted. When we got back to camp we found that Spender, who had been surveying on the opposite side of the valley, had watched our strange manoeuvres inverted close-up, through the telescope of his theodolite, and had been hopelessly mystified by our curious behaviour.

After breakfast, we packed up and started towards the pass. The porters were carrying enormous loads of meat. The Baltis halted repeatedly to make a fire of yak dung and to cook some tit-bit.

The grass banks above the lake were now covered with pink, blue and mauve flowers – sloping meadows of colour. I had become very attached to this place, and was most reluctant to leave. But one day I shall go back there, prepared for a long stay, to gain a real knowledge of the range.

From the pass, it was a pleasant run down to our last camp in the Shaksgam valley. On his way down, Spender found a camping-ground, where there was a dead horse. This was proof that the pass had been used recently, though for what possible reason we could not imagine. We were relieved to find that the Shaksgam river had sunk to its previous level. Presumably the recent cloudy weather had been a check on the melting of the great glaciers which flow into it, though it was clear that the subsidence was temporary, and that it would not be long before all the rivers would rise to their normal summer level. The Shaksgam would then become unfordable until the late autumn. At the camp we found a note from Auden, written in verse, telling us that his party had finished its supply of food and had taken advantage of the opportune fall of the river to return to Suget Jangal. The enjoyment of an unlimited supply of meat that evening was spoilt by the lack of salt. We had run short some days before, and our desire for it had become a craving. Having never been without salt before for any length of time, I had not realised what an extremely important item of diet it is. But now I could understand why countries had become depopulated because of the lack of it.

Spender climbed 3,000 feet up the side of the valley on the morning of 5 July, while we lay in bed discussing plans until he returned at 11.30. He had seen traces of camping grounds which suggested that there was an old route going up the Shaksgam valley. We wondered if this could possibly have any connection with the remains that we had found in the Zug Shaksgam, and seriously considered spending several days in looking for a pass which would connect the two rivers. But we decided that it would be tempting providence not to cross the Shaksgam while the river was low. This we did without much difficulty, and camped in a jungle on the other side.

On 6 July I was roused at 5.30 by a large plateful of fried liver thrust at me by Tilman. At that hour of the morning I found it rather repulsive.

We walked a long way up the Shaksgam valley that day for survey purposes. From opposite the place that Younghusband had called Durbin Jangal, we looked up a wide side valley to a snow saddle at its head. We fancied that this saddle might lead over into the last of the tributary valleys that we had crossed in the Zug Shaksgam. We had to ford the stream several times on our way up the valley. In the afternoon we climbed 1,500 feet up, but rainclouds prevented us from seeing much and a biting wind soon sent us down. The return to camp, that evening, was an unpleasant business. A surprisingly ferocious wind whirled sleet into our faces. We got thoroughly drenched in fording the rivers, and the wind intensified the painful numbness that accompanies these aquatic sports in glacier rivers.

The next morning we started down the Shaksgam. Spender surveyed as we went, and it took us two days to reach Suget Jangal in the Sarpo Laggo valley. There we found Auden, Lhakpa Tensing and Mahadi. Auden had been employing the fine intervals of the last few days in geological work in the neighbourhood, while the two porters had been up to Mone Brangsa to fetch more food. We were two days overdue, and Auden had been concerned about us. He and his men had just set out in search of us, when they saw us coming over the col between the Shaksgam and Sarpo Laggo valleys.

Suget Jangal was a perfect resting-place, for it had a quality of serene peace, rare in this country of stern severity. Some tall shrubs which grew beside the shallow blue pools were now covered with pink blossom. The song of small birds, the splash of a brook which welled from a crystal spring, the young hares running shyly across the meadows, all welcomed us, and we lay on glades of soft green grass, half hidden in shady caverns of willow branches.

When Auden had left us on the 21 June with Lhakpa and Mahadi, he had descended the Surukwat to a camp six miles above its confluence with the Yarkand river. He left Mahadi in charge of the tent and continued with Lhakpa towards the Yarkand river. After travelling four miles they found a much larger river, almost the size of the Shaksgam, joining the Surukwat from the east. It seemed clear that this would prove to be the Zug Shaksgam. The water was chocolate in colour, a fact which agreed with Mason's account of the higher reaches of the river. Mason had been reluctant to assume that the Zug Shaksgam joined the Yarkand river. The only possible place for such a confluence would have been together with the Surukwat near Bazar Dara. There was some evidence to show that this was unlikely. Wood's 1914 survey showed admittedly a river joining the Surukwat only three miles from the Yarkand river, but the height of its confluence with the Surukwat was given as 12,550 feet, and it was shown to fall very steeply from the mountains to the south. Spender has shown that this height was probably a misprint, since the rest of Wood's heights are only 300 feet too high, while this is 1,300 feet in error. Had Mason known that his river could fall to 11,270 feet before joining the Yarkand, and had he realised that the topography of the river joining the Surukwat was incorrect, he would probably have assumed, as the present expedition has shown to be the case, that this latter was the valley of the Zug Shaksgam. The difficulty of gradient in supposing that the Zug Shaksgam joined the Yarkand thus did not really exist.

Another two and a half miles brought Auden and Lhakpa to the flat gravel terrace of the Yarkand river, sticking out of which were small hill outcrops of slate. While eating lunch on one of these hills, Lhakpa noticed many figures appearing from the west. Knowing the fears of the Baltis about robbers, and impressed by Younghusband's accounts of his two journeys in Central Asia, both of them felt slightly apprehensive. The field-glasses resolved these figures into two men and a herd of yak. Lhakpa was sure that the men would be armed, and was in favour of moving quickly back to their camp. However, they walked towards the herd, which seemed to become smaller and smaller the closer it approached. Eventually two small Yarkandi boys and a flock of goats appeared over the brow of a gravel ridge. The boys were quite unconcerned until the camera was taken out of the rucksack, but were comforted by being given two boxes of matches. Lhakpa tried Nepali and Tibetan on them, but they gave no intelligible reply.

Auden and Lhakpa then returned to their camp, alarming Mahadi by telling him that a band of robbers was on its way up the Surukwat. They then went back to the junction of the east and west Surukwat rivers, which have a height of about 13,700 feet. It was here that Younghusband's guides were undecided in 1887 about the route up to the Aghil pass. Auden and Lhakpa climbed a rock peak 17,950 feet in height (peak 5,462 metres of Spender's survey) in order to see if there was any route over the Aghil, leading out from the west Surukwat. Only one col appeared to be easy, and they crossed this two days later, on 27 June, after first ascending a peak of 19,000 feet in order to obtain a round of compass bearings. The weather was perfect, and the view from this peak towards K2, twenty-six miles distant, was magnificent. The descent of the south-west side of the col turned out to be difficult, since the scree, which was at an average angle of about fifty degrees, was so cemented with ice that it proved very resistant to step-cutting, and necessitated delicate balancing with heavy loads. Mahadi had evidently profited during his two off-days by eating more than his share of the food, and for the remaining five days they had to live on short rations. After making a compass sketch map of the complicated glacier system at the foot of the col, they descended over the gravel flats of a wide and barren valley for ten miles down to its confluence with the Shaksgam. This valley, for which Auden suggests the name Skam Lungpa (Balti for barren valley) on account of its barren nature, proved to be that erroneously shown in the Italian map as leading up to the Aghil pass. They then ascended the Shaksgam to a point three miles south of Durbin Jangal, where, in two places, they discovered interesting fossils. The weather got worse on 30 June, and, by the time their food supply was exhausted on the morning of 3 July, the Shaksgam had again become fordable. They reached the dump-camp in the Sarpo Laggo on 4 July, crossing from the Shaksgam to the Sarpo Laggo by the 14,200 feet col previously used by Desio.

12   K2

We did not spend long in luxurious idleness at Suget Jangal. The very next day, 9 July, we again split up into groups, each with a separate task. Seven porters, under the charge of Angtharkay, were sent up the Sarpo Laggo glacier to Mone Brangsa to relay all the loads that had been left there down to the junction of the Sarpo Laggo and Crevasse glacier valleys. I estimated that this would take a week, and our plans were arranged to coincide with this. Spender, with Angtensing and Nukka to help him, was to accompany the porters up the glacier, and from a suitable base he was to explore and survey the country to the east, between the Sarpo Laggo glacier and the main watershed. Auden, Tilman and I, with Lhakpa Tensing and Ila, were to spend a week exploring the glaciers rising about the northern flanks of K2, and to connect up with the Duke of Abruzzi's surveys at the head of the Baltoro glacier, and those that Spender had planned.

The other two parties left Suget Jangal in the morning, carrying a large supply of fuel. Tilman and Auden and Lhakpa went with them to our main dump, three miles away, to fetch food, warm clothes, spare films and tobacco that had been left there. Ila and I spent a delicious morning lazing on the grass in the hot sun. Later we attended to various domestic jobs, such as airing sleeping bags, washing and mending clothes, until the others returned. We packed up and started after lunch; this required a considerable effort of will.

We followed the same route that we had taken when we had been hunting bharal nearly four weeks before. On the way I visited a nest that I had seen on that occasion, and found that the young birds had flown. We crossed the high ridge into the K2 nullah, contoured along a thousand feet above the stream, and camped when we came to a deep gully containing a trickle of water.

We climbed 2,500 feet the next morning, to a rocky point about 16,300 feet high. It commanded a view up the K2 glacier to a wonderful circle of ice peaks in the country ahead of us. In the opposite direction we could see an enormous distance to the west, far up the Crevasse glacier. The weather was clear and still and we stayed for a long time, taking a wide round of angles and photographs, and discussing lazily the many questions that are raised by any view into unexplored country. Not far below us on a little saddle there was a herd of bharal, grazing peacefully on a meagre pasture. The descent to camp took us only a few minutes of swift scree-running.

After a short halt for a meal of tsampa and tea, followed by a pipe, we packed up and climbed down to the valley, carrying a supply of firewood besides our usual loads. When we reached the snout of the glacier, we climbed into a corridor between the ice and the valley-side, which served us as a road for several miles. We camped late that evening by a small lake in the ablation valley above the glacier.

By way of contrast with the peace and sunshine of the previous day, it was snowing when we woke on 11 July, and we could not see far. We kept to the true left side of the valley for half a mile, and then crossed the glacier. It did not take us more than an hour to do this, which was good going, for the glacier was nearly a mile wide and its surface consisted of the usual tortuous wilderness of moraine-covered ice. On the previous day we had seen a peak, about 20,700 feet high, which stood well detached from the main range of giants to the south. Its summit would obviously command a superb view of the whole district, and we decided to spend two days in attempting to climb it. We pushed on another mile or so up the true right flank of the glacier and halted on a flat shelf at the foot of a small side nullah. It had stopped snowing and the weather had showed signs of a sudden improvement. So, after a meal of bread and cheese, we started up the nullah towards the peak carrying equipment for a light camp for the three of us and food for two days. Bearing to the right, we climbed up an easy slope for 3,000 feet and camped on a ridge at an altitude of 17,700 feet. The Sherpas descended to the dump by the glacier, with instructions to spend the next day bringing firewood up there from below. The view from the ridge was very fine. The great peaks of the K2 massif were beginning to stand up in their true perspective, and the glaciers looked like gracefully sweeping trains at their feet. The camp made a splendid survey station, but being on the ridge it had one disadvantage – that there was no water at hand. Snow had to be melted for cooking and drinking purposes, which always takes more than twice as much time and fuel. We were using a Primus stove for cooking. On the way up, Auden had been feeling ill. He did not eat any supper for evening, and he had a bad night.

By sunset the sky was clear. Only torn ribbons of mist swathed the mountains to the south, their soft colour giving promise of fine weather. The delicately carved flutings of the snow peaks flushed with the same coral glow before the ghostly grey of night enveloped this lofty world of ice.

I woke as the sun touched the summit of K2. The glaciers below us were still sleeping in frozen darkness. We heated some tea and tsampa. Auden was running a temperature and stayed in his sleeping bag, while Tilman and I climbed sleepily on to the ridge. It was a cloudless morning. We mounted quickly along the ridge over snow-covered rocks. Higher up, in spite of an intensely cold night, the snow was very bad, and when, after climbing for two hours, we reached a sloping glacier plateau, we began to sink in up to our hips. It was surprising to find such bad conditions, for it was already nearly the middle of July and the weather in June had been more than usually fine. We began to wonder if in these parts the snow ever consolidates in the normal way. But in spite of the very hard work, we climbed quickly, and three hours after leaving camp we reached a bergschrund at the foot of the final pyramid of the peak, only 400 feet below the top. There we had a short rest to eat a chunk of 'emergency ration'. I took off my boots to thaw my feet in the sun, as they had lost all feeling. Meanwhile Tilman cut steps across the bergschrund and up the slope above. We found this to be a great deal more difficult than we had expected. It consisted of hard ice, set at an exceedingly steep angle and covered with about nine inches of powder snow. At each step the snow had first to be cleared away before we could cut into the ice. It was terribly hard work and we advanced ridiculously slowly. We took the lead in turns of about twenty minutes each, while the man behind anchored the rope as best he could and speculated what to do in the event of a slip. We were climbing in a wide gully coming down from a ridge which led along the skyline to the top.

After we had been cutting for about two and a half hours, I was about fifteen feet below the crest of the ridge when I missed my stroke and hit myself violently on the knees with the pick of my axe. This made me feel very sick, and Tilman had to cut the rest of the way to the ridge. We had hoped that when we reached this the rest of the climb would be comparatively simple. But the ridge was very narrow and was crowned by a snow cornice which curved like a breaking wave over a terrifying drop on the other side. It led to a square tower of rock which formed the summit of the peak. The top was so close that we could have thrown a stone on to it. But the prospect of the ridge and the tower was so alarming that we nearly abandoned the climb. Tilman led along the ridge flogging away the cornice as he went. After some exceedingly delicate work he reached the rocks. As he took in the rope I followed along the ridge and we climbed together on to a little platform. This was the first place where we could rest since we had left the bergschrund, and we had a bite of food before tackling the final pitch. It was my turn to take the lead and I did not much like the look of it. But it was not quite as bad as it appeared, and in short time we were sitting astride a sharp rock which formed the summit.

The view from the top was astonishing; well worth the trouble and difficulties of the climb. To the south were the colossal northern faces of K2 and other peaks of the main watershed, a breathtaking panorama of sweeping ridges, lofty summits and hanging glacier terraces, dazzling in the midday sun. For a stretch of fifty miles, the Aghil range filled our northern horizon. We could trace the course of the Shaksgam valley almost from its source to its junction with the Yarkand river; while across the Aghil pass we could see far into the barren ranges of Turkestan. To the west were the peaks of the Crevasse glacier, whose intricacies were to occupy our attention during the next two months.

Among these mountains 'The Fangs' stood out clearly, and another beautiful rock peak which came to be known as The Crown. Beyond these, to the south-west, peak after peak rose in jagged profusion of rock spires.

Immediately below us to the east, between the peak we had climbed and the southern wall of the Shaksgam valley, we were surprised to see another ice stream, nearly as big as the K2 glacier. It rose at the foot of K2's massive neigh-bour, Staircase peak, and the river which issued from it flowed into the K2 nullah through a narrow gorge. We called it the Staircase glacier. Staircase peak has now, by a decision of the official Karakoram Names Committee, been called Skyang Kangri.

In spite of all the fascination of this gigantic panorama, we did not stop long on the summit, for a cold wind was blowing and there was too little room for comfort. We slid down a doubled rope from the summit tower. This is a method frequently used when climbing down difficult places and usually it saves a lot of time. But we had arranged the rope carelessly, and when we had tried to recover it we found that it had jammed in a crack. We struggled with it for a long time without success, and I was just about to repeat the climb up the tower when it yielded to a final tug. The ice slope was much more difficult to descend than to ascend. Our steps had been obliterated by snow sliding down from the above. Tilman went first, while I gave him what support I could from above, I followed when he had gone the whole length of our eighty-foot rope. But it was impossible to anchor one's axe in the ice owing to the powder snow on top, and we both had to work with the greatest possible care to avoid a slip which would have been disastrous. When Tilman had only got fifty feet to go, the step I was standing in gave way. Leaning heavily on my axe, I managed to break into a standing glissade, and to keep my feet, though I went down past Tilman at a tremendous speed, and shot over the bergschrund into the soft snow below it. Tilman followed my example, and we stood at last on the gla-cier, having taken seven hours to go up and to come down the last 400 feet of the peak. The remaining 2,000 feet to camp was pleasantly easy.

We found that Auden was no better, but he was anxious to go to the lower camp and started down ahead of us. After a meal of tsampa and sugar, washed down with melted snow, we followed. Though we were both tired, we were obliged to carry heavy loads. But the descent was mostly down easy scree and we reached the lower camp at eight o'clock, to find the two Sherpas waiting for us with tea and hot bread and a thick brew of pemmican. It had been a glorious day and I was very sorry that Auden had not been able to share it with us.

We were lucky to have had such perfect weather for the climb, for snow was again falling when we woke on 13 July. It was pleasant to have an excuse to lie late in bed. But my morning peace was disturbed. Breakfast was served unnec-essarily early, and while I was trying sleepily to deal with a plateful of watery porridge, I upset the whole lot into my sleeping bag.

Auden's fever still persisted, and it was decided that he should stay where he was for the next two days, while Tilman and I went up to the head of the glacier, to reach the great north face of K2, which promised to be something very remarkable. We took both Sherpas with us and sent one of them back to Auden from our next camp. This was at the foot of a great rock ridge which screened the upper part of the glacier from view. On the way we had to cross the only tributary of the K2 glacier coming from the east. It showed signs of recent and substantial decrease in size. Our camp was on a little grassy alp, covered with flowers and set in a wilderness of black boulders. The weather had cleared by the evening, and we climbed a thousand feet on to the rock ridge to reconnoitre the upper part of the glacier and to do a survey station.

It was snowing again early next morning, but this time without much determination, and soon rifts in the clouds gave us hope of better things. Tilman's watch had finally succumbed to the rough treatment it had received while crossing rivers, and when the sky was overcast we had no means of telling the time. I do not think it had been light for long when we started. Ila came with us, carrying the theodolite. We climbed obliquely up to the rock ridge and crossed it over a low shoulder. Heavy mists hung in the upper glacier basin. Above them the summit of K2 appeared, floating at an incredible height above our heads. While Tilman went on, I waited with Ila on the ridge for nearly an hour in the hope that the mists might clear enough for me to photograph the whole north face. The pattern of cloud was constantly changing as it drifted across the mountain, revealing for a moment some new ridge or corrie in its gigantic structure and altering its apparent shape. But though we waited a long time this shifting drapery of cloud still clung to the mountain, and we had to leave the ridge without a clear view of the stupendous north face.

We ran diagonally down scree slopes to the glacier and walked easily along by the side of the ice. But before we had covered a mile we were stopped by cliffs rising sheer above the side of the glacier. Tilman was sitting disconsolately on a ledge wondering what to do. The ice was broken up into a complicated maze of those serrated pinnacles which are a common feature on the glaciers of the northern side of the main watershed both in the Karakorams and in the vicinity of Mount Everest.

These northern glaciers are nearly always divided into four distinct zones. Firstly, there is the upper *névé*, or snow basin, from which the glacier rises. Then follows a section of smooth ice, free from a covering of permanent snow and moraine deposits. Below this the ice stream merges gradually into the pinnacled zone. Farther down the pinnacles increase in size and decrease in numbers, until a few isolated towers are left standing out of the lower section of the glacier, which is so covered with gravel and boulders that very little ice can be seen.

It is an interesting fact that these pinnacles very rarely occur on the glaciers of the southern side of the watershed, whereas the middle section of those on the northern side of the range are always pinnacled to a remarkable extent. I have never heard a satisfactory explanation of the phenomenon. On the large glaciers, moraine-covered troughs, caused by the junction of tributary ice streams, run down through the pinnacled areas. Such a trough provides an easy route up this difficult section of glacier. But if it is necessary to cross from side to side one is forced into a labyrinth of pinnacles. We now had the choice of climbing four miles along difficult cliffs, or crossing a few hundred yards of pinnacled ice into a trough where we might expect to find reasonably easy going. There was some difference of opinion as to which course we should take, but after much discussion we decided to try and reach the trough. We were soon immersed in the usual blind maze of narrow corridors enclosed by smooth walls of ice as much as 150 feet high. It was difficult to maintain a sense of direction and impossible to work out a route for more than a few yards ahead. No corridor led far without interruption. Sometimes the way was blocked by a cul-de-sac, sometimes by a vividly blue lake, with sheer sides, unfathomably deep. Occasionally it was possible to surmount these obstacles by chipping steps laboriously up the ice walls. More often we were forced to go back and try another route – balancing along the crest of a knife-edged ridge, sliding down on a rope over a vertical cliff, squeezing through a tiny opening into a slit of a gorge, or jumping over a chasm, with a river thundering in the unseen depths below. Except for the appalling length of time that it takes to cover any distance, the work of finding a way through these pinnacles is very fascinating. The ice scenery is most beautiful. It is like being in a deserted city built to satisfy the whims of a fantastic imagination. The shapely church spires are supported by slender buttresses of translucent crystal; the walls of the streets are carved with intricate tracery, and the alleyways are spanned by delicately balanced arches and fragile bridges – all of ice.

When eventually we reached the trough it was past midday. We left Ila to wait for our return, and hurried on over moraine-covered ice between the rows of high pinnacles. After an hour we reached the smooth ice of the upper part of the glacier, and were able to travel more swiftly. As we went, the valley gradually opened into a great cirque at the foot of the north face of K2. In the midst of this, on a wide plain of ice, I halted, while Tilman went on to collect a specimen of rock from the mountain.

The afternoon was fine, and nothing interrupted my view of the great amphitheatre about me. The cliffs and ridges of K2 rose out of the glacier in one stupendous sweep to the summit of the mountain, 12,000 feet above. The sight was beyond my comprehension, and I sat gazing at it, with a kind of timid fascination, watching wreaths of mist creep in and out of corries utterly remote. I saw ice avalanches, weighing perhaps hundreds of tons, break off from a hanging glacier, nearly two miles above my head; the ice was ground to a fine powder and drifted away in the breeze long before it reached the foot of the precipice, nor did any sound reach my ears.

To the right of K2 lay the famous Savoia saddle which had been reached twenty-eight years before by the Duke of Abruzzi from the Baltoro glacier. It presented a formidable appearance from this side. To the left of K2 was a bewildering mass of peaks and glaciers whose existence I had not suspected. Sitting alone gazing at the cirque forming the head of the K2 glacier was an experience I shall not forget; no mountain scene has impressed me more deeply.

It was an hour before Tilman returned, and we hurried back down the glacier, for it was late in the afternoon and we had a long way to go. By the time we reached Ila, the weather had made a sudden change for the worse. Great billows of cloud were rolling over the peaks from the south and a cold blustering wind blew up the glacier. Before everything was blotted out, we managed to erect the theodolite, to fix our position and to take angles to some important points at the head of the glacier. Instead of crossing to the side of the glacier at once, we went several miles down the trough, hoping to find an easy way through when the pinnacles had thinned out. We had passed below our camp before we found a hopeful line. We tried several passages, but each was filled with an impassable lake. It began to look as if we should have to spend the night without food in the middle of the glacier. At length, just before dark, one of us hit on a possible route, and we climbed through to the side of the glacier. The long pull up from there to our camp was a severe penance at the end of a long day.

The weather had broken badly. We went down, in steadily falling snow, on the morning of 15 July, to Auden's camp. His fever had gone, but he was still rather weak. Ila and I accompanied him slowly down the glacier to our first camp in the K2 nullah. In spite of the weather, which was becoming worse, Tilman went with Lhakpa Tensing up the eastern tributary of the K2 glacier with the intention of crossing a saddle at the head of it into the Staircase glacier basin which had interested us so much when we saw it from the top of the peak we climbed.

It snowed all night and did not stop until eight o'clock the following morning. The snow was lying thick upon the ground when we started traversing round the hillside toward Suget Jangal. As it was still early in the day, and we had not far to go, we did not bother to put on snow-glasses. When we got round the corner out of the K2 nullah, we saw a herd of a dozen bharal. They had seen us and were running away up the hill. Ila and I dumped our loads and followed them, while Auden went on down to Suget Jangal. The animals had disappeared from view, but it was easy to follow their tracks in the snow. We climbed for several thousand feet, creeping cautiously over each bit of the convexly sloping ground expecting to find the bharal on the other side. It was an exhilarating chase, and, with the cries of innumerable snow pheasant echoing across the hillside, reminded me pleasantly of following game over winter snow in Europe. I was enjoying it so much that I quite forgot that we had left our snow-glasses in our loads.

The bharal led us over some very difficult country, and we did not see them again until the middle of the afternoon. I shot one, and, while Ila dragged it down to the main valley, I returned to our loads and carried them down to Suget Jangal. Auden was not there, and, having skinned the bharal, we were just about to start on to the main dump as dusk was falling, when he arrived. He had been to the dump, but had found no one there, nor any food. He had seen a camp across the Sarpo Laggo river, about a mile away, but he could not attract attention. Also the river was in flood and he could not cross.

We settled down on the grass before a blazing fire, and cooked a mixed grill of liver, heart and kidneys which would have satisfied the most fastidious epicure. The weather had cleared; we sat talking, and feeding the flames with dead willow branches until eleven o'clock, under a moonlit sky flecked with soft fleecy clouds. I congratulated myself on having escaped the usual dreaded penalty of spending a day amongst snow without snow-glasses. But, as I got into my sleeping bag, I began to feel some slight discomfort. At first I thought it was the smoke from the fire that was making my eyes smart. However, in a few minutes the pain increased so much that I found it impossible to sleep. It felt as though the inside of my eyelids had been lacerated and then filled with sand. Any movement of the eyelid over the eye aggravated the pain. The continual flow of tears made it difficult to keep my eyes open for long without blinking. The muscular quivering caused by closing my eyes gently was extremely unpleasant. I found that the only way of obtaining any slight relief was to hold my eyelashes down with my fingers. In the morning I found that Ila had been suffering in the same way. It was not a severe attack of snow-blindness, and though neither of us could see very well, we were able to walk over the sand flats to the dump.

When we got there, we saw someone on the other side of the river trying to attract our attention by waving a coat. He walked downstream, evidently indicating the way to a possible crossing-place. Having left a note for Tilman at the dump, we followed. We went a long way down before we came to the crossing-place. Even at this early hour it was by no means easy to ford the Sarpo Laggo river, which, a month previously, had not given us a thought, even late in the afternoon.

Spender came out to meet us, and conducted us back to a comfortable camp, where both the other parties were waiting for us with all the loads that had been left at Mone Brangsa early in June. Spender had completed the mapping of the glaciers to the east of the Sarpo Laggo. It was very interesting to compare and fit together the results of our respective explorations. Ila and I spent the rest of the day bathing our eyes in a saturated solution of sugar and water, an ineffective remedy prescribed by Angtensing.

The next morning Tilman arrived. He had managed to reach the Staircase glacier and to follow it down. In the bad weather he had seen very little, but it was an interesting trip, and his compass bearings have been a help in plotting that section of the map.

13   The Crevasse Glacier

We could now give our whole attention to the problem of getting supplies up the Crevasse glacier into the ranges to the west. Looking back, now that their geography is known, it is difficult to recapture our feelings while we were working out plans from the slender data that was then available, but I well remember, long before the expedition started, poring for hours over the existing maps of that part of the Karakoram, and trying to visualise the probable lie of the ranges and glaciers in the unknown regions that we were now about to penetrate.

We knew that it lay immediately to the north of that remarkable knot of mountains which gives rise to several of the largest glaciers in the whole range. Among these were the Hispar, Biafo, Virjerab and Panmah. In 1892, Martin Conway ascended the Hispar glacier and crossed the Hispar pass at its head. In describing the view from there, he wrote (in *Climbing in the Himalayas*): 'Before us lay a basin or lake of snow. From the midst … rose a series of mountain islands, white like snow that buried their bases, and there were endless bays and straits as of white water nestling amongst them.' Later he referred to the phenomenon as the 'Snow Lake', though how much more importance he intended to be attached to the name I do not know. He was not able to explore it, but from there he descended into the Biafo glacier, which he followed down to Askole.

Dr and Mrs Bullock Workman, who ascended from the Biafo to the Hispar pass in 1899, used Conway's name for the great basin that they saw from the Hispar pass, retaining the capital letters. By degrees the Snow Lake developed a great importance in geographical speculation. In fact it was recently expected that there might exist a vast ice cap, such as was unknown in the Himalaya, and from which flowed, besides the Biafo, a number of glaciers whose sources were unexplored. Certainly the area of 300 square miles mentioned by Conway suggested something of the sort.

In the account, read to the Royal Geographical Society, of his expedition to the Shimshal area in 1925, Dr Visser expressed the view that the Virjerab glacier had its origin in the Snow Lake. It had also been suggested that the Crevasse glacier rose in this fabled ice cap, and also a great ice stream, that Younghusband had seen in 1889, flowing towards the Shimshal pass. The lower reaches of this glacier had been visited by Colonel Schomberg in 1934, and called by him the Braldu glacier.

In 1933, Gregory and Auden had made an expedition up the Biafo glacier with the object of investigating the Snow Lake, but circumstances prevented them from reaching it. So, in 1937, our knowledge of the area was limited to the reports of Conway and the Workmans who, in 1908, had again seen, but not explored, the Snow Lake.

The idea that the Crevasse glacier would lead us on to this strange ice cap was an intriguing one. By carrying a fortnight's food up the glacier and travelling as quickly as possible, and given good weather, we could no doubt have solved the problem of its source. But in the first place we wanted to be able to survey the glacier, its tributaries and the surrounding ranges, as accurately as possible; secondly, we wanted to be in a position to make a thorough exploration of the country at its head, and to attempt to clear up the problem of the sources and all these great glaciers, and to fix their geographical position; and thirdly, it would be a waste of time to be compelled to return by the way we had come, and we hoped to finish the expedition by descending, either to Shimshal or to Hunza, or to some place as remotely distant from our starting point. So I had decided that when we finished our work in the Aghil range and on the northern glaciers of K2, we should start up the Crevasse glacier, carrying all the supplies that were left.

A stock-taking on the morning of 18 July showed that we had 1,500 pounds of food; enough to last for another fifty-four days. In addition to this we had 700 pounds of equipment and packing; three journeys were necessary to move everything forward to each camp on the glacier. As time went on, our food supplies would become lighter, and we would be able to reduce the number of relays to two. Even so, I estimated that it would probably take us a month to get everything within striking distance of the head of the glacier. But time would not be wasted by this slow rate of progress, as there would be more than enough exploration and survey work to be done on the way.

Travelling over difficult glacier country, when it is necessary to work from a base which is entirely out of reach of any outside assistance, presents a very different problem from that of an expedition for which some sort of transport and supplies, however bad, are available. I found, as I had expected, that cutting ourselves off from such support, for a period of more than three months, threw a considerable strain on the party.

As Spender had fixed our position, we knew roughly the direction that we had to follow to reach the country surrounding the Snow Lake. But whether we could keep going in that direction depended upon where the glacier led us. The views that we had seen up the Crevasse glacier from the heights above the Sarpo Laggo valley showed us that our course would, at first, lie due west. Ten miles up, however, the valley split into several branches, each filled with a very large ice stream. We called their point of junction the First Divide. From that distance it was difficult to see which was the principal glacier, and we would not forecast the direction of our route beyond the First Divide.

Our main worry was fuel. We had brought twelve gallons of paraffin with us. So far, we had been very lucky in finding wood, and we had used the Primus stoves a great deal less than we had expected. But the containers in which the fuel was carried had been badly battered in transport, and more than half of the oil had leaked away. We now had less than five gallons and even that was leaking. It is difficult to estimate how much oil will be used by a party when it is working beyond reach of wood fuel, as so much depends on conditions. But only a small proportion of the food that we had with us could be eaten without being cooked, and although we might never be compelled to melt snow for drinking purposes, we could not exist for long without fuel. Much depended upon how far up the glacier we should find wood, for we could not afford the time to transport it for any great distance.

On 18 July, the morning after Auden and I arrived, we sent seven men, under the charge of Angtharkay, to make the first dump on the Crevasse glacier. I told them to choose for themselves the best route, and to go as far as they could. The rest of us spent a busy day doing our various jobs. Our camp was in a little sandy bay at the corner formed by the junction of the Sarpo Laggo and the Crevasse glacier valleys. Nearby there was a large collection of huts. In one of these we found the remains of a quite recent fire. The Baltis were as puzzled as we were and could offer no explanation of this extraordinary discovery.

Angtharkay's party was very late in getting back. The sun was setting when we saw them coming across the mile of river flats which separated us from the snout of the glacier. They appeared to be moving very slowly, and with the aid of field-glasses we saw that they were dragging something between them. In the dusk we could not make our whether there were six or seven of them, and we feared that there had been an accident. But, as they approached, their cheery shouting reassured us, and when they arrived we found that the object that they were pulling along was a fox that they had managed to capture on the glacier. The poor creature was very frightened and made vicious attacks on anyone who went close to it. We photographed the animal and set it free, and it ran off amid roars of cheering from the Sherpas. Angtharkay reported that the going on the glacier had been difficult, but they seemed to have covered quite a lot of ground, and he said there was plenty of fuel above the dump.

After supper that evening Spender took advantage of the weather to make some more astronomical observations for Azimuth while I booked his angles, lying in a warm sleeping bag. Unfortunately the Wild theodolite had been seriously damaged and he had to work with the smaller Watts instrument, which was not accurate enough for a latitude observation. This place became known as Azimuth Camp.

The next day, Spender, Tilman and all the porters carried loads to Dump I. Spender stayed up there alone to survey while the others came back in the evening. Auden stayed in camp with a recurrence of his fever, and I spent a most enjoyable day hunting bharal in the hills behind. The weather was perfect, and as I climbed to a great height I had some wonderful views of the surrounding country. I found a herd and shot two very good heads. When Tilman returned in the evening he told me that Spender had fixed the position of Dump I on his plane-table and found it to be five miles west of Azimuth Camp. This was surprisingly good progress, even though a mile of the way was over gravel flats. I began to hope that we might reach the head of the glacier very much more quickly than I had expected.

The carrying of the last relay to Dump I was complicated by the new supply of meat that had resulted from my hunt. However, the meat so cheered the Sherpas that they did not mind how much they had to carry, nor how far they had to go. There was keen competition amongst them to make up the biggest pack, and it was regarded as riotously funny when the load was so heavy that its carrier collapsed under its weight. The Baltis regarded this frivolity with mournful resignation. They were never able to understand the buffoonery of the Sherpas. But in justice to them in this case, it must be admitted that they could not benefit from the extra meat on account of their religious scruples.

It had been decided that Auden should go down the Shaksgam with Mancho and Buddha to continue the survey and his geological work in that direction. We left a fortnight's food with him and arranged that his party should catch us up while we were working up the Crevasse glacier. Then we went, with all the remaining loads, to Dump I, which we reached on the evening of 20 July.

On 21 July, while I was helping Spender with the survey among the mountains of the north, Tilman conducted another carrying forward to Dump II. He managed to get on to a moraine shelf running along the northern bank of the glacier, and succeeded in going four miles before depositing the loads. I had not expected to be able to put the dumps more than two miles apart on the lower, broken part of the glacier, so this rate of progress was extremely satisfactory. Another relay was carried up the next day, and on 23 July we camped at Dump II with all the loads.

From Dump II on 24 July we were able to reconnoitre the confusion of glaciers at the First Divide. There was no doubt as to which of the branches we should follow. To the south, a gigantic fan of icefalls descended from the vertical cliffs of the main watershed, and united into one ice stream, which joined the main glacier in a jumble of pinnacles. Even if our route had lain in this direction, it would have been practically impossible to get far up these broken icefalls. A mile or so further up a big tributary came in from the north. As it seemed to flow roughly from the direction of the Crown, we called it the Crown glacier. We were surprised at its size, for it came from the range of mountains dividing the Crevasse glacier from the Shaksgam valley, and we had not expected to find any very extensive glaciation there. The main valley, we were pleased to find continued on a bearing only ten degrees north of west. Ten miles farther up there was a confluence of glaciers. We called this the second divide.

The junction of the pinnacle crown glacier prevented any further progress up the Northern flanks of the Crevasse glacier. On 25 July, while Tilman and Spender were surveying, I set out with the men to cross the glacier, carrying the first relay of loads for Dump III. We had not gone far before we got into trouble. Our way was barred by a wide stream flowing down the glacier. It had cut a deep trough in the ice, through which it slid with such velocity that there was no chance of fording it, and it was far too wide to jump. We followed it up for some way until we got involved in the pinnacles of the Crown glacier. At length we came to a place where the stream was spanned by a remarkable bridge. In order to get across this, we had first to climb through a tunnel in the ice and cut steps spirally upwards, while the torrent thundered through the enclosed canyon fifty feet below. It was a sensational and very beautiful place. The exit at the top of the tunnel was made by a somewhat dangerous step from one ice cornice to another. Having been granted such a dramatic and unexpected way out of our difficulties, I thought there would be no further trouble in reaching the other side of the glacier. But soon we were held up by a smaller stream, and, when it seemed that we were almost across the glacier, another big river confronted us. For five hours we hunted for a way of getting over this obstacle. First we explored downstream until we could get no farther; then we went up until we became entangled in a network of pinnacles amongst which we were continually losing ourselves and our companions, and even the river itself. At length Angtharkay and I found an ice bridge, and reached it by cutting steps down a steep slope and sliding down a rope over an ice cliff. But although we could cross the bridge, it led us into a cave twenty feet high, from which there was no exit.

Meanwhile Sen Tensing had found a place where the near wall of the canyon overhung the river, and he thought he could jump across to an ice cliff on the opposite side. It was a formidable distance, with only a tiny ledge on the other side on which to land, while below there was a nasty drop into the torrent at the bottom of the ravine. I should not like to have undertaken the jump myself, but Sen Tensing insisted he could do it. We tied a rope to him and he started to make elaborate preparations. When it came to the point, he did not like the prospect, and kept walking to the brink and back again. Angtharkay was doubled up with laughter at Sen Tensing's mounting nervousness and discomfiture. Though the victim had my full sympathy, it certainly was very funny to watch, and I had some difficulty in maintaining an air of grave concern. But at last he hurled himself across the abyss and landed on the ledge on the opposite wall.

He swayed backwards for a second and I thought he must fall; but he recovered his balance and clung to the ledge. From there he was able to climb to the top of the wall.

We worked downstream until we found a suitable place for a rope bridge. A treble strand of rope was fixed from a high ice bollard on our side of the river to a point lower down on the opposite bank. We used for a runner a piece of bent wood that was carried by one of the Baltis instead of an ice axe, and the loads were easily hauled across the river by Sen Tensing. It had been my intention to leave them there and to return to camp by the way we had come, as by now it was late in the afternoon. But we could not get Sen Tensing back across the river as we could not haul uphill across the bridge. So I decided that Angtharkay and I should join him, and, while the others went back, we would look for a route much lower down the glacier. We entrusted ourselves to the flimsy contraption and were hauled across. Neither of us was very successful in concealing his alarm, but Sen Tensing displayed admirable generosity and restraint!

We stacked the loads, waved goodbye to the others, and set off down the glacier, taking a tin of pemmican with us against the probability of being benighted. We soon discovered that we were on a narrow tongue of ice with a river on either side, gradually converging towards each other, so that we should soon be forced to cross one of them. It also transpired that Sen Tensing had sprained his ankle in his heroic leap and he could not get along very fast. Angtharkay and I went ahead, looking for a new way across either of the rivers. The one on our right was the smaller of the two, but it was out of the question to think of fording it. We found a place from which we could do a downward leap of about fifteen feet, on to the farther bank, but it was a difficult landing and unlikely that Sen Tensing could manage it on one foot. Eventually we were cut off by the confluence of the two rivers. Here, luckily, there was an unexpected way out of the difficulty. Two ice pinnacles, leaning out from the opposite banks of the right-hand stream, almost touched one another. I chipped steps to the top of one and from it jumped over to the other. The distance from one to the other was small, but the pinnacles were so slender, and they were leaning at such a dizzy angle, that I was afraid that one of them would collapse under my weight. However, we all three got across safely.

From this place we reached a high ridge of moraine which had been swept right across the main glacier by the big ice stream coming in from the south. Angtharkay and I went ahead again, as fast as we could, to find a route before it became too dark to see. We built small cairns every hundred yards or so, to guide Sen Tensing. We encountered no more difficulties, and reached camp before eight o'clock. The other porters had got in nearly two hours before us. We had now found a good way across the glacier, but I cursed my stupidity for not having spotted the difficulties of the other route before having embarked upon it. This had wasted much time and a great deal of energy. However, to make up for it, Spender and Tilman had done a very successful day's work.

For the next two days a thick haze made visibility so bad that survey was impossible. But during this time the rest of the baggage was carried up to Dump III, which was established three and a half miles farther up, on the southern side of the glacier. Also the loads that I had left by the river were rescued and brought along, so that on the evening of 27 July everything was at Dump III. We were now twelve and a half miles west of Azimuth camp, and we had been working up the glacier for only ten days. As we were already over the most difficult part, and we expected soon to get on to smooth ice, the position was very satisfactory.

On 28 July, Tilman and I, with the porters, all carrying big loads, pushed forward towards the Second Divide. For the first two miles the way was complicated and difficult, but we were able to keep to the moraine at the side of the ice, and so to avoid the worst of the pinnacled section of the glacier. Beyond this we found wide troughs of smooth ice in which we were able to walk at a considerable speed. As we approached it, we saw that the Second Divide formed the junction of two huge ice streams of equal width, one flowing from the north-west and the other from the south-west.

It is difficult to think of suitable names for geographical features in unexplored country. But from the explorer's point of view it is better to give unsuitable names than to give no names at all. It is irritating and confusing, for instance, to speak of 'The glacier coming in two miles below Dump III', 'The peak we climbed the day so-and-so was ill', or 'The valley that puzzled us when we were doing our first station in the Shaksgam'. Generally the first name suggested, however unsuitable it may be, comes to stay. In this way, to the annoyance of scientific societies and survey departments, important features of newly explored country come to be known by such frivolous names as Cockeyed peak and Lousy valley, and occasionally by names that would hardly pass the censor.

In a moment of exasperation, I called the range of high peaks, lying between the two glaciers beyond the Second Divide the 'Father Christmas' group. The name was adopted by my companions without comment, and it soon lost its ridiculous sound. The northern branch became known as the 'Father Christmas glacier', and the highest peak of the group was 'Father Christmas'. The southern branch was regarded as the main Crevasse glacier, for no better reason than that we thought our ultimate route would lie up it.

We succeeded in establishing Dump IV at the inside bend of the Main glacier, between an icefall and steep rock cliffs. There was a division of opinion as to the actual site of the camp. We had to choose between a stretch of soft sand that had been deposited at the foot of the cliffs by a glacial stream, and the broken surface of the ice where a platform would have to be cut. There was no doubt about which would be the more comfortable place, but most of us thought that the sand flat was in danger of being bombarded by stones from the very rotten crags above. The sybarites in the party ridiculed this idea, and despite their minority they had their way. We returned to Dump III in bad weather. We paid later for the foolish choice of this camp site.

We were so well in advance of our schedule that we decided to strengthen our position by bringing up wood from farther down the glacier. This job occupied 29 July and 30th. On 31 July, Spender, Tilman and I went up to occupy Dump IV, and on 1 August, the porters brought all the remaining loads to that camp. Also Auden arrived with his Baltis at this opportune moment. At each dump we had left him a sketch map and detailed instructions of how to get to the next. In this way he found no difficulty in following us up the glacier when he had finished his work in the Shaksgam valley.

14   Survey and Adventures

Apart from the insecurity of the camp site, Dump IV was an ideal base from which to reconnoitre the various possibilities that were now taking shape. Spender's survey showed how the lower part of the Crevasse glacier system fitted into the blank space that we were exploring, and we were able to calculate, with some degree of accuracy, our position in relation to the mapped country on the southern side of the main range. Even allowing for a considerable discrepancy in these neighbouring surveys, most of which were known to be very unreliable, it was clear that we must be approaching that high network of watersheds in which the Snow Lake was supposed to lie.

The dullness of relaying all this food up the glacier had been relieved by the excitement of speculating where the glacier would lead us. But our impatience had increased as we approached the upper basin. Now at last we were in a position, still with many weeks' food at our disposal, to make a prolonged exploration of this exciting country, and to indulge in that most absorbing of all forms of mountaineering – the search for passes which lead from one unknown region to another.

But there was a very large field to be covered, and so many alternative plans, that it was hard to choose between them. For this reason, we decided to split up into three self-contained parties, each with its separate objective. The main survey party, consisting of Spender and myself and five Sherpas, was to concentrate on making its way to the north-west. If possible, we were to try to find a route into the Braldu glacier system and follow it down to the country that had been traversed by Younghusband, and later by Schomberg, to the north of the Shimshal pass. In comparison with the rest of the Karakoram, this region was extremely inaccessible, and it was important to take the opportunity of exploring it thoroughly. Tilman, with two Sherpas, was to find the Snow Lake, and having explored it, to work his way back to Skardu, across the little known ranges to the south-west of the Hispar pass. Auden, who had to get back early, was to try to find a pass that would take him into the Panmah glacier, or failing that, he would accompany Tilman and make his way down the Biafo glacier, from the Snow Lake. He was to take the four Baltis with him.

Whether it would be possible to achieve any of these ambitious plans, or whether we would be forced, by the difficulties of the country, to retreat ignominiously down the Crevasse glacier, was our chief concern. And it was enough to cause us some anxiety, for, although we were in an unusually strong position as regards food, it had to be remembered that very few passages had been made across the main ranges of the Karakoram.

A reconnaissance from a high ridge above Dump IV, on 1 August, helped us to decide upon our immediate plans, and gave us a superb view of the north face of 'The Fangs' which swept upwards for 5,000 feet from a vast glacier basin, in a beautiful glistening arc, curving up to the summit ridge like the crest of a gigantic wave, frozen as it was about to break. Both the 'Father Christmas glacier' and the Main glacier bent round to the west again, and were lost to view several miles north and south of the Second Divide.

On 2 August, Auden, Tilman and I, with Ila and Angtharkay, took a light camp up the Main glacier, intending to make a rapid reconnaissance of its head, and to look for a way of starting our respective journeys. Meanwhile Spender, with the rest of the porters, went up the 'Father Christmas glacier' to extend his survey in that direction; for it seemed less likely that we would find a route so far north, so it was best to take this opportunity of mapping the area.

Progress was so easy on the smooth ice of the Main glacier that we must have kept up an average speed of nearly two miles an hour. Strewn all over the surface of the glacier we found a large number of dead birds, some just skeletons, some still with all their plumage. They mostly belonged to the duck family, though I found one big bird with legs longer than my arm. This phenomenon was not confined to the Crevasse glacier. We found these frozen birds in the upper basins of most of the big glaciers that we visited in this part of the range. Presumably they had perished during migratory flights, though it is hard to understand why they should choose such difficult routes from Central Asia to India, when there are many lower passes over which they could fly across the main range. As a reason for this it has been suggested that the ancestors of these birds began their flights before the present range existed, and, as the mountains rose gradually out of the plains, the birds, instead of flying round the new obstacle, preferred to fly over it. But it seems to me that this is carrying the reputed conservatism of birds too far.

I asked Auden how deep he thought the ice might be at this point on the glacier. He surprised me by saying that it was probably at least 2,000 feet thick. It seemed hardly credible that if two Eiffel Towers were placed vertically on top of each other on the bed of the glacier, the topmost one would not appear above the surface of the ice.

In a remarkably short time, we reached the point where the Main glacier bent round at a sharp angle to the west. We camped at this corner in a wide hollow, partly filled by five small lakes. In the evening we climbed several hundred feet above the camp to a sharp ridge of disintegrating marble that formed the actual corner of the valley. The weather, which had been bad all day, cleared at sunset, revealing a splendid view of the upper part of the glacier, which ran up at an easy angle to a snowbasin enclosed by sharp peaks. We saw no less than four saddles leading over the watershed formed by these peaks. Each of these saddles lay at the head of a small tributary glacier, and was accessible from this side. We took compass bearings to these saddles and made a guess at their distance so as to be able to plot their rough position on our chart. The gathering dusk put an end to our work, though the sky was still luminous with the soft colours of evening. In my mind was a curious mingling of peace and impatient excitement. That night I dreamt that Angtharkay and I succeeded in crossing a pass which led down to a glacier flowing between beautiful woodlands. At the snout of the glacier we met an Englishman, who invited us to a cocktail party at his house. Angtharkay was opposed to this idea, as he said it was late in the afternoon and we would be benighted on our way back. However, I was weak-minded, and we went into a crowded drawing-room for a 'quick one'. I asked where we were, and my host replied, 'Braldu of course, didn't you know?' We took a taxi back up the glacier to the foot of the pass, but even so we were too late, and night had fallen before we got back to the camp. The dream had a grain of prophetic truth.

In spite of the fine evening, it started to snow lightly before we slept, and had not ceased when we awoke next morning. But we started early, and soon there was a temporary lull in the falling snow. We had numbered the saddles that we had seen the night before from right to left, beginning with the one farthest up the glacier. I had elected to explore No. 2 saddle with Angtharkay, as my calculations of its position had suggested that it would lead in the right direction for my purpose. The others were bound for No. 3 saddle, which was farther to the south and a great deal higher.

The two parties kept together for an hour and a half, and then our ways separated. We passed some fairly large tributaries coming down from the 'Father Christmas' group, which probably connected with the country that Spender was surveying. Angtharkay and I kept going steadily for another three hours before we made a brief halt. After that the weather changed for the worse. Visibility was restricted to a few yards and snow was falling heavily. But we had seen the ground ahead of us, and with a compass we had no difficulty in keeping our course. When we reached the saddle (about 19,000 feet) we were met by a violent wind, which doubled us up and lashed our faces with hard, frozen snow. The only hope of seeing anything seemed to be to cross the saddle; there was a chance that we might find shelter from the bitterly cold wind on the far side. But a few cautious steps forward took us on to a very steep ice slope, of unknown depth and covered with a thick deposit of fresh snow. We waited for a few minutes, but I got so cold that I started cutting steps down the slope into an inferno of whirling snow and mist. Once we had started we had to go on, taking the work in turn. I could not make up my mind which was the more unpleasant job: the infinitely laborious task of cutting steps through deep snow into the ice, blinded by the strong upward swirl of frozen particles, or standing above trying to brace one's body against the possibility of a slip, while the wind did its best to blow one over, and froze one's limbs into useless numbness. We had no idea whether the bottom of the slope was twenty feet below us or two thousand. The work seemed to go on interminably, and I was about to give it up when we reached a bergschrund, below which we could see a gentle snow slope. We crossed the bergschrund in a swift sitting glissade.

It was 1.30 by Angtharkay's watch, which kept fairly good time, providing it was wound up every six hours. A slight rift in the clouds gave us a vague view into a deep and complicated valley system below us. To the south, a great wall of peaks stretched away for a long distance. This meant we couldn't be above the Panmah glacier, while the void below did not suggest the proximity of the Snow Lake.

We made our way down through soft snow, and before long we emerged below the clouds. We found that we were in the upper basin of a small glacier which was one of many flowing from an immense cirque, which in its turn was obviously the head of a large glacier system. The main glacier could not be seen, but there were indications that it flowed in a northerly direction. The view to the north was blocked by a high rock ridge running west from the watershed we had just crossed. It was high time to turn back, but the temptation to see over this ridge was too great, and we made towards it as quickly as we could. Angtharkay entered into the spirit of the hunt with his usual enthusiasm, and led the way across steep ice slopes. It was slow work and we took a long time to reach the foot of the ridge. We climbed to the top of a rock pinnacle, and saw below a great glacier flowing away to the north. Judging from its position, direction and size, there could be no doubt that this was the Braldu glacier, and from where we stood it would be easy to reach it. For me it was an exciting discovery, as it gave us access to the ranges of the Shimshal pass.

I drew a sketch map and took a round of compass bearings. Then we started back, hurrying as much as possible. We were both tired, and although the track was already made, it took us nearly two hours to reach the bergschrund at the foot of the pass. We had a lot of trouble in crossing it to reach the ice slope above. There we found that our steps had been obliterated by the driving snow; and had to be recut. I thought that we should never reach the pass, but it was easier to cut steps uphill, and by now the blizzard had ceased.

By the time we had regained the pass, the mountains to the west were clear, though great masses of storm cloud still hid the high peaks. The view was magnificent, but very perplexing, and there was not time to try to understand it. I managed to identify the saddle that the other party had been aiming for, and saw that it also led into the Braldu basin, though a tremendous ice cliff on its north-west side made it impossible to cross. I had been lucky in my choice; from what I had seen it was plain that there was no route over Saddle No. 1.

The peaks on the other side of the Braldu basin looked a tremendous distance away, and there was no sign of the ice cap that we had expected to find.

It was doubtful if we could reach the camp before it was too dark to see; everything depended upon the state of the snow on the glacier. It was a relief to be going gently downhill, and we ran madly along. At first the snow was good, but soon we came to a very bad patch, and as we floundered slowly across it, we realised that we were going to be beaten by the oncoming darkness. However, the conditions soon improved, and we swung down over the hard surface with a peaceful sense of unreality induced by physical fatigue and by the fading evening light. But the innumerable crevasses that crossed our path were real enough and were becoming increasingly difficult to see. I fell up to my head in one of these, and heard the ominous tinkle of icicles as they fell into the void below my feet. A welcome drink from a glacier lake refreshed us. It was another fine evening, and after night had fallen there was still enough light to grope our way along.

The ice became smoother, and we stepped out with more confidence. As we approached the corner we heard a shout from someone who had evidently come to look for us. Suddenly I felt the ground give way from under my feet and found myself falling through space. It seemed an age before a tug came from the rope, and I had time to wonder whether it really was tied round my waist! But at length my fall was checked with a sudden jerk; it felt as if the rope had nearly cut me in two. It was difficult to judge how far I had fallen. The ragged patch of starlit sky, at the top of the hole through which I had dropped, looked very far above me. I found that the crevasse was just narrow enough for me to get my feet against one ice wall and my back against the other. By this method, known to climbers as *chimneying*, I climbed up for a short way. But I soon became exhausted, for it is no easy matter to obtain sufficient friction on ice to *chimney* between vertical walls. In the dark I thrust my foot against an icicle that gave way, and I fell again, this time into a deep lake at the bottom of the crevasse. I tried to find some purchase below the surface of the water, but could find nothing but loose bits of ice floating about. I was becoming very cold, and there was not much time to waste before numbness would make action impossible. I found an ice bollard jutting out of one of the walls, a few feet above the water. I managed to get my left arm over this, and, with some help from the rope, to hoist myself out of the water. The bollard did not feel very safe and I was afraid that it would collapse; by this time I had little strength left for further efforts.

When only two men are travelling together on a glacier – a stupid practice at the best of times – it is wise for the man behind to carry a spare length of rope. Fortunately Angtharkay was doing this. I shouted to him to send down an end with a loop tied in it. At first I could not make him hear, and it seemed a long time before the rope came dangling down. Having found it in the dark,

I slipped my foot into the loop, and, using it as a stirrup, stood in it. Angtharkay then pulled in the slack of my waist rope. It was rather difficult to make him understand which rope to make fast and which to pull in, but eventually I was brought to the surface of the glacier, and climbed out of the crevasse. I sat gasping on the ice while Angtharkay banged and rubbed my limbs, which had lost all feeling. In his excitement Angtharkay put one foot down the crevasse and very nearly fell in himself. I had lost my ice axe.

The incident was a well-deserved lesson; firstly, for being so rash as to get benighted; secondly, for travelling over an unknown glacier with only one companion; and thirdly, having taken that risk, for not having made certain that he had a full understanding of the 'stirrup rope' method of getting a companion out of a crevasse. I was lucky to have got off so lightly.

We groped our way on to the corner. Here we met the other three on their way up to search for us. Apparently it had been Tilman whose shouts we had heard just before I fell into the crevasse. Angtharkay had shouted back rather incoherently, and Tilman had gathered that something was wrong. Not knowing what was the matter, he returned to camp to fetch the others, and to bring spare clothing, food and ropes. We all went down to the camp together. I stripped off my water-logged clothes and was soon in my sleeping bag with hot tea and a pipe.

The other three reported a completely blank day. They had reached their col, which was 19,500 feet high, at about midday. It was blowing a gale and snowing heavily. As far as they could see, there was no chance of getting down the other side, and there was only a narrow corniced snow ridge to sit on and wait for a possible clearing. So they gave it up and returned to camp, expecting to find us already there. When by evening we still had not returned, they became anxious, and Tilman had climbed to our view point of the previous evening to look for us. As it turned out, their failure to see anything from their col did not matter, as we had been able to settle the question of its farther side.

Next morning, the other three went off to explore Saddle No. 4. Angtharkay and I stayed in our sleeping bags. It was a fine day, but I had no regrets at my laziness, for I was tired and more than satisfied with the previous day's work. Also I had a pain in my back, a souvenir of my adventure in the crevasse. I slept most of the morning and, in the afternoon, I lay in the sun and read copies of the *Calcutta Statesman* four months old, that Auden had brought for wrapping up geological specimens. I derived as much enjoyment from them as if they had been that morning's issue. Angtharkay washed his long hair with great care, then he oiled it and twisted it up into a neat plait, which he wound round his head. He loves to do this, in the sunshine, whenever he has any spare time.

The other party returned in the evening after a successful day. They had reached the saddle which was 18,000 feet high. From the top they looked down into what they at once recognised to be the basin of the Nobande Sobande glacier, which is the principal tributary of the Panmah glacier on the southern side of the main watershed. These glaciers had been explored by Professor Desio, of the Duke of Spoleto's expedition, in 1929. Crossing a small tributary glacier on the other side of the col, Tilman, Auden and Ila had climbed on to another col about 18,100 feet high. From there the view to the west was very extensive. They looked for a great distance along the main continental water-shed, which, as we had now discovered, separated the Braldu and the Nobande Sobande basins. Far beyond they saw a range of pinnacled rock peaks, which must lie, they supposed, near the head of the Biafo glacier and the Snow Lake. This view enabled them to make tentative plans.

The reconnaissance of routes from the head of the Crevasse glacier had taken less time than we anticipated. In spite of the fine weather, which per-sisted on 5 August, we retreated to Dump IV, though we regretted having to waste the day by going down the glacier instead of breaking new ground. Tilman, Auden and Ila, taking with them a light camp and food for three days, went on to investigate the Crown glacier, the source of which we had not yet placed. The next day Angtharkay and I went up the 'Father Christmas glacier' to find Spender and to hear his report of the country he had been surveying. We had trouble in crossing some surface streams which had cut deep troughs in the ice, and a line of ice pinnacles at the junction of the two glaciers delayed us. But on the 'Father Christmas glacier' we walked up a medial moraine that was as smooth as a high road. We met Nukku coming down with a note from Spender, and he conducted us far up the glacier to Spender's base, which we reached that evening. Spender had been luckier than we in the timing of his work.

He had employed the two days of bad weather, August 2nd and 3rd, in marching up the glacier. The three succeeding days had been perfect and he had accomplished an amazing amount of work. He had completed no less than three high stations on each of these days. In this way he had not only mapped in detail the whole of the 'Father Christmas glacier' system, but he had fixed the position of many distant peaks which had come into view. What was more, he had discovered a route to the north, over a comparatively easy pass, into a deep valley running east and west, which he supposed to be a trib-utary of the Braldu glacier. After discussing the question in detail, we decided that it would be more profitable to attempt this route than to cross the pass that I had discovered into the upper basin of the Braldu glacier. The difficult ice slope on the other side of my pass, and the extraordinary simplicity of travel on the 'Father Christmas glacier', were additional arguments in favour of this plan.

That night the fine spell broke, and on 7 August, leaving behind a small depot of stores, we returned to Dump IV in rain and falling snow. We got very wet and had difficulty in cooking our evening meal. We sat up late; I was just dozing off to sleep at about ten o'clock when a boulder, falling from above with a series of sharp retorts, set my nerves tingling. This was followed, ten minutes later, by louder crashes near the camp. Obviously something had to be done. It was snowing steadily and the night was warm. If it were to freeze later, an enormous mass of rock would probably be dislodged, and might wipe out the whole camp. But it was pitch dark, and the glacier lantern was somewhere outside in a dump of loads that was buried in snow. The candles that we burned in our tents would not stay alight for a second in heavily falling snow. I was discussing the situation with Spender when there was a prolonged and deafening roar, which became louder and louder, and was accompanied by the whirring sound of flying splinters. This culminated in a noise like a clap of thunder within a few yards of the tent, which was followed by absolute silence. It was difficult to believe that none of the camp had been hit, but after a moment of frozen suspense I heard shouts and laughter from the Sherpas whose tent was twenty yards away. This bombshell had the effect of bringing the whole party to its feet, except for the Baltis, who did not seem unduly disturbed, and were quite indignant when we dragged them out from under their blankets. It was a long, cold business shifting our tents and sleeping bags on to the ice hummocks out of range of the bombardment. We got very wet. It was impossible, in the dark, to cut platforms, but somehow we succeeded in erecting the tents with sufficient floor-space for everyone to lie down.

When dawn broke we found that a foot of snow had fallen, and it was still coming down in large soft flakes. At midday, when there was still no improvement in the weather, we began to get rather worried about the other party. It would be difficult to get through pinnacled ice with all this new snow, and by now their food and fuel would be nearly finished. Visibility was practically nil, and until it improved it was no use setting out to look for them. At about three o'clock it stopped snowing and diffused sunlight filtered through the clouds. We were preparing to start down the glacier when we suddenly saw the others approaching the camp. They were all very tired, having covered a lot of difficult ground during the last three days. They had obtained sufficient data for Spender to be able to place the Crown glacier, which was twelve miles long, on the map. This helped us considerably in our subsequent attempt to unravel the intricacies of the mountains lying between us and the Shaksgam.

It started snowing again in the evening and continued heavily all night. Although it cleared up at about ten o'clock the next morning and became brilliantly fine, there was too much snow for us to move up the glacier, and we were confined to the camp for another day of inactivity. It was an annoying waste of time, but when we considered that it was the first time that we had been seriously held up by bad weather during the whole season, we could not complain.

There is a good deal of talking during these occasional days of forced idleness. I recorded in my diary a list of subjects of conversation on a similar occasion: Organ playing compared with engine driving (Spender was a bit of an expert at both); national characteristics; farming at home and in Africa; art and literature for love or money; life in Berlin and Vienna; winter in Norway; food (always the most enchanting of subjects); why men go to sea; civilised and primitive culture; Tolstoy – from which to strategy and luck in war; sensitiveness and callousness; asceticism and indulgence; that dinner we had in Paris on the way out; and so back to food – with special emphasis on dripping!

On 10 August Tilman and Auden started on their journeys. Tilman had with him Ila and Sen Tensing, and took food enough for twenty-three days. Auden had the four Baltis, and took food to last for a fortnight. Spender and I, and two of our Sherpas, accompanied them to our camp up the Main glacier, while Angtharkay, Lobsang and Nukku started relaying our thirty days' food up the 'Father Christmas glacier'. Travel on the upper glaciers was very different from what it had been a few days before. Now, in the deep new snow, we had to work hard for every yard of progress. At the upper camp we said goodbye to Auden and Tilman, whom we did not expect to see again until we got back to England.

15 Panmah Journey
by J.B. Auden

My last view of Tilman and the two Sherpas was on 15 August through the theodolite telescope from a survey station at 17,300 feet. They were black specks on the top of the Faith col. The day was fine and, as the two Baltis whom I had sent on the 12th to reconnoitre a route had reported that there was an easy way down to the Nobande Sobande, I did not hurry, but lazed by the theodolite admiring the view and thinking of arriving back in England after nearly four years' absence. But our feet were wet, and at midday we started our descent to the main glacier. It was out of the question to go down the icefall of the side glacier, but the Baltis had stated that there was a gully on the west side. This gully unfortunately led down to a precipice, necessitating a horizontal traverse before descending with the rope some couloirs in the limestone cliffs. The Nobande Sobande was reached at sunset, and we saw to our dismay that it was far more crevassed and broken up than had been apparent from above. The Primus stove had always been a failure, and as it would not light at all on the night of the 11th, I had already thrown it away to lighten our loads, and had given the paraffin to Tilman. We therefore spent our second night without hot food.

The next day we tried to get on to the main glacier, a short distance above our camp, but were held up thirty yards from the edge by blocks of tumbled ice. There was only one ice axe between the five of us, so that it was not possible to split up into two reconnoitring parties. An unsuccessful attempt was then made to cross the side glacier leading down from the 18,000-col, after which the main glacier was penetrated by a route just below the camp. After several hours amongst an intricate system of small valleys in the ice we had advanced about 600 yards into the Nobande Sobande, but crevasses had so split up the glacier into isolated wedges and towers that further advance was barred. It was now about three o'clock and despondency was setting in. It would have been possible to return next morning up the cliffs by which we had come down, cross the 18,000 col glacier above its icefall, descend to the Nobande Sobande from the east side, but by so doing two days' rations would be used up, without having gone more than half a mile towards Askole. We climbed a certain way up the mountain-side to get a revised bird's-eye view of the crevasse system cutting the col glacier late in the evening. There was a little dry grass here, but not enough to cook a hot meal. Hussain was diligent with his prayers, and Allah was invoked throughout the night.

The next day we kept to the left wall of the Nobande Sobande, sometimes along an ablation valley, and sometimes, where the ice pressed against the rock wall, traversing along the cliffs above. The first flowers were seen just west of the Drenmang glacier. Mahadi put some in his hat and began singing at the prospect of an early release from his hardships. He became more subdued when we reached the Drenmang. The broken ice of the Nobande Sobande lay against the valley wall and appeared to offer no route. I climbed about 1,500 feet hoping to find a gully descending to the Drenmang, but all the gullies ended in difficult couloirs. On returning to the others, I gave Mahadi and Hussain my ice axe and sent them to explore an alternative route. Two hours went by, and once again imagination invented the worst disasters. But they returned radiant and covered with mud. They had found a route through tunnels in the ice where the highly broken-up margin of the glacier joined on to the cliff, and had cut steps in all the difficult places. We had to hurry, since the ice the whole way along this route was discharging its boulders in the evening sun. Once on the Drenmang glacier the going was easy, and we reached the moraine on the south-east side whilst it was just light enough to see grass, flowers and wood in plenty. We at once lit a fire and had our first warm food since breakfast with Tilman sixty hours before.

The next day was perfect. While I went up at dawn to a station 15,230 feet in height with the theodolite, the Baltis roasted some fresh satu from our stock of flour. From Drenmang to Skinmang our route was over a grass-covered hill-side. About one and a half miles from Skinmang and at least 800 feet above the glacier we found a well-built cairn. Desio shows no itinerary on his map through this place, and it is probable that the cairn had been put up by Baltis, at a time when the Nobande Sobande presented fewer difficulties than now. After crossing the Skinmang glacier, we descended another five miles, following a bear track down an ablation valley and being occasionally bombarded by boulders dropped from the overhanging ice. Camp was pitched at the foot of the Eriole valley by flowering rose bushes.

Five minutes after crossing a ravine entering the Dumordo valley by the snout of the Panmah glacier, a mud-flow swept down, carrying with it immense boulders. I had often read of these flows, known as swas in the Punjab, and knew abstractly of the size of the boulders that are moved. But here was an actual demonstration, for one of the boulders must have weighed about 120 tons. The Baltis considered this escape to be one more proof that God exists and was favourably disposed.

The rest of the journey to Srinagar via the Skoro La and Deosai plains saw the fulfilment of long anticipated pleasures. Tobacco and eggs at Askole, apricots at Skoro, over three months' mail at Skardu, the grassy uplands of Deosai, and silver birch above Birzil. I arrived at Bandipura on 3 September and was welcomed by a letter from Lady Clutterbuck and a hamper of food. She had sent her car, which took me the next day to the trees and shady lawns of Srinagar.

16 Legends
by H.W. Tilman

11 August was another glorious day. Auden, with the four Baltis, myself, and my Sherpas, went up to the col that we had reconnoitred on 4 August. I dumped my loads on the far side and returned, while Auden, after doing a theodolite station on top, camped on the other side of the pass. The food for twenty-two days which my party was carrying, and our equipment, made up loads too heavy for the two Sherpas and myself, so we had to relay. Meanwhile Shipton and Spender were finishing the survey of the Crevasse glacier. On the 12th I left them at a station on my way to the col, or pass, as it had now become. Crossing quickly we found Auden's camp and a note, and at the same time saw his party moving down the glacier ahead of us. We joined forces and dropped down on to another tributary glacier lying north-west; having gone a little way up it, we camped on the ice.

Opposite was another short glacier leading to a col on the Nobande-Braldu watershed which we had already marked down as worth a visit. However, next day, we went above this col, by climbing an easy peak (18,770 feet) overlooking it from the west. From the top there was a remarkable view, but Auden was ungrateful, because there was no concrete bed, or its equivalent, for the legs of the wretched theodolite, and the sky was rapidly clouding over. He explained at some length, and with great warmth, that readings taken as the theodolite sank slowly into the snow might be accepted by nitwits like myself, but certainly by nobody else, and that some observations should have been made lower down, when the visibility was good.

Stunned though I was by this verbal storm, it was impossible not to enjoy the view which I, at any rate, had come for, and which was all the better for not being looked at upside down through the telescope of a theodolite. We could see the Ogre (23,900 feet), a triangulated peak whose position relative to the Biafo had always been a puzzle, Kanjut peak (25,460 feet), a great area of the upper Braldu, the Crown peak, the Drenmang, Chiring, upper Panmah, and Nobande Sobande glaciers, together with a confused jumble of peaks to the south, amongst which the mighty Masherbrum was alone distinguishable. From here I could see a route to the west across the two main arms of the Braldu. If there were a pass from the westernmost, it must lead either to the Biafo or the Virjerab; I hoped and believed it would lead to the former, but anyhow I made up my mind to try it.

The next day we all went up the glacier leading to the same col which later was called Faith pass. Auden turned aside to geologise, while I pushed on to the col with the two Sherpas and one Balti, all laden. This glacier was as badly crevassed as any I have seen, and the price of safety, as of liberty, was eternal vigilance. Approaching the col, the weather, which had been threatening, developed into a blizzard. We struggled on, hardly knowing the top when we reached it, dumped the loads there, and started back. In the driving snow it was difficult to keep even an approximate direction, and when the snow froze on our glasses it would have been impossible to see a haystack at a yard, let alone the half-concealed crevasses through which we had to thread our way. Removing my glasses every few yards, I led on, expecting every instant to be engulfed. Nothing happened. We got clear without putting a foot through; perhaps a benign Providence watches over the blind as well as the drunk.

The following day, 15 August, we separated, Auden making for the Panmah with the four recalcitrant Baltis; the two Sherpas and I for Faith pass and the Braldu. It was a brilliant morning, our tracks of yesterday were in places faintly recognisable, but in spite of that I fell into two crevasses in quick succession. The Sherpas held me, but in one my snow-glasses were swept off as my head went through the snow. My luck was in, for they were caught on a ledge. I was lowered to the ledge and managed to retrieve them.

Somewhat shaken by these untoward happenings, which made us marvel still more that we had escaped disaster under the unfavourable conditions of the previous day, we pushed slowly on to the dump on the col. Because of our small fuel reserve, we had exercised such strict economy since starting to use the Primus four days ago, that we had cooked nothing but tea and pemmican. The Sherpas at this inopportune moment complained of hunger and suggested opening a tin of pemmican to eat raw. Sen Tensing thought we ought to camp and make a real meal. Neither of these motions could be accepted by the Chair, and, having pointed out a distant rock outcrop by a glacier lake as our objective, I turned to find a way down.

Once down on the glacier, which was a tributary of the Braldu, we pressed on without stopping, camping finally at the appointed place on one of the main arms of the Braldu. The rocky spur on which we wanted to camp was rather high above the lake, and the question was whether to camp coldly on snow close to the water, or warmly on rock some distance from it. As I should not have to fetch the water, and also had a casting vote, we went to the rocks. That evening we made some satu on the Primus, and Sen Tensing's face assumed a less lugubrious look.

Sen Tensing was rather a character. He had attached himself to the Everest reconnaissance party in 1935 on the East Rongbuk glacier at Camp II, having turned up, unannounced, from Sola Khumbu in Nepal. He was so pleased with the clothes we gave him, or rather his appearance in them, that he never again took them off. Down in the valley under a blazing sun, miles from any snow, Sen Tensing could be seen fully attired in a windproof suit, gloves, glasses, boots, puttees, and Balaclava helmet, ready apparently to battle with some imminent and terrific blizzard. So fond was he of dressing the part of the complete mountaineer that I dubbed him the Foreign Sportsman, and the name stuck.

He is as broad as long and somewhat stout, very willing, cheerful, and talkative, full of his own importance, and by no means regardless of his own comfort and general wellbeing. For instance, at this very camp, I found that he had made himself an extra sleeping bag out of the canvas food bags that had been emptied and discarded from time to time. Most of us had collected one or two, but the Foreign Sportsman had 'won' six, cut them up and sewn them into a sleeping sack. Having got over his earlier passion for looking like the complete mountaineer, he now no longer wears the clothes he receives at the beginning of an expedition, but keeps them for sale or barter, and appears dressed like a country gentleman. This year he favoured a grey flannel suit with thick white stockings worn outside the trousers. He is for ever chanting interminable Tibetan prayers – at least the patience with which the other Sherpas suffered this chanting led us to suppose they were prayers and not smutty songs. He reads and writes Tibetan characters, and manages to do rather less than his share of the menial work without protest from the others; this, taken in conjunction with the prayer-chanting, leads us to suppose him an unfrocked Lama.

The following day I decided to risk a reconnaissance instead of first bringing the remaining loads down from the col. The dawn was not promising, so there was the risk of not seeing anything and thus wasting a day. Moreover, most of our food was still lying on the col, and I, no less than the Foreign Sportsman, was haunted by the thought that a prolonged spell of bad weather might prevent us from reaching it.

However, all went well. Starting very early while the snow was crisp, we followed a tributary glacier to the west, crossed the low but steep col at its head which took us down to the other main arm of the Braldu, crossed that, and made for a low snow ridge three miles away to the west. So wide was the saddle on this ridge that we had to go on for half a mile down a swelling convex slope before we could see anything below. There was much cloud about and more was rolling up, but we were in time to see and recognise the strikingly bold peaks of the Biafo west wall and the end of what the Workmans called the B15 ridge, all of which we had looked at so often in their photographs. With our eyes on the lowering clouds we hurried back, afraid of being caught by a storm similar to that of two days ago. No storm came, and by evening the weather looked more promising.

But it was snowing briskly when we left early on the 17th to fetch the loads, and visibility was poor. The crevasses on this tributary glacier were comparatively few, but there were enough to make us wish to avoid groping our way back in a blizzard. Conditions on top of the col and over the Panmah side were similar to those of the earlier storm, but once we started back the weather improved, and fitful gleams of sunshine brightened our return.

All we ever learnt about this Karakoram weather was that it is unpredictable. I remember on the Crevasse glacier, on the fifth day of a very fine spell, a sun halo was observed, and all our weather prophets tumbled over each other in haste to predict a change. Two more fine days followed, while the evening of the third appeared so settled that the prophets now spoke contemptuously of sun haloes and promised more fine weather. It was not surprising, therefore, that we woke the next morning to find it raining and blowing hard. It proved to be one of the only three really bad days we had. I say 'really' bad, though it was merely unpleasant – but there appear to be two sorts of bad weather – ordinary bad weather and surveyor's. Any day that is not clear, cloudless, still and warm, is for them 'bad' weather.

I hoped this would be our last relay. We had eaten forty pounds of food, a few odds and ends could be jettisoned, and by carrying very big loads, everything could be moved in one shift. When we arrived back I got the Sherpas to build the father and mother of all cairns which, before we left, I crowned with a tin containing a note. I had to climb the cairn to reach the top. It was likely that the pass which the main body were to cross would take them into the Braldu a long way down; they would have to come to the head for survey purposes, and I hoped they would spot our cairn, as in fact they did.

The promise of a clear night was this time realised. At dawn, mist spread up from the Braldu, but to the west, whence most of our weather came, it remained clear, and at 8 a.m., when we sat on the halfway col (Hope pass), it was brilliantly fine. The Sherpas were carrying seventy-five pounds each and myself fifty pounds, but we got safely down over the bergschrund and began the long plod, going very slowly, the snow rapidly softening.

The wide saddle (Charity pass) was reached at 1 p.m. There was not a cloud anywhere, so it was much easier to recognise the familiar landmarks of the Workmans' photographs. Unmistakably conspicuous was the Ogre, which was now seen to lie on the eastern end of the so-called B15 ridge, which itself formed the southern boundary of a long eastern tributary of the Snow Lake itself. This now lay below us, and it was already clear that it was a large *névé* field, the upper basin of the Biafo.

The descent was easy except when we got caught in some desperately soft patches of snow, but we soon set foot on dry land, on what might truly be called the shore of the Snow Lake, and camped about 3.30 p.m. Another blazing hot day followed. We left the camp standing and walking across the *névé* field to the south wall, a distance of about four miles. Two feeder glaciers, besides the one that we had descended, flow in from the east; one leads apparently to the Nobande Sobande where the watershed seemed difficult to cross, and the other and more southerly to the Choktoi, the pass to which looked very easy. This latter feeder is about three miles long, and its south wall is the remarkably high, precipitous, straight ridge carrying the Ogre, the peak almost overlooking the col. Some nine miles in length, this ridge terminates where the Snow Lake ends and the main Biafo begins its south-easterly course.

While contouring round the foot of the ridge between these two feeder glaciers, we saw in the snow the tracks of an Abominable Snowman. They were eight inches in diameter, eighteen inches apart, almost circular, without sign of toe or heel. They were three or four days old, so melting must have altered the outline. The most remarkable thing was that they were in a straight line one behind the other, with no 'stagger' right or left, like a bird's spoor. A four-footed animal walking slowly puts its hind foot in the track of its forefoot, but there is always some mark of overlapping, nor are the tracks immediately in front of each other. However many-legged it was, the beast or bird was heavy, the tracks being nearly a foot deep. We followed them for a mile, when they disappeared on some rock. The tracks came from a glacier pool where the animal had evidently drunk, and the next day we picked up the same spoor on the north side of Snow Lake.

The Sherpas judged them to belong to the smaller type of Snowman, or Yeti, as they call them, of which there are apparently two varieties: the smaller, whose spoor we were following, which feeds on men, while his larger brother confines himself to a diet of yaks. My remark that no one had been here for nearly thirty years and that he must be devilish hungry did not amuse the Sherpas as much as I expected! The jest was considered ill-timed, as perhaps it was, the three of us standing forlorn and alone in a great expanse of snow, looking at the strange tracks like so many Robinson Crusoes.

I have no explanation to offer, and, if I had, respect for ancient tradition would keep me silent. They were not the tracks of one of the many species of bears which seem to haunt the Himalaya, either Isabillinus, Pruinosus, or 'Bruinosus'; for naturalists, like stamp collectors, are keen on variety. There was no game of any kind, nor grass, within fifteen miles, and the nearest village was forty miles away. A few days later, lower down in the Cornice glacier valley, bear tracks were common and were recognised as such by the Sherpas and myself. A one-legged, carnivorous bird, weighing perhaps a ton, might make similar tracks, but it seems unnecessary to search for a new species when we have a perfectly satisfactory one at hand in the form of the Abominable Snowman – new perhaps to science but old in legend. All respecters of tradition must have noticed with surprise and regret how a certain great newspaper allowed the hospitality of its columns to be used, or rather abused, by the iconoclasts for a determined attack upon the very existence of the Abominable Snowman. No great harm, however, was done. Bear tracks (species not agreed) were in the course of a column and a half successfully proved to be made by bears; wolves and otters were found to make tracks after their kind, and when the dust had settled the Abominable Snowman remained to continue his evasive, mysterious, terrifying existence, unruffled as the snows he treads, unmoved as the mountains amongst which he dwells, uncaught, unspecified, and not unhonoured.

On the 20th we struck camp and crossed the Snow Lake to the west, walking first on *névé* and then on bare ice. The descent was almost imperceptible. The area of this nearly flat eastern basin of the Biafo I should put at about six miles by three; at the most twenty square miles instead of 300. It is a disappointingly small area for such a grandiose name, and though one might wish secretly to find the first impressions of earlier and better travellers confirmed, a discrepancy of that size is difficult to overlook.

Another strange feature that had caused a good deal of dispute among geographers was the Workmans' Cornice glacier. According to these explorers they had found a glacier which had no outlet, being completely surrounded by mountains. This remarkable glacier lay in the angle formed by the Hispar south wall and by the Biafo west wall, and although never actually reached, yet it had been observed from all sides. Sir Martin Conway denied the physical possibility of an enclosed glacier, on the ground that for thousands of years snow must have been pouring into it, and that either the resulting ice would have piled up and overflowed the barrier wall, or melted and found an outlet as water. The Workmans retorted that they had observed correctly, and appealed to the argumentum ad hominem – Sir Martin Conway 'not having seen the glacier in question nor its barriers' – leaving the controversy to be renewed by us after a lapse of nearly thirty years. Shipton and Spender had derided the idea of a completely enclosed glacier, while Auden and I supported the Doctor and Mrs Workman – more, perhaps, from chivalrous motives than for any scientific reason. So upon me lay the task of establishing (I hoped) the truth of the Workmans' assertion and of confounding the scientific sceptics – a consummation always desirable, if seldom attainable.

Five miles from our camp of 20 August we reached the main Biafo glacier. To our right we looked up a northern extension of it to the watershed of what must be either the Virjerab or Khurdopin glaciers. Facing us to the west was the gentle rise to the Hispar pass some three miles away, while on our left the main Biafo glacier flowed in a broad stream to the south-west. We crossed it here, where it is, perhaps, two miles in width, and camped on some rocks at the foot of the western wall just below the point where this bends to form the southern wall of the Hispar glacier. On the way over we noticed a deep gash cut in this great wall, some two miles below the spot where we pitched our camp. It looked somewhat like a col shown on one of the Workmans' photographs, which now proved to be close to camp. I had studied this photograph hopefully, but the col itself proved to be quite impracticable. Lying between this impassable col and our camp was a short tributary glacier leading to a high saddle and to a snow peak, from which it seemed likely that a view of what lay behind the west wall could be obtained. Somewhere behind the wall lay the Workmans' Cornice glacier, on which we meant to set foot.

We tackled the peak next day. Having left camp very early, we presently became involved in the intricacies of a difficult icefall. When at length found, the route was amusing, passing through a tunnel under a mammoth block of cold, blue ice, and beneath beautiful but dangerously unstable séracs which were just beginning to catch and reflect the light of the rising sun – a fact which made one mentally resolve to return by another route if that were possible. A mile beyond, another and steeper icefall held us up until overcome at last by means of a series of snow bridges, which no reasonable man would have contemplated had there been an alternative crossing.

From the snow plateau above we gained a footing on the peak which 'went' pleasantly enough until within about 200 feet from the top, when our ridge became icy, and narrowed to what climbers like to describe as a knife-edge. It is an expressive term, but the knife-edges of some, probably my own, are blunter than those of others. There ought to be some kind of definition for those knife-edge ridges, those ice walls, and overhanging rocks, which are climbed with such distressing ease and frequency. However, we left this particular knife-edge ridge alone. There was some excuse for this faint-heartedness – one of the soles of my boots was flapping loose, and to my mind the Foreign Sportsman and Ila climbed with too much abandon to be desirable companions on such a place.

We descended to the plateau and ascended the saddle whence another ridge of our peak beckoned invitingly. On closer inspection it proved more formidable than the first, but from a short way up we got a reasonable view.

Immediately below, at the bottom of a deep chasm, was a glacier flowing south-west, to be joined after a short distance by two other valleys. We could not see into them, but they obviously contained glaciers flowing from the Biafo west wall. Beyond the glacier was a tumbled sea of peaks that would have defied the topographical sense of a homing pigeon. The head of the glacier abutted against the Hispar south wall, and a remarkable feature was the grass and juniper wood which we could see growing in the valley unusually close to its head. To our ice-weary eyes the vision was tantalising, and prospect of reaching wood so quickly fired the Sherpas with a mighty longing to get down to it. It was clear that the glacier was either the Cornice glacier itself or a branch of it. There was no way down to it from the saddle, and a descent from the Hispar wall looked doubtful, so before investigating that, we decided to try another low col we had noticed further along the Biafo wall, which very probably led to one of the two tributary glaciers whose presence we guessed. It would be far more satisfactory to enter the Cornice glacier at its head and follow it down, or better still remain imprisoned in its fastnesses, than merely to view it from afar, as the Workmans had done, or to search for its outlet.

For our return on so hot an afternoon it seemed wise, if possible, to avoid the two icefalls. The attempt was unsuccessful. After a long snow trudge we came to an impasse, and after thus wasting an hour and much energy, found ourselves trusting once more to the precarious bridges of the steep icefall, which were weakened now by the hot sun. This mistake rather lessened the allure of new routes, and although the next icefall could have been avoided by a long climb, when I put the proposal to the Sherpas, pointing out the increasing risks from the séracs and the ice tunnel, they replied that my imaginary perils would be passed in a few minutes while the climb might take hours – a very unsound argument but one with which, at the time, I heartily agreed.

On 22 August we went down the Biafo to reconnoitre the gap in the west wall. There was no approach by any side glacier, for it was simply a deep notch cut in the high, precipitous rock ridge which bounds the Biafo on that side. To reach it we had to climb up a long avalanche cone of ice debris directly beneath the hanging glacier from which this had fallen. Frequent creaks and groans seemed to portend another fall. There was little difficulty in gaining the col, perhaps seven or eight hundred feet above the Biafo, but at first glance the chances of getting down the other side looked exceedingly slim. The unknown glacier, whose surface was bare ice, lay nearly 2,000 feet below, shut in by tremendous cliffs. After about a mile it disappeared out of sight round a corner, but I was confident that this was the glacier on which the Workmans had looked from the Sosbun and Hoh Lungma cols, and, moreover, that it joined the glacier we had seen the day before from the peak. We stood on a narrow gap between two frowning rock walls. On our right only 100 feet of smooth rock separated us from a negotiable slope of snow below, but we could not climb down, nor was there anchorage for an abseil, even if we had sufficient rope. On the left a narrow corridor of snow dropped steeply to end in a snow wall above an icefall, but after studying the wall for some time we detected a break in its defences. Some grass which we could see just above the corner drew us like a loadstone; we felt that the Cornice glacier was as good as reached, and that the icefall must be difficult indeed to stop us.

While we were walking back to camp, a white, filmy look in the sky indicated the end of another fine spell. Dawn of the 23rd was thick and snow was falling lightly. We packed up and hurried down the glacier, having some difficulty in locating our col in the gathering mist. The fractured ice above groaned ominously as we panted up the ice debris, sweating profusely with the fear of its falling and with the haste we made to get clear before it did. The sweat fogged our glasses so that we stopped often to wipe them, and though this made us realise the foolishness of hurrying, yet it was difficult to move slowly under the threats of immediate extinction from above. That day the narrow gap was a forbidding spot. Mist drove across it and swirled about the great, gaunt cliffs which lowered blackly at us as though grudging our passage. We built a cairn before descending into the mists, and by midday we were looking back at it from the Cornice glacier. I had tried to impress upon the Sherpas the peculiarities of this glacier – that no river issued from it – that presently we should come to a blank wall and find ourselves entirely shut in by mountains. They listened politely but incredulously, evidently entertaining more respect for my imagination than my veracity. Their belief in the strange behaviour of the glacier was no greater than mine in the man-eating propensities of the Yeti.

As we rounded the first corner, the mist turned to rain, and we pressed on in search of the wood that we were confident we should soon find. On the abrupt cliffs of the north side – the south-facing wall – grass grew wherever it could cling, and presently we camped in a little meadow, lying at the foot of a crag, where there were flowers, birds, the hum of insects, and much spoor of bharal; all commonplace things, but giving unbounded pleasure to us after five long weeks of glacier travel. Down the valley a high ridge, seen dimly through the rain, appeared to block the way, but if I ever had indulged any hopes that the glacier might outrage natural laws, the rapidity of its fall dispelled them. Nevertheless our situation was not without charm. We could sing that night as we used to sing in France, trundling across country in a troop train to some unknown destination: 'We don't know where we're going, but we're on the way'.

After our usual breakfast of tea and satu, eaten by a less usual wood fire, we continued down the north bank, our direction lying slightly north of west. To our starved senses the vegetation seemed tropically lush; in the moraine trough were rose bushes, and juniper, while long grass covered the hillside to a height of several hundred feet. Traces of bear and buck abounded. Five or six miles from our pass we came to a slightly bigger glacier flowing south-west, and in the corner between the two glaciers was an old unused grazing camp, a sight which greatly excited us, as traces of human life in wild country always did. We crossed the mile-wide glacier, finding on the far side a path and recent signs of cattle. I was sure that this was the glacier we saw from the peak, but to make certain I went up it for a mile. The vegetation here was equally profuse. On the hillside grassy bays ran up for 500 feet above the ice, and there were even a few birch trees growing within two or three miles of the Hispar watershed. I reached a point far enough up to see the peak on which we had failed, but the short glacier which must lie below it on the south was still hidden.

After I rejoined the Sherpas we followed down the right bank, passing great logs of juniper which made me long to camp and start a fire. After a fortnight without wood, I felt quite guilty at passing all this fuel without adding some to our loads, forgetting that we were going down the glacier and not up. Two miles on we reached the snout of the glacier and a grazing village of tumble-down stone huts. Conversation with the inhabitants was not easy, but we managed to get a few eggs and learnt that the village from which the shepherds came was Bisil in the main Basha valley. We could now identify the nullah we were in as that marked on the map as the Kushuchun Lungma. It is difficult to understand how the Workmans failed to suspect some connection between the large stream issuing from this nullah and their Cornice glacier, when they affirmed so positively that it had no outlet. In a drab world it would be refreshing to report the discovery of a glacier flowing uphill, or even of one which did not flow at all. It gives me no pleasure, therefore, to have to affirm that this glacier behaved as others do. To many – schoolmasters and parents, editors and politicians, for instance – correcting the mistakes of others is a congenial task. As it is more usual for me to give than to receive opportunities for performing this pleasant duty, I ought to have rejoiced, but I can honestly say that to tramp down the Cornice glacier, hoping every moment to reach an impasse and finding none, was as sorry a business as any that has fallen to my lot.

The path down the nullah was rough, and having crossed the river by a snow bed, we began casting about for a camp site still some miles short of the main valley. One promising site had to be abandoned because the sparkling spring which first attracted us proved to be impregnated with sulphur.

Early next morning we dropped down to Bisil, but before reaching the village we stopped to admire a beautiful, pointed snow peak to the south-east which I identified on the map, wrongly as it happened, as Ganchen (21,100 feet). From that distance it looked climbable, as most peaks do, and I set my heart on it. From the village itself two more snow peaks on the same ridge, but farther north, came into view. The northernmost appeared to be the highest of the three and was called Ganchen by the men of Bisil. Later, viewing the range from the opposite side, I thought the second peak the higher – which agreed with the Workmans, who had named that Ganchen.

There can be no more delightful village at which to arrive after four months in uninhabited wilderness than Bisil. Yellowing wheat fields, pale pink buckwheat, shady walnuts and stately poplars gladdened my eyes, and in the centre of the village a stone tank fed by a bubbling hot sulphur spring waited to refresh my body. Though I was watched by the whole astonished populace, man, woman, and child, I lost no time in undressing, but before I was ready to leap into this heavenly tank a curious conversation took place between the Sherpas and the village headman. 'How many are there in your party?' the headman asked. 'We porters and a Sahib.' 'Yes, I see, but' (looking hard at me) 'where is the Sahib?' This pleased the Sherpas immensely, and I kept the thing going by assuring the headman that the Sahib was a bit tired but would arrive shortly.

Flour, eggs and potatoes were forthcoming, also some apples, which, though watery, woolly, and everything an apple should not be, tasted to me, at that moment, like a Cox's. The Basha valley with its pleasant villages was a scene of peace, made beautiful by the changing greens and yellows of the ripening crops. We were, of course, the subject of much curiosity because no one could understand by what route we had come.

Six miles down, at a village called Zil, we struck up the hillside to the left in the direction of our peak. The elevation of the valley is only about 9,000 feet, so there was clearly some stiff climbing in front of us to get within striking distance of a 21,000-foot peak rising so close to the valley; nor would it be easy, now that we were so close underneath it, to find the best line of approach. When we had climbed high enough to dislike the idea of turning back, we discovered that the nullah we were making for was closed at its head by a high rock ridge, apparently cutting us off from the peak. Above us was a grazing village, to which we climbed disconsolately, and there we camped. What our next move should be I had no notion, but at any rate the hundreds of cows, yaks, goats, and sheep grazing on the hillside assured us of a drink of milk. We got our milk and with it some information, the locals assuring us that the forbidding rock curtain at the nullah head could be climbed easily. They had no name for the fine peak close above, radiantly lit by the last rays of the setting sun, though it surely must have impressed itself upon their imaginations, if they had any. They had never heard of Ganchen, but paradoxically, the man who did all the talking, knew all the principal cities of India.

In the morning, leaving Sen Tensing to guard our few possessions, Ila and I set out to reconnoitre. After a climb of about 3,000 feet we reached the foot of the rock ridge and found it scored with a number of easy gullies invisible from below. Having selected one of these we had no difficulty in reaching the top, some 4,000 feet above camp. Only a few hundred feet below, on the other side, was the meeting place of two small glaciers descending from our pointed peak and from the next peak to the north, Ganchen of the map. There was a high, but apparently possible col on the ridge south of Ganchen, but neither peak could be climbed either from there or from the glaciers. Descending 1,000 feet and climbing another gully, we looked into a nullah on the south. From there, too, our peak was inaccessible, so I decided to curb ambition and try the col. We had to get back to Askole, but to go round by the valley was dull, whereas if we crossed this Ganchen range we should find ourselves in the Hoh Lungma valley, whence we could climb one of the Workmans' cols and thus make sure that the glacier they saw was the same as that which we had traversed. The possibility that somehow we had mislaid the Cornice glacier had just occurred to me, so I determined to make sure. Opponents of the 'enclosed glacier' school, of which, as I have said, I was a warm supporter, would no doubt have derided me for clutching thus at straws.

Sitting perched on the ridge in warm sunshine, debating these matters of high policy, we saw an old grey-bearded ibex stroll unsuspectingly beneath us within spitting distance. Ila, of course, wanted to hurl a volley of stones; any moving animal, whether ten or a hundred yards away, seems to excite the stone-throwing proclivities of the Sherpas.

We got back about 4 p.m., to find the village unoccupied except for one old man and a boy. I feared that the Foreign Sportsman had somehow been the cause of this wholesale exodus, but was relieved to find they had merely gone down to the valley to work in the fields for the day. They returned at dusk and all gathered round our fire; with them was the much-travelled ex-bearer who had already entertained us with his travels from Bombay to Rangoon. The sub-ject he unfailingly returned to was his last master, whom he called a 'bhot-baksheesh-deni-wallah sahib', which is to say, a very open-handed gent. The hint, however, was not taken, and I gave him no opportunities for invidi-ous comparisons. Like the headman of Bisil, he, too, on first seeing us, had asked where the Sahib was, but in this case the mistake was more reasonable, because it is conceivable that the sahibs he saw in Bombay, Calcutta and Rangoon were less shaggy and better dressed than I was.

On one or two occasions earlier in the year Shipton and I had almost come to the conclusion, directly contrary to that of the textbooks, that time spent in reconnaissance is always wasted, but if you do choose to waste (or save) time by reconnoitring a route it is not at all a bad plan to follow it. However, Ila and I thought better and decided that by crossing the ridge, which divided us from the glaciers, much farther north we should save ourselves some steep climb-ing. So next day we traversed gently upwards for a mile and a half, gained the ridge at a reasonable height, and then looked down a most unmanageable drop, which, had we attempted it, would have brought us into the nullah at a point several thousand feet below the glacier we were trying to reach. Comment was unnecessary, even inadvisable. Sorrowfully retracing our steps to the gully of yesterday, we toiled up it with our heavy loads, dropped down the other side, and camped on grass just above the glacier descending from the pointed peak. It was a pleasant camp, with fresh water, enough wood for cook-ing, and a great view, comprising most of the Hispar peaks including Kanjut (25,460 feet) and one which might have been Dasto Ghil (25,868 feet). From the ridge above camp we had seen in the far distance the huge white mass of Nanga Parbat.

Next day, the 25th, we started for the col, fully laden. Quickly crossing the first glacier, we reached the other descending from the south slopes of Ganchen and our col. The surface was bare ice, and in spite of the gentle slope, the Sherpas had difficulty in standing. Arriving at the foot of the long and steeper rise to the col, we halted to take stock. The route seemed easy, the angle perhaps thirty degrees, but it was either bare of snow or thinly coated with what had once been snow but was now turned to slush by the midday sun. At first it was not bad and I hoped that we should be able to keep our feet without cutting steps, but when deeply committed, with the angle gradually steepening, I began to realise that we should have to cut the whole way. On the easy slopes near the bottom the Sherpas disdained a rope until the Foreign Sportsman slipped and slid down pretty violently for some way before coming to rest on a shelf just above a crevasse. The Sherpas were not happy on the ice, nor was I. Their boots had few nails left in them and mine even less. On my left boot only the inner sole remained.

Only the Foreign Sportsman's dignity was hurt. We gathered him up and his belongings, put on the rope and climbed slowly on through an icefall, cutting steps the whole time. Twice we had to haul the loads after us, up steep ice pitches, but about 3 p.m., when my arms were rather tired, the slope eased off, enabling us to rest and have some food. Still hoping to reach the col, we carried on until 6 p.m., when we camped; the col looked close enough, but we were the best part of 1,000 feet below it.

Prolonged step-cutting with a load is very chastening, so next morning I decided to go up to the col for a look before taking the camp up. We had to cut nearly all the way, and at last when we stuck our heads over the top at 9 a.m. a glance showed us that it was hopeless to try to get down the other side. A very remarkable view slightly tempered this keen disappointment, for it is not often possible to see two such mountains as K2 and Nanga Parbat at the same time. All the Baltoro giants were there, the Ogre too, the Chogo Lungma glacier, and the peaks of the Hispar. Immediately below, a glacier led north-east to the Hoh Lungma, whose wide valley we could plainly see.

On returning to camp we began looking for another way down; none of us much liked the look of the ascent. After some search, we concluded that the only alternative was a rather sketchy route by some rock on the south side of the icefall; we decided to try it. Before packing up we made another journey to the col to take a photograph, as I had stupidly left my camera behind the first time. The Sherpas philosophically accepted the double journey imposed by my carelessness.

Our new route began well. There was not much step-cutting and the rocks were easy, but below the halfway mark it was less accommodating. I was inspecting a gully, so loose that I devoutly hoped we should not have to use it, when I brought down a rock which nearly pinned me by the leg. On beating a hasty but cautious retreat, the Foreign Sportsman, who was supposed to be safeguarding me from above, let loose a small avalanche of rocks, one of which caught in the rope and almost dragged me off. However, he managed to support the rock from his end while I feverishly untied and severed my connection with this new and unwelcome addition to the party. Finally, we avoided the gully by an abseil and the rest was easy.

This repulse only made me the more determined to get over this ridge between us and the Hoh Lungma, and to spend a month over it rather than go tamely round by the valley. I decided to go back up the Basha valley to Bisil and then to strike up one of the nullahs there. This move would bring us on to the range near Ganchen, so that besides searching for a pass we could have a look at the peak.

Our camp was in a nullah leading directly down to the village of Zil, but we took an unconscionable time reaching it next morning. We spent several hours locked in a fierce struggle with some stubborn bush which was so thick that we could not even fall through it, though it grew on a steep slope. At Zil we had some food, but the difficulty was water, for although irrigation channels led everywhere, they were full of silt and useless for drinking. Fruit was the best substitute, so the Foreign Sportsman went off to buy apricots, and presently returned in triumph with a hatful on which he had squandered half an anna. I thought they were dear at that price because they were all green, and the Sherpas had my share as well. The villages through which we had passed a few days ago made no attempt to conceal their astonishment at our return. We had come from nowhere and were now on the way back; perhaps they thought us disembodied spirits doomed to perambulate the Basha valley, like the Flying Dutchman, to the end of time.

Every nullah we passed was examined briefly and discarded. To select the right one, with so many to choose from was a difficult problem; we could not see far up any of them, and the locals seemed to know as little about them as ourselves. It was another brilliant day; every day had been fine since the rain on the Cornice glacier; the heat in the bottom of the deep valley was tropical. We passed many streams, but all were the colour and consistency of Turkish coffee.

We camped a mile short of Bisil, near a small village which provided eggs and a few potatoes, and the next day I sent the Foreign Sportsman to Bisil to see what he could get. The Sherpas were 'tough' that night and slept out, or perhaps they found the tent too stuffy even for them. Except for the night on snow I had been sleeping out since leaving the Cornice glacier, partly because I enjoyed it and partly because of the Foreign Sportsman. He is not a good sleeping companion – singing far into the night is his least offensive habit. The previous night, although I was lying some distance from the tent, I had to ask him to sing under his breath.

The whole of next morning was occupied playing 'Sister Anne', Ila and I taking the name-part alternatively, but at 1 p.m. the Foreign Sportsman returned from Bisil where he had spent the morning and three rupees. For this we got fifteen pounds of flour, two pounds of potatoes, two dozen eggs, an ounce or two of salt, and (displayed with pride) a hatful of green apples. The waste of time was even more annoying than this ineradicable preference for unripe fruit, and we began to rush violently up a steep path under a grilling sun in a mood even sourer than apples.

In the course of a couple of hours the path took us to a grazing alp, but above it ended in a gully. A trickle of water, coming down, encouraged us to climb until at length the trickle ceased, darkness came on, and we camped at the spot where the water failed, on the steep, rocky bank of the gully. It was an unaccommodating site and we had to dig three separate shelves for ourselves and one for the fire. The Foreign Sportsman atoned for his morning's work by digging a particularly large and luxurious grave for me.

The path had vanished completely, and this was the more astonishing because last evening I had seen a few cows grazing high above this point. I stuck to the gully while the Sherpas chased an ephemeral path which took them into a nullah blocked at the top by the high, smooth snout of a glacier. They were forced to rejoin me, and another 1,500 feet of climbing brought us out on to the glacier well above the snout. South-east were the two big snow peaks; the northernmost called Hikmul by the Workmans, and the other Ganchen. Straight ahead to the east was another glacier descending from a col on the ridge of Hikmul, which looked as if it might 'go'. Crossing the first glacier we came suddenly to a steep drop of seven or eight hundred feet, at the bottom of which flowed yet another glacier from the western slopes of Hikmul. These two glaciers joined. It is annoying to lose height during an ascent, but there was no help for it, so down we went and camped on moraine by a small lake. A dull, cold afternoon presaged the end of one more fine spell.

The only flour we had left now was the fifteen pounds bought at Bisil, so I reduced our flour ration from two pounds to one pound per man, to make it last five days. In addition we ate one pound of pemmican daily between the three of us, and a little satu.

On the following day, 2 September, we went up to look at the col. There was a fairly straightforward route on bare ice most of the way, and the short slope to the col was of good, hard snow. As we were beginning to discover, this was rare so late in the season, for most of the slopes were of bare ice. My first glance down the other side to a tributary glacier of the Hoh Lungma was not reassuring, and a more leisurely inspection confirmed the view that it was an exceedingly nasty place. A steep and very loose gully led to a snow. slope which ended in a gaping bergschrund. The upper lip of the 'schrund was an ice cliff which could be seen only imperfectly, but it was clear that to overcome the difficulty we should have to employ roping-down tactics. Such methods usually take a long time, and in this case would have to be carried out while exposed to rockfalls which the gully apparently dispensed with some prodigality, for the snow slope below was littered with dirt and stones. The judgment of the Sherpas does not usually err on the side of rashness, but in this case I think they failed to see the bergschrund, the ice cliff, and all that it implied, because they seemed as keen to try this interesting route as I was loath to risk it.

Farther north was another glacier tributary of the Hoh Lungma; the two were separated by a narrow ridge, so we retreated from the col and moved round the low glacier cirque to the north. From here we climbed to another col, cutting huge bucket steps hopefully on the way, in the belief that we should want them next day. The descent to the northerly glacier looked more practicable, but at the top was a difficult bit of ice-glazed rock, on which I spent some time preparing it for the morrow. The glacier below led north-east and joined the Hoh Lungma much farther north than the other, a point which was rather to our advantage if we wanted to reach the head of that glacier. The thoughts of the Foreign Sportsman, however, were directed more to the lower end of the glacier and the valley, and he suggested that much time would be saved if, having got down, we then crossed the narrow dividing ridge back to the glacier we had first seen. It was difficult to treat this suggestion kindly because, apart from the fact that we were not going home yet, the ridge in question was the sort of place one climbs only in nightmares.

We were back in camp by 1 p.m., so after some food the Foreign Sportsman and I went up the glacier which flowed beneath the western slopes of Hikmul. This peak I had inspected closely, deciding that it was not for such a weak party as ours. At the head of the glacier, however, a low col seemed to give access to the slightly easier Ganchen. A trudge of two miles up the glacier brought us to the col only to find a sheer drop of several hundred feet cutting us off effectually from the peak. As, from the col, Hikmul looked even less inviting, I decided to cross to the Hoh Lungma without further delay.

We started early on 3 September in mist and snow. Snow had fallen in the night, so that even the great bucket steps that I had cut on the approach to the col took some time to find. On top a bitter wind chilled the Sherpas, who waited patiently while I recut the steps down the bad bit to a rock rib. Having rejoined them on top, I lowered them down and then the loads. We then picked a careful way down 700 feet of loose snow-covered rock, crossed a bergschrund by an ice bridge, and, without a pause, hurried down a much crevassed glacier to its junction with the Hoh Lungma which we reached about noon.

Relying on the old map, I had assumed, perhaps unwarrantably, that we were on the Evi Gans glacier, and was prepared for a walk of some eight miles up the Hoh Lungma before reaching the col at its head, from which the Workmans had looked down upon the Cornice glacier. But to my great surprise, on turning the corner, we found that the Hoh Lungma ended in a pinnacled rock cirque a bare half-mile from where we stood. Two miles farther down it was joined by a big glacier from the east, and thinking that this was the Hoh Lungma and that the short, wide arm on which we stood had been ignored by the map-makers, we went down to it. Proceeding up this glacier, which began to trend north, we camped on the bend.

Whether we were on the Hoh Lungma or Sosbun glacier, the map led me to expect a march of seven or eight miles to reach the head. Allowing a day to get up, another day to climb the col and return, on the third day we must make with all speed for the nearest village because our remaining two days' food would then be finished.

Starting next day with a one-night camp and reconciled to a day of glacier travel, we had not gone more than two miles before it became evident that the head of the glacier was not far away, for a mile farther on there was a sharp bend to the north-east, after which it ended abruptly in an unpromising rock wall crowned with jagged towers. There seemed to be little hope of climbing this wall, but leaving our loads we pressed on, and as we advanced the head of the glacier gradually opened up, revealing a low snow col on the extreme right of the rock wall. We had still about two miles to cover, but the glacier (which I still thought was the Hoh Lungma) was a gentlemanly one with neither crevasses nor streams to hinder us.

We soon reached the foot of the col, now about 500 feet above us, and began climbing the slope which, though not very steep, was icy. A third of the way up was a wide and deep bergschrund, fortunately bridged, whence we cut diagonally to the left. Fully conscious of this yawning receptacle below, and of the Foreign Sportsman's carefree methods, I cut the steps very big and safe. It took a long time, but at length the final step was cut, the few feet of rock wall crowning the top scaled, and we were gazing at a most unexpected sight. At the bottom of a 2,000-foot cliff, so sheer that we could drop a stone on to it, lay the head of the Cornice glacier, and across the void, barely a mile away, was the col which we had crossed from the Biafo a fortnight ago. I had expected to look on to the Cornice glacier, but from a point very much farther west. The explanation was, of course, that the glacier we had ascended was the Sosbun and not the Hoh Lungma. Anyhow, from one point of view it was a very satisfying conclusion, and that very startling topographical phenomenon, an entirely enclosed glacier, had gone the way of the Lost City of Atlantis and the Loch Ness Monster.

We descended, picked up our loads, and returned to camp. With the unexpected saving of this day the food situation was easier, so we indulged in a mild orgy of chapattis.

Starting at 6 a.m. on 5 September, we crossed back to the right bank of what we now knew was the Hoh Lungma. The crossing of a glacier sounds very easy on paper, but in the Himalaya it is not to be undertaken lightly. The opposite side of a glacier always looks easier than the side one is negotiating, and though it looks close it seldom takes less than an hour to reach – an hour miserably spent climbing out of one hollow in order to get into another. Four miles down, we had to cross the combined glaciers descending from the Ganchen group, and on the moraine, on the far side, we met a shepherd with a dog looking for three lost sheep. He was neither startled nor curious, but promptly asked us for 'baksheesh'. We might have been lifelong residents of the Hoh Lungma. It was gratifying to be recognised as a sahib, but it was disappointing to find the hardy hillman differing so little from men of the plains and the city.

In the course of the afternoon we reached the first village, Chokpiong, where we had camped on the way up in May. It was, I remembered, remarkable for a toothless but vociferous lambadar (headman), an unusual number of cretins who gibbered at us, horrible goitres, and dirt. They were all still there, and next morning I was not sorry to see the last of Chokpiong and the sad numbers of goitrous, eye-infected morons. The principal idiot sat by our fire half the night mowing at us, and was the first of a long string of similar admirers who visited us before we were up.

From here to Askole the way is long, tedious, and difficult; the difficulties centred in the two rope bridges by which we crossed and recrossed the Braldu river. On the march up, these bridges were avoided by a short rock traverse along the north bank, but now the river was too high to permit this, and the bridges had to be faced. The first of these was the less trying of the two because it was well made, and we had the assistance of a local man who crossed backwards facing us, partly, I suppose, to give us something slightly less frightening to look at than the river, and also to spread the handrails when necessary. These bridges are merely three thick fibre ropes; the centre one, which is for the feet, hangs a little below the two handrails. At the anchorage at either end these three ropes are wide apart and on the same level, but farther out the foot-rope hangs at a more or less convenient distance below the other two, which are then close together and have to be kept apart with two sticks. Even so they are much too close to be comfortable for a man carrying a load. The whole bridge sags so badly that there is a steep hill at each end. Every few feet the three cables are secured in their relative positions by a connecting rope, and fifty feet below the flimsy structure the dirty grey waters of the river roar through the ravine with a cold fury horrible to contemplate.

To watch a Balti on one of these bridges is a lesson in confidence. He rests his hands lightly on the handrails and walks boldly and quickly across. Not so the novice, who clutches frantically at everything within reach and fearfully shuffles each foot forward a few inches at a time. It would be less trying if one could get a real 'Thank God' hold of the handrails, but these miserable things, while not thick enough to inspire confidence, are far too thick to grip properly, so that if a foot did slip off, one would not have a dog's chance. I was surprised to find that the Sherpas liked these atrocities as little as I did, for I imagined they must have used them in their own country. They assured me that this was their first experience, and, watching the Foreign Sportsman, I thought at times that it was going to be his last. His caution was almost excessive. He attended to the placing of each hand and foot as though climbing very difficult rock, and by the time he got over, his face was a pale saffron.

The second bridge was much worse, because it had a permanent cant sideways as well as a very deep sag, nor had we any Balti to encourage us. The most ticklish part, the 'mauvais pas', is where you have to get over the stick which keeps the handrails apart. The stick is, of course, at the same height as the rail, which means that you have to balance on one leg, hoist the other high enough to clear the stick, and then bring the first after it. This manoeuvre is performed twice.

But this was our last adventure, and from Askole we returned to Skardu by a shorter route over the Skoro La, which was now open, and, journeying across the Deosai Plains, we reached Srinagar at the end of September.

17   Which Way Out?

While Tilman and Auden were starting on their interesting journeys, connecting up the mountain ranges surrounding the Crevasse glacier with the partly explored, though very little known, country to the south of the main watershed, Spender and I were continuing to reap the benefit of the abundant supplies that we had brought so laboriously from our Sarpo Laggo base. Three fine days of intensive work enabled Spender to complete the survey of the upper Crevasse glacier, and to fix the position of remote ranges on the Panmah-Biafo-Braldu watersheds. I had intended to employ the time by climbing some of the peaks on the main divide, but I found the survey so absorbing that I escorted Spender to his stations to help him to reach them and to give him what assistance I could in the survey work. It was enthralling to disentangle the geography of the region, to arrange the peaks and valleys and glaciers in their true perspective, and gradually to learn to know them with an intimacy and understanding that, for me, is the basic reason for mountaineering.

Again we were lucky with the weather, for it kept fine until this part of the survey was finished. Angtharkay's party had worked hard, and when we got back to the Second Divide we found that they had relayed nearly all the loads to a dump at the foot of a side glacier leading to Spender's pass. We ascended the 'Father Christmas glacier' in a blizzard, and by the evening of 15 August everything was in readiness at that dump.

The head of the 'Father Christmas glacier' was enclosed by precipitous peaks, and there seemed to be no possibility of forcing a route across them. But a narrow tributary glacier, flowing in from the north, offered the unexpected line of escape that Spender had discovered. His reconnaissance had made it possible for us to reach the col in bad weather, and on 16 August, in spite of wind and snow, we carried the first batch of loads up to it. We made a dump on top of the pass, and looked for a moment into the ravine where we hoped to find a route, but we were driven back by a bitter gale.

I felt rather like a schoolboy, at last beginning a holiday full of exciting possibilities which had first begun to take shape months before, but which, as the term dragged on with maddening slowness, had receded to an unattainable but infinitely enticing dream. The Shimshal pass, the people of the lower Braldu valley, and the unknown ranges that surrounded it, had been discussed by us for so long, that it seemed impossible that we should ever get there. Now at last we were on the threshold of this region, ready to cross its passes and to grope our way through its unmapped valleys.

17 August was another day of bad weather. We trudged up the side glacier again, carrying the remainder of the loads. Though in fact we made much better time than on the previous day, we seemed to be going irritatingly slowly. It was extremely cold on the pass, and the visibility was poor. On the other side of the pass, we found a fairly steep slope of soft, deep snow. At the bottom, this slope ran into a flat snow plateau which extended for several hundred yards before the glacier entered a steep gorge. We hurled all the loads recklessly over the edge and slid down the slope after them. We then tried dragging the loads behind us, but the snow was too deep and soon we had to abandon this method. We had intended to take half the loads down to a suitable camping place, and to return the following day for the rest; but the Sherpas disliked the prospect of struggling back uphill through the deep snow as much as we did, and after much rearrangement we managed to take the whole lot. The Sherpas were then carrying *over 130 pounds each.*

Lower down, the glacier became very badly crevassed. A thick covering of new snow made it exceedingly difficult to detect the crevasses. My adventure of a fortnight before had made me very cautious, particularly as it would have been extremely dangerous if one of the Sherpas had fallen when carrying such a tremendous load. I prodded the snow in front of me with my ice axe at every step; my slow progress was very tiresome for the Sherpas, for it was almost as difficult for them to stand still as to walk forward, being so heavily laden. At length we reached a place where the glacier plunged down for nearly 1,000 feet over a sheer icefall. We camped on moraine just above this point.

In the evening the heavy mists cleared from below and we went to the brink of the icefall to reconnoitre. We soon saw that it was impossible to climb down the chaos of contorted ice cliffs that fell in a sheer precipice, gashed by a network of black fissures. But fortunately a slender gully, which contrived somehow to run unbroken between the glacier and the sheer crags which bounded it on the right, offered us a heaven-sent way out of the difficulty. Below the icefall, the glacier was joined by another in a confusion of pinnacles. Below the junction, the ice stream ran in a north-westerly direction, and to our amazement, seemed to end about three miles farther down. Below this, we had a thrilling glimpse of grass and bushes. But we were worried about the direction of the lower valley. At first it seemed that it swung round in a right-angled bend to the north-east. This was not at all to our liking, for, although we still had three weeks' food, the country was difficult and we could not afford to be led far out of our course.

Though, next morning, the sky was overcast, there were signs that it might clear. So, while a relay of loads was being carried down the gully, Spender,

Angtensing and I climbed a peak lying to the east. Bad snow conditions made the climb laborious and dangerous, but we reached the summit (19,000 feet) at half-past nine. The weather had become beautifully fine and windless, so that we got a clear view of our immediate surroundings, and Spender worked for nearly two hours with his plane-table. We saw, to our relief, that we were mistaken about the valley below us, and that, below the snout of the glacier, it continued to run in a north-westerly direction. We saw the whole of the glacier that joined our glacier from the east; but the country beyond to the north and east, was terribly complicated, and we decided to go up this glacier to spend a short time exploring in that direction. This decision required considerable resolution, for we were very impatient to find out where our valley would eventually lead; and the green grass and bushes that we had seen lured us to lower altitudes.

When we returned to camp, we found that the Sherpas were already back. The gully had not belied its promise and had taken them quickly and safely down past the twisted cliffs of the icefall. We packed up and started down immediately. At the junction of the two glaciers we made a dump, and then, taking with us sufficient for a light camp, we started up the valley to the east in the late afternoon. For nearly two hours we worked up badly crevassed ice which threatened to stop us, but after that things became easier and we were able to camp as far up the glacier as we wished. It was a beautiful, peaceful evening, and from where we lay we could see for many miles down the valley to a far-off range of placid rounded mountains which were a restful contrast to the rugged country piled around us. Spender called the highest of these the Jökul, which is the word used for the ice-capped volcanic cones of Iceland.

It was a bitterly cold night, followed by an even colder dawn. We struggled petulantly with the leathery chapattis that were provided for breakfast and with our boots that were frozen in impossible shapes, and started with Nukku and Lhakpa Tensing, at 6.30. I had a severe stomach ache which was not improved by the biting wind which blew down the glacier. I climbed in a doubled-up posture until we got into the sun. With the warmth my belly ceased to ache and I was able to climb upright and enjoy the brilliant morning.

The slope was easy and we climbed as fast as we could, racing against the clouds that we imagined would soon blot out the view. Four thousand feet above the camp, at an altitude of more than 20,000 feet, we reached a sharp ridge, surmounted by a heavy cornice that overhung a tremendous precipice to the north. We cut an aperture in the cornice and set up the plane-table on a precarious rock platform. Spender and I trod delicately between the legs of the tripod, trying not to disturb its balance nor lose our own, while Lhakpa Tensing held the umbrella above the instruments, and Nukku sat below holding the ropes attached to each of us, like a showman controlling the antics of a group of marionettes. I should explain that the umbrella, peculiar though it may look on a mountain, is a necessary adjunct to the survey equipment. Spender used a neat lady's parasol with an elegant blue ribbon loop, that he had obtained from Messrs. Marks & Spencer for 3s. 11d. It looked somewhat incongruous held by a grimy hand, shading a bearded, sun-scorched face.

From this high station we looked down on to the head of the Crown glacier, and were able to disentangle much of the country towards the Shaksgam river. But it was the distant views that compelled our attention. Many of the peaks that we had been amongst a month earlier, including K2, The Crown and 'The Fangs', were to be seen. To the west, the great peaks of the Kanjut range and Dasto Ghil, provided us with new food for discussion, and a fresh vision of the incredible size and majesty of the Karakorams. North-west of us were the snow domes of the Shimshal mountains, and beyond them stretched range after range into the blue distance of Kashgar and the Hindu Kush. The wind of the early morning had died and, when the work was finished, we sat for some hours trying to understand this limitless tangle of country. Then we plunged down at a thrilling speed over snow and scree to the camp.

Angtharkay's culinary genius had produced a lunch of sandwiches of toasted cheese-rind and curry powder between large soggy chapattis. While we were munching these the camp was packed up, and we then ran down the glacier in high spirits. Most of the new snow had melted from the ice, which simplified the passage of the crevassed section. We picked up more loads at the dump and camped a mile down the lower glacier, in a narrow rocky passage which ran for several miles like a street between high walls of ice. The crystal turrets glowed with the soft colours reflected from the evening sky, and after dusk shone like silver in the brilliance of a full moon.

The next day, 20 August, we reached grass and flowers and wood-fuel, and camped on 'dry land' for the first time after a month of glacier travel. This seemed to mark a further stage in the complex experience of this slow journey.

Four Sherpas went back to the dump on 21 August to fetch the remainder of the loads. Spender spent the day surveying high up on the valley sides, while Angtharkay and I went in search of game. My stupidity in spurning some animals with poor heads lost us an opportunity that never recurred, of securing plentiful meat. But it was a day full of the delicious freedom of movement that had been denied us during our sojourn on the glaciers. In the evening we succeeded in shooting a couple of snow-cock. With a rifle it is necessary to stalk these creatures and to shoot them sitting. This method might not meet with approval in some circles, but it provided us with a memorable meal.

The next day we managed to shift all the loads at once, though some of the Sherpas had to carry over a hundred pounds each. We tried to follow the course of the river, but soon it entered a narrow ravine and we were forced to leave it. Ancient river terraces, whose cliffs rose several thousand feet above the present river level, cut by side streams into grotesque canyons, caused us endless trouble, as they had done in the Aghil range. We were obliged to climb higher and higher in our search for a route, and before long we lost sight of the river. Although we were gradually evolving a technique for dealing with the obstacles presented by these conglomerate deposits, it was still a frightening business negotiating them with a heavily laden party. For two days we made lamentably little progress. At length the terraces became so broken that it was almost impossible to make any headway. We climbed down a long and diffi-cult gully, and on the evening of 23 August we camped on the shore of the river. The weather was bad during this time, and, as there had been no sun to melt the snow, the river was so reduced in volume that we found that we could make our way along the bottom of the gorge by wading through it. At eleven o'clock on 24 August we reached the end of the valley and walked out on to the wide gravel flats, which we at once recognised to be part of the Braldu valley. Immediately to the south was the great moraine-covered snout of the Braldu glacier, and we realised that the valley we had come down was the one men-tioned by Colonel Schomberg in his book Unknown Karakoram, and called by him Wesm-i-Dur. At the junction of the two valleys we found the sheep-fold and huts that he had reported. They were in good repair. The Sherpas were in a great state of excitement and examined the buildings with a profes-sional interest to see whether there were signs of recent occupation.

I have often wondered exactly what the Sherpas think during these long journeys in uninhabited mountain ranges so far from their own homes. On earlier expeditions they often seemed worried, but now they accepted the sit-uation with philosophical resignation, and displayed a touching confidence in our ability to find the way to inhabited country before the food ran out.

25 August was an off day. Spender, as usual, employed it in intensive survey work, while the Sherpas settled down to a long session of a strange game called Barachu. Always popular, this pastime had, during the last month, become an obsession, and every moment of the day, when the party was not actually on the march, there was a game in progress. It is a kind of Ludo, played with a pair of dice and a collection of stones and match-sticks. Though I have often played, I have never been able fully to understand the rules, which may be the reason why I have never won! The game requires a strong voice and a quick wit. The dice cup must be slammed down with as much force as possible, while the player either screams a cat-call or gabbles a mystic incantation, according to the state of the game. When the cup is lifted from the dice it is important to move the pieces before anyone has time to question the action. Little atten-tion is paid to the actual fall of the dice.

We had enough food left to last us for another sixteen days, but there was still a great deal of work to be done. The most important job was the explora-tion and mapping of the Braldu glacier, which was the only great glacier in this part of the main Asiatic watershed that was still unexplored. In order to round off the survey, too, it was important that it should be carried right down the Braldu valley to join up with the lower Shaksgam river, and also up to the Shimshal pass, whose exact geographical position was still unknown. We had hoped that there would be time to go into the unknown ranges to the northwest. In fact, we would both gladly have spent the whole winter in these parts, but I had agreed to join the 1938 Everest expedition and had to get back before the passes to Kashmir were closed for the winter. Two minor considerations were the state of the party's boots, which were now practically useless, and the possibility of not being able to obtain fresh supplies of food. But without the other obligation these difficulties could doubtless have been overcome, and there was a very strong temptation to continue our life in this interesting country. However, we consoled ourselves with the reflection that we had at least learned to understand some of its problems, and that we might someday be privileged to return to use that knowledge.

We started up the Braldu glacier with food enough for eight days. If we were to finish the job we would have to travel with all possible speed, and to be blessed with a spell of fine weather. The lower part of the glacier was the usual wilderness of broken moraine-covered ice. On the way over this we passed a very remarkable ice arch, which must once have formed part of a tunnel cut by a glacier stream. In spite of the rough going we succeeded in covering six miles on 26 August, and camped that evening on a beautiful grassy alp on the western flank of the glacier, just below its pinnacled section.

Recent bharal spoor enticed Angtharkay and me into a hunt before breakfast the following morning, while Spender was plane-tabling. We found a place where a herd had spent the previous night. From there we tracked the animals for miles over difficult country, expecting each moment to find them feeding in a nullah. After four hours we discovered that a pack of six wild dogs was stalking the same herd. In the confusion that resulted the bharal escaped unharmed, and we returned to camp still breakfastless, and disgusted at having wasted most of the morning.

We got into difficulties farther up the glacier, but in the middle of the afternoon we reached a corridor leading through the pinnacles for several miles, without interruption, so that by nightfall we found that we had covered another five miles, and were approaching the smooth ice of the upper part of the glacier. On 28 August we camped in the middle of the vast glacier basin into which Angtharkay and I had descended on 3 August. We had come up the glacier a great deal more quickly than we had dared to hope.

During the next three days the weather was perfect, and we wasted none of our precious time. Angtharkay, Lhakpa and I reached a high saddle at the head of a branch glacier on the west. It was not situated on the main watershed as I had hoped, but from it we were able to climb a small peak (about 19,000 feet high) for a round of photographs and compass bearings. Again I was able to see the great peaks of the K2 range, and this time my view extended past the Mustagh Tower to Masherbrum and the pinnacles of the lower Baltoro glacier, whose acquaintance we had made in May. Conway's Ogre and its sculptured satellites were now close at hand, and, seen from this angle, they looked more than ever astonishing. But all this was of small interest compared with the fascinating newness of the world we were in.

While surveying on the glacier to the south, Spender saw, through his telescopic alidade, a large cairn. We sent two Sherpas to investigate this, and found that it had been built by Tilman's party to mark the site of one of their camps. There was a letter in it, telling us of their movements up till 18 August and of their discovery of a route to the Snow Lake.

The Braldu glacier proved to be a large ice stream with a great number of branches in its upper part. The heads of some of these branches were twenty-two miles from the snout of the main glacier. The basin of the Braldu abuts on those of the Virjerab, Biafo, Nobande Sobande and Crevasse glaciers, and its bounding walls form a considerable part of the main Asiatic watershed. With the help of his survey of the head of the Crevasse glacier, and the fine weather, Spender succeeded in completing a detailed survey of this basin in the very short time that remained, but he had to work at high pressure to achieve this.

A forced march enabled us to reach the shepherd's huts below the snout of the Braldu glacier on the evening of 1 September, with our job done. On the way down Angtharkay had shot two snow-cock, a gratifying result of the rifle instruction that I had been giving him. A sumptuous dish of roast fowl and rice made a fitting feast of celebration at the end of a strenuous week of work and deep enjoyment.

We started down the following morning, making for a point, about six miles away, where the Braldu valley made a right-angled bend to the east and was joined by the stream coming down from the Shimshal pass which lay to the north-west. We were all in a state of suppressed excitement, as we expected, that very day to make contact with some sort of habitation. But for three miles Spender and I lost interest in this intriguing prospect, being absorbed in an argument about the ethics of Empire. The debate was only temporarily checked when my opponent fell head first into a muddy side stream.

The river which flowed down the valley was an alarming size, certainly a great deal bigger than the Shaksgam when we had last seen it. We were uncomfortably aware that in order to reach the nullah leading to the Shimshal pass we would be obliged to cross the Braldu river. Lower down, flowing over gravel flats nearly a mile wide, it broke up into five or six streams. I decided to attempt the crossing here, for it was still early, and later in the day, even if we found a better fording-place, the river would probably be greatly swollen. I started alone, and crossed the first stream fairly easily. But I failed to cross the second one direct and went a long way down before I could negotiate it. The third was a desperate struggle, and I emerged on the other side feeling very cold, humiliated and alone. The idea of going back was so unpleasant that I felt prepared to go to great lengths to get over the fourth stream.

A bitter wind started to blow down the valley bringing with it clouds of dust. I tested the next stream in several places by throwing boulders into it, but each time I heard the ominous dull sound produced by deep water. My better judgment prevailed at last and I turned to face the return journey. The third stream gave me a very bad time on the way back, as my numbed limbs were not easy to control. The mad, merciless rush of water, surging giddily round one, trying with ceaseless uneven thrusts to throw one over, is the most frightening thing I know. Near the side, I fell into a deep pocket, but fortunately it was in a slight back-water and I was able to scramble out. At length I got back to the rest of the party, having made a complete fool of myself.

When I had changed into dry clothes and restored life to my legs, we continued on our way. Just before the corner of the valley the river spread out, nearly covering the gravel flats. On the other side we could see trees and grass. We recognised this as the grazing ground marked Chikar on Schomberg's map. In spite of my lesson, we decided to try to cross the river again.

It was here that we evolved a simple but effective technique for crossing these rivers. One man is tied to the end of a long rope; the rest of the party anchor the rope at a point upstream, preferably above the outside of a bend. Leaning, if necessary, his full weight on the rope, the first man then advances through the water swinging pendulum-wise on the rope. Except for the last man, the rest of the party carrying the bulk of the loads have the safeguard of a rope stretched at right angles across the river, as well as the pendulum rope. The last man crosses in the same way as the first, though this time with the others holding him from a point farther up the opposite bank. The support of the pendulum rope enables one to withstand the force of the water to an astonishing extent.

In this way, we got across the streams without an accident, and reached a lovely oasis of willow thickets and meadows. We found a number of stone huts and signs of old cultivation. We were disappointed to find no evidence of recent occupation. But the sight of glades, the smell of growing things, and the song of many birds filled us with a great joy. The grass was gay with flowers, despite the lateness of the season. The most common and most lovely of these was a little blue flower, with a tall stalk, which closed its petals at dusk and when the weather became cold or stormy.

The evening and a huge wood fire brought peace, and we slept on luxurious beds of deep grass.

18　Conversation Piece

I woke on 3 September with a delicious sense of comfort and wellbeing, and, lying on my soft bed of grass, with the willow branches swaying above my head, lazily watched the dawn break over the storm-clouds which now filled the valley of the Braldu. It was a great temptation to indulge in this new luxury.

In spite of the unpromising weather, Spender decided to attempt the high station on the Jökul, which we had planned from above, and with a great effort we managed to get away at 7.15. Angtharkay and I took the rifle with us in the hope of being able to relieve the food situation. As we climbed, the weather became worse. All the country we had hoped to see was hidden by cloud, and a bitter wind harried us. It was obvious that a high station would be of no value, and after climbing for 2,000 feet, Spender stopped to do some range finding to points down the Lower Braldu valley. Angtharkay and I found some spoor a fortnight old and followed it over into a big glacier nullah. The ground was difficult and I had a good deal of trouble in moving about over it because of the deplorable state of my boots. Higher up, the wind was very fierce and made things so unpleasant that we abandoned the hunt, and returned down an impressive gorge, soon after midday.

Coming round the corner of a willow thicket, we saw a horseman riding away from our camp. The idea crossed my mind that the camp had been raided, but when the man saw us he dismounted, came over to us, and shook us cordially by the hand. He was the first human being outside our party whom we had seen for nearly three and a half months. It was at once evident that we had no common language. Angtharkay tried Tibetan and Nepali, which were as useless as my Hindustani and English. The subject of food was uppermost in our minds and it was an easy matter to communicate this to him. He indicated that he had none to spare, but made it clear that he wished to be friendly with us. He then remounted and rode off towards the river. When we reached camp, I learnt from Spender about the arrival of our visitor. He appeared from across the river and had come right up to the camp before he saw it. The discovery appeared to give him a shock and he tried to bolt. Lhakpa, however, managed to get hold of him and somehow persuaded him that we had no evil designs. He consented to come and have some tea in the camp. Though for us the arrival of a stranger was an exciting event, the other three Sherpas, being engrossed in a long session of Barachu, hardly noticed it, and from the depths of the willow jungle came the sound of the slapping of the dice-cup and loud appeals to the God of Chance. This must have puzzled our guest a good deal, but he was very polite about it, and joined in a sign conversation with Spender and Lhakpa. It appeared that he had come from down the valley where he and others were engaged in working a salt deposit. Why he had left the rest of his party on the other side of the river we could not discover, but he took his leave saying that he was going to fetch them. We watched him cross the river, which for a man on horseback held no terrors. We continued to observe his activities through field-glasses when we reached the other side.

Besides him we could see three men and four yaks. After much fuss, they shifted their loads to a sheep-pen and came across, riding on the yaks and the horse. It was entertaining to watch them coaxing the animals into the swift stream and hunting for the places where the water was most broken. When they arrived, after a round of formal introductions, we settled down with Lhakpa and Angtharkay to a lengthy conference. During this the Barachu continued uninterrupted. Not even talk of food, the main subject of discussion, drew the players from their game. Conversation was difficult and laborious, as we had first to establish a system of conventional signs which were mutually understood. Lhakpa had a few words of Turki, but these did not take us far. However, our friends were intelligent and had a great sense of humour, so that things went better than might have been expected. It appeared that flour was not obtainable this side of Shimshal – four days' march away – but that sheep and butter could be got more readily. Our friends agreed that one of their party should ride across the Shimshal pass as fast as he could and bring back some of these provisions. But they first demanded that we should write our names on a bit of paper. I wrote our two names and was then told to write those of our Sherpas. This done I had to add their own names: Dildorbik, the old man who had first visited us and who seemed to be in charge of the party, Mohi Bacha, Mohamad Ali and Sour. Then I had to state, in any language I pleased, whence we had come and where we proposed to go. We could not understand the reason for all this, but we were obliged to comply with their wishes. The precious document was then wrapped very carefully in a bit of cloth, unwrapped and wrapped up again and then entrusted to the youngest member of their party, who was to be the messenger. We paid the price of one sheep, six rupees, as security. This sum was counted half a dozen times by each of them, which incidentally taught us how to count up to six in Shimshali. The youth then mounted the horse and departed, encouraged by the promise that he would be rewarded with one of our empty flour-bags, if he returned in two days. The idea of two days was conveyed in our sign language by placing the palms of the hands together in an attitude of prayer and then twice laying one's head on them, to indicate sleep. This primitive transaction took quite two hours to complete.

The other three Shimshalis deposited their few belongings in one of the huts and joined us round our fire. The conversation which followed was much more difficult than it had been before. It is easy enough to capture a man's sympathy and understanding when discussing affairs of the stomach, but it is a different thing to keep the party going with small talk when neither side can understand a word the other says. Nor was it easy to learn much about their country. However, we began to compile a small vocabulary of their words, and by the time we had been in the valley a week we had learnt something of their culture.

Darkness put an end to the Barachu, which had been in progress since morning, and the three players joined the circle. We cooked and ate our supper of pemmican and rice, but we did not invite the Shimshalis to join us. A dinner invitation is one of the easiest things to put across without the help of a common language – if one has enough food! But we were uncomfortably aware that our supplies were dwindling and that shortage of food was likely to curtail our work before we had completed all that we had planned. So Western hospitality went by the board; but it was comforting to remember that they probably thought we were Chinese! Besides, we imagined that they were well provided with the usual dirty but plentiful Shimshali food. They sat silently round us in a circle and watched us eat. We thought that they eyed our heaped plates rather hungrily; but perhaps rice, and even pemmican, look wildly exciting if one seldom sees them! When the meal was over two of them left; apparently to cook their own food. Soon they came back to borrow one of our cooking pots, and later returned to ask for some curry powder. After a long time they came to summon Dildorbik. We accompanied them to their hut, as this appeared to be the correct procedure, and we hoped that politeness might atone a little for not having asked them to share our dinner. On the floor we saw one cold round of leathery bread, leaning unappetisingly against our smoke-blackened cooking pot, in which they had heated a little water and coloured it with curry powder. Someone suggested hopefully that this might only be the hors d'oeuvres, but we soon discovered that it was their complete menu, and that they had eaten nothing since the previous night. They were positively cheerful about it; as if the curry powder had transformed bread and hot water into an extra special debauch! We reluctantly upheld the hospitable traditions of the British Empire and supplied them with some flour. But we felt that they had given us a lesson in the real meaning of 'travelling light'. Even those of us who have a reputation for 'toughness' make far too much fuss about the danger of running short of food.

Our belated hospitality had finally dispelled the Shimshali's mistrust of us, and next morning Dildorbik offered to show us some game, if two of the Sherpas would help with the transport of the salt which they had dumped on the other side of the river. One of the yaks, being a young one, was given an off day. Lobsang, Nukku and two Shimshalis mounted the other three yaks and the cavalcade set out, looking rather like a party of holidaymakers nervously embarking on a donkey-ride at Margate. The rousing send-off that we gave them made the Sherpas look painfully self-conscious and nearly caused a disastrous stampede among the yaks. Angtharkay, Dildorbik and I forded the stream coming from the Shimshal pass and climbed the steep hillside beyond, in search of meat. Before we had gone far, the old man made Angtharkay exchange his black coat for my buff-coloured sweater, so as not to be too conspicuous. We traversed into a big side valley, at the foot of which was a collection of huts and sheep-pens. The valley was filled with wonderful pasturage which would support many thousand head of sheep. We spotted a herd of bharal on a ridge 3,000 feet above us. Dildorbik urged us to remain in hiding until the animals came down to feed and drink. In a deep ravine he curled up and went to sleep, while we shivered through some dull hours of waiting. This proved to be the wrong policy, for instead of coming down towards us, as we had hoped, the herd went off down the other side of the ridge. We spent the rest of the day hunting for them among the crags without success. However, before we returned to camp Angtharkay secured a hare with a remarkable shot. Spender had put in a useful day's work surveying the valley. His measurement of the distance to the Braldu-Shaksgam junction showed that both Younghusband and Colonel Schomberg had greatly underestimated the length of this valley.

That evening, from the warmth of our campfire, we watched a mighty storm raging over the peaks of the Braldu glacier. But the next morning was cloudless and still. Shafts of sunlight filtered through the willows, and bits of thistledown and cobwebs floated in the frosty air. Spender left early in order to get a high station on the Jökul, while I went to have a look at the valley with Mohi Bacha and Sour. We kept to the left bank of the river and passed through many oases of lush grass and willow clumps like the one where we had camped. Hundreds of birds flitted in and out of the thickets; the most common of these was the hoopoo, with its quaint lolloping flight. We also saw many different kinds of water-birds near the clear river pools.

At each of these oases I found clusters of huts, and my guides showed me water-mills for grinding corn, and various contrivances for making butter and cheese. I was told that these places were only inhabited in the winter, when they were used as grazing grounds by the people of Shimshal. The season was not due to begin for another month. This explained the mystery which had been puzzling us since we had arrived in the valley. It is an unusual state of affairs to find winter migration to higher pastures. Presumably it is due to the smaller precipitation on the northern side of the watershed. It would be most interesting to travel in these parts in mid-winter. The occupation of these high valleys would probably make it possible to live off the country to an unusual extent. Rivers would not present the almost insoluble problem which they do in the summer. With the help of skis one might be able to undertake long journeys into the unexplored glacier regions.

The Shimshalis were most instructive and attentive. Whenever we stopped they took off their coats for me to sit on, and they were quite unnecessarily helpful whenever we came to the slightest difficulty on the route. They were extremely eager to explain everything about the country. It exasperated poor Mohi Bacha that we could not converse more easily. He kept holding his tongue and tugging it, in a gesture of despair at its impotence!

We got back to camp in the late afternoon, to find things in a great state of excitement. Spender's party was back, and the youth had returned with two sheep and some butter. He had brought with him two more Shimshalis, who had come mainly out of curiosity. We spent a merry evening feasting off liver and blood sausage. The latter is a very favourite dish of the Sherpas, and they gorged themselves preposterously. This gory delicacy is made by stuffing the entrails of the animal with a mixture of blood and tsampa. Conversation with the Shimshalis was now becoming much easier. Lhakpa Tensing was our most successful linguist. He had been very assiduous in making a list of words and their meanings, which he wrote laboriously on a dirty scrap of paper, in Tibetan characters. He looked rather like a tourist abroad grappling with some difficult situation with the aid of Hugo's 'All you want in France'. He had made wonderful progress in the last two days.

The next day we lazed in the sunshine until late in the morning. We had arranged to make a journey, with Dildorbik as our guide, down to the junction of the Braldu river with the Shaksgam . We were just about to start when a small army was seen approaching down the hill. Three of the party rode ponies and wore smart frock coats and bright pink shirts. The visitors proved to be the Lambadar of Shimshal and his party. The Lambadar was now in residence at Shuijerab, a grazing village just at the other side of the Shimshal pass, and on hearing news of us from our messenger had brought a strong force with him, presumably to exterminate us if we were enemies and to honour us if we were friends. The party had come from Shuijerab that morning, and must have started very early. I went out to greet the Lambadar, and as I shook him by the hand he addressed me in some language that I could not understand. I replied in Hindustani, which did not seem to mean anything to him. Blankets were spread on the ground, and we all sat down to wrestle with a difficult interview. The Shimshalis were now in huge force. I again addressed the Lambadar in Hindustani; whereupon he expressed great surprise, and speaking that language very badly and with evident difficulty, asked in amazement if we were Indians. When we told him that we were 'Angrezi' (English), he displayed violent emotion – probably relief. The assembled multitude leapt up for an orgy of strenuous handshaking. I am sure that they had thought we were Chinamen, and that the language in which the Lambadar had first addressed me was Turki. Probably the messenger's description of the Sherpas and their pigtails had led them to that conclusion. We now got on splendidly and were able to learn all that we wanted to know about the lower Braldu valley and the route across the pass to Shimshal. The Lambadar took great interest in our recent journey, and expressed polite amazement at our intrepidity and hardihood. The Sherpas produced a particularly filthy brew of tea, with which our guests struggled for some time before good manners gave place to nausea, and they handed it on to their followers. I thought that the session would go on all day, but the Lambadar cut the proceedings to an almost European brevity by taking his leave, again addressing me in Turki to make quite certain that we were not playing him false. The Shimshali party went over to the huts and had a meal. Presently a plateful of apples arrived. Of all possible gifts this was the most welcome. We returned the compliment with one of our ropes, apologising at the same time for our impoverished condition, which we put down to the difficulties of our journey. This, of course, brought forth a further flood of compliments. We asked our friend if he would send down to Shimshal for flour and any other form of food he could get. For our proposed trip down the valley he provided us with two ponies and his two pink-shirted attendants. We were also given two yaks for our equipment, so that nobody should have to carry loads. Angtharkay's digestion had not survived last night's feast, and now he was suffering for his greed. We left him behind with Lhakpa and set out at noon.

The river had gone down tremendously since we had last forded it, and with the ponies and yaks to help, it caused us no trouble. When we reached the other side we rode ahead, with the two pink-shirted gentlemen in attendance. The three Sherpas followed driving the two yaks – a reminder of home, which they much enjoyed. We were making for a place called Darband, which we imagined was where Dildorbik's party had been extracting their salt.

The way led through a country of vivid contrasts. The gaunt flanks of the valley and the barren gravel flats made a sombre and forbidding background to sloping lawns of delicate green. These meadows were astir with life amongst the bleak sterility of the surrounding crags; and the springs of clear water which danced through them were sun-flecked and gay compared with the turgid, muddy river that slid down the valley below. As in the Aghil range, it seemed to me that, with a little ingenuity, a great deal more of the valley could be irrigated into fertility and made to support a permanent population.

At four o'clock, we reached a grazing ground known as Sar-i-Laksh, and our guides told us that we were nearing Darband. We left one of the pink shirts here to wait for the yaks and rode on over the next rise. From the crest of the hill we saw ahead of us a round stone tower. When we reached it we found that it was part of a long rampart built above a ravine. In fact it defended the only approach to the upper part of the valley. As the other side of the main stream was bounded by a vertical cliff, anyone coming up the gorge would find the way barred by the rampart. In the middle of this there was a great wooden gate barricaded by a heavy beam. It was a great surprise to come upon this relic of former wars, and to find it still in a perfect state of preservation. There were two towers in the rampart. We were taken into one of them, very like a chamber in the turret of a Norman castle, with small windows overlooking the ravine, through which the defenders could shoot arrows against an attacking force. Our guide demonstrated how the archers used these slits, and also produced for our inspection an incredibly ancient matchlock gun. There was evidence that the gun was still used, for hanging from the beams was a bharal skin, and joints of dried meat. On a shelf were stored balls of fermenting yak-milk cheese. We tasted these but found them too sour to be appetising, We did not discover to whom all this belonged; there was no sign of life in the place, save for a solitary yak grazing on the far side of the ravine. We were then taken through a trapdoor on to the roof of the tower. In its low walls were more narrow slits. Looking down across these ancient battlements, and over the grim gorge beyond, gave us a vivid sense of the present mediaeval state of Central Asia. We returned to camp at Sar-i-Laksh, our guide having first carefully barred the gateway in the fortress, as if expecting a night attack.

The next morning, while Spender climbed to a high station from which to survey this part of the Braldu valley, I rode down the valley, with one of the pink shirts, whose name was Abdulla. He looked very like a brigand chief in his short riding boots of rough brown hide, with off-white plus-fours bagging over them. His costume was completed by a frock coat, and a round woollen hat perched jauntily on the side of his head. We let ourselves through 'the gateway to Central Asia', and led our ponies across the gorge by a precipitous path. We then rode on down the valley, over a wilderness of boulders, which is evidently part of the ancient terminal moraine of the Braldu glacier. Above this the river flows over gravel flats, below, it falls into a spectacular canyon, whose vertical rock walls are so close together that in one place the narrow gap is spanned, 200 feet above the torrent, by a flimsy wooden bridge, not more than five yards long. It felt weirdly exciting to be riding down this sinister ravine, towards the Shaksgam, with my barbaric retainer.

In about an hour we reached a grove of tall willows, growing in a grassy swamp. Here we found one of the salt diggings. My guide demonstrated the method of salt extraction. A large pit is dug and filled with water, and the salt-bearing earth is churned about in the pit until it becomes a saturated solution of salt and mud. The mud is allowed to settle. Meanwhile in a long trench a fire is made, small V-shaped vessels of slate and clay are placed across it, and filled with the salt solution. The water is evaporated by the heat, and the salt is left behind in long bricks.

There is a Tibetan proverb which says: 'If your horse cannot carry you uphill, it is no horse; if you do not lead it downhill, you are no man,' but the latter half of the statement does not seem to hold good in these parts, for we rode down the most precipitous places, and our sure-footed ponies did not turn one hair of their shaggy heads.

Towards the junction of the Braldu and the Shaksgam the country became grimly forbidding. Vast masses of black scree welled from tiny fissures in the pale limestone cliffs. To the north the view was blocked by the mountainous desolation of the Aghil range, vividly striped by broad wavering bands of black and yellow strata. An intensely green oasis on the other side accentuated the rugged austerity of the scene. We rode along the shingle flats at the junction of the two rivers and turned eastwards, following the Shaksgam for a mile up its gorge. Great bleached boulders bore witness to the river's higher channel in former years.

We ate our lunch imprisoned in the depths of this gloomy canyon. Then I climbed 2,000 feet up its precipitous side, and from there could see the river as far as its junction with the Oprang. My view upstream was restricted to a few miles. It seemed to me that it would be possible for a lightly-laden climbing party to force a route up this gorge, without having to ford the river, which, except in mid-winter, cannot be crossed. The rocks up which I was climbing were covered in clay, which tended to peel off and made me very scared. Queer cactus-like plants clung to the crannies, and added to the nightmare quality of the place.

When I had rejoined my companion, we rode back to the junction and retraced our steps back up the Braldu valley. We lingered for a while among the willows. The afternoon sunlight slanted through their swaying branches, and made patterns of light on the grass. The cool air was murmurous with the sound of the stream and the rustle of leaves. And yet only a few yards away we were surrounded by stark desolation.

We reached camp late that evening to find that Spender had done a good day's work on the hills above the fort. Early the next day we rode back up the valley through the lush meadows of Karmush and Kuz, where pools of transparent jade held the morning sunlight. Spender stayed behind to complete his survey of the valley, while Abdulla and I rode ahead. We had some good gallops across the sandy flats, and finished up on the other side of the river, racing each other back to camp through the meadows of Chikar. An exciting finish was greeted by a rousing cheer from Angtharkay and a group of Shimshalis.

I lazed the golden afternoon away, drinking innumerable pints of tea.

19   Marching Back

We started on the first stage of our homeward journey soon after seven o'clock the next day, with three Shimshalis carrying our loads. Dildorbik, Abdulla, Spender and I rode ponies. They took us at a fine pace up the steep hillside. In this way, we avoided the gorge above Chikar and reached the upper valley. The country here reminded me of the approach to so many Tibetan passes, except for the great Dolomite spires which stood like watch towers above the gently undulating ground. Two hours' riding brought us to the junction of three flat valleys. We halted here and lit a fire of yak dung and waited an hour for the porters to arrive. The views in every direction across this plain were magnificent. The limestone peaks to the south-west rose sheer out of flat glacier beds and looked twice their height. In contrast to these, the Jökul peaks, to the north, showed their gently rounded ice caps. When the porters arrived, Spender did a station and Angtharkay cooked some meat pies over the smoky yak-dung fire. We rode on to a village called Shuwert, Abdulla leading some breakneck gallops over uncertain country. His clothes, especially his boots, had the real Cossack look about them, and his reckless speed and wild cries would have been rewarded with volleys of applause at the Cossack display at Olympia.

Shuwert was quite a large place of about four dozen houses. At this time it was quite deserted. A surprisingly large glacier, rising in the country behind the Jökul peaks, fed the main stream of the valley up which we had come. The Shimshal pass itself lay to the left of this on a mass of ancient moraine material. It formed such a gentle and indefinite curve, that as I rode up to it I found it hard to believe that it really was the pass that was such an important link in the main Asiatic watershed, which we had explored through eighty miles of rugged intricacy. Our companions were fully aware of the significance of the pass, and kept repeating what we already knew, that the water on one side flowed into India, while that on the other side made its way into Turkestan, later to be lost in the deserts of Central Asia.

I sat for a long time on the crest of the pass, caught up in the magic of the view. Away to the south-east many of the peaks with which we had been so familiar during the past month, and to which we had given such strange names as 'Flat-Iron', 'Father Christmas' and 'The Fangs', rose up as if to give a last friendly salute before receding into the past with other expedition memories. My contentment was shadowed with regret.

Below the pass on the other side was a great blue lake, a square mile or more in area. Beside this was an extensive plain known as Maidan Abdulla Khan. Across this I was made to race against Abdulla and Dildorbik. But for the fact that Abdulla's hat blew off half-way across I would have come in a very bad last, though they had given me the biggest and strongest mount. Soon we came upon large herds of yak and sheep, and heard the melodious calls of shepherd children. Then a steep descent took us suddenly out of this charming world into the steep-sided barren valley of Shuijerab. Our friend the Lambadar came across the bridge to meet me, accompanied by an enormous retinue of villagers. They brought with them apples and apricots, from Shimshal, and a vast bowl of curdled milk on which I fed while exchanging compliments and platitudes. This went on for some hours, until a combination of food and the hot afternoon made me commit the social error of dozing. The situation was relieved by the arrival of Spender, who had put in a terrific day's work winding up the survey and fixing the geographical position of the Shimshal pass.

At sunset, we made a conducted tour of the village, which was then a busy hive of activity, in which the women and children played the chief parts. The women greeted us in their usual manner by waving their hands round above their heads. The huge pens were filled to overflowing with sheep and goats. We watched some infants supervising with extraordinary skill the herding of the enormous flocks. There were innumerable lambs, each of which had to be placed by its mother. The children worked until long after nightfall, settling the disputes and attending the bleating complaints of the sheep.

The following morning we made a late start, owing to the lengthy business of giving presents to our hosts. Also the Lambadar made strong efforts to dissuade us from leaving. The reasons given were various and disconnected, and most of them we could not understand. His excessive hospitality led him to refuse to provide us with men to carry our loads in order to induce us to stop another day. However, when we demonstrated that we were quite capable of carrying all our kit ourselves, he yielded, and men were forthcoming, and refused to allow us even to carry light rucksacks. We made fruitless efforts to photograph some of the rather picturesque women of the village. As in other parts of Central Asia, they were terrified of the camera, and could not be induced, even by their men-folk, to submit to the ordeal. But they, in company with the whole village, turned out to see us off. I was particularly sorry to say goodbye to our old friend Dildorbik, who was a most delightful character.

The Sherpas got on extraordinarily well with these people. They shared the same boyish sense of humour and love of the ridiculous. After a very short acquaintance they were playing the fool with one another, as if they had been friends all their lives. On the march below Shuijerab, they were continually putting stones in each other's loads, having weight-lifting matches and splashing one another with water as they crossed the streams, quite regardless of how long they had been marching, or how much they had to carry.

The going was easy at first, as we kept to the floor of the valley. But soon the river began to cut its way through limestone and conglomerates and disappeared far below, while we continued along the hillside, keeping on top of one of the ancient river terraces. These terraces were more imposing than anything we had seen on the northern side of the watershed, and formed country of which it is difficult to give an adequate description. Evening brought us to the edge of the most fantastic ravine carved out of these alluvial deposits by a side stream. Angtharkay remarked, with some truth, that had we encountered it in unexplored country it would have presented an unsurmountable obstacle. As it was, a stairway had been engineered through it with astonishing skill, and it was an easy matter to descend the 1,500 feet into this fearsome gorge. When this path was first constructed I do not know; it may have been perhaps 200 years ago. The pioneers of the route must have had remarkable determination, for anything less promising than the way they had chosen would be hard to imagine. Halfway down we passed through a wooden doorway without a door, which was built into the cliff. It appeared to serve no purpose but to add to the eeriness of the ravine. I am inclined to believe, however, that it was an artistic expression on the part of the path-builder. We camped at the bottom of the chasm and built a huge bonfire, that lit up the extravagant pinnacles and gullies which towered 1,000 feet above our heads. Below, the stream thundered through a bottle-neck so narrow that it must almost be possible to touch both sides at once. It then plunged in a waterfall to the main river below.

On 11 September, we were faced with a long day's work, which included the crossing of two high passes. Although we were now only about five miles from Shimshal, the gorge below us was so bad that not even the ingenuity of the natives, with hundreds of years at their disposal, had been able to construct a way through while the river was at its summer level. In mid-winter it is possible to get through the gorge by walking along the river bed itself, but now we were forced to take a circuitous route over the Shach Mirr and Zard-i-Gar passes and into the Shipodin nullah, which joins the main valley below the gorge. We started the day with a long climb out of the ravine. This took us back on to the river terrace, and level going for a short way, until we had to plunge down into the next side nullah. From here a steady climb of about 3,000 feet took us to the first pass, from which we looked across another ravine to the second, 1,000 feet higher. We found it most interesting to see how the natives dealt with this terrific country. We had so often been faced in the last few months with the problem of making our own route over this type of ground. The day was cloudy, which prevented us from seeing the wonderful view of the great peaks of this part of the Karakoram, which these passes must command. However, I thoroughly enjoyed the journey through the gorges, without the worry of finding a way. But by the time we had climbed 2,500 feet to the next pass, we had done quite enough uphill work for one day, and were glad to run swiftly down a steep scree-slope into the broad, open Shipodin valley. We camped here at five o'clock in a threatening snowstorm, which deposited most of its venom on the crags above us. The morning of the 12th was brilliantly fine. The great peaks across the Shimshal valley, including the Kanjuts and Dasto Ghil, which stood over 25,000 feet high, were ethereal in the early morning light. Before we were up, a large troop of men, horses and yaks was seen coming down the valley towards us. To our great astonishment, the new arrivals turned out to be our friends from Shuijerab, including the Lambadar himself and Abdulla. They had left the village on the previous morning, and must have travelled at a tremendous speed in order to overtake us. We could not understand the reason for their journey, but we imagined that it was connected with us. They had probably discussed the situation after we had left, and come to the conclusion that we must be kept under friendly arrest, until word had been received from the Mir of Hunza, to whom news of our arrival had been sent as soon as they had heard of us in Shuijerab. The messenger who took this news was still under the impression that we were a party of Chinese. We all went down together through a steep gorge to the main valley. The Lambadar hurried along with Spender and me, and became very fussed when by some scree-running, I got a long way ahead.

When we reached the main valley, we saw Shimshal a mile or so farther downstream, on the other side of the river. It was a gladdening sight, after the bleakness of the conglomerate gorges, to see the village climbing the hillside in terrace upon terrace of green and gold. The river was spanned by a rope bridge, grouped at both ends of which a large gathering was awaiting our arrival. Before we reached the bridge we were met by our old friend Mohi Bacha, bringing with him a great quantity of apricots and some excellent cakes. He seemed delighted to see us again, and insisted that we should sit down and eat his food there and then, before facing the perils of the rope bridge.

This type of rope bridge consists of several strands of yak hide wound together into a single cable and slung across the river on two tree-trunks, which are built into great piles of boulders. A horseshoe shaped wooden runner is placed over the rope. The two ends of the runner are tied together and pulled across the river with a load, human or otherwise, attached to it. I have crossed these bridges in Tibet without using the runner, but the friction caused by the contact of one's legs on the rope, throws a far greater strain on the arms than that produced by climbing a rope hand over hand without using one's feet. There is considerable danger therefore of dropping into the river from sheer exhaustion. Tied to the runner, however, it is not difficult for an active man to pull himself across with his hands. The rope bridge at Shimshal was about 200 feet long. While our loads were being hauled across, the yaks and horses of the Lambadar's party were driven into the river and made to swim to the other side. They were carried several hundred yards downstream by the force of the current before they could reach the opposite bank. Before we were allowed to try our skill on the rope bridge several exhibition crossings were made by the natives. The cable was very knotted, which, in spite of assistance from the other side, added greatly to the work of pulling oneself across. The Sherpas put up a bad show, which caused a good deal of merriment among the Shimshalis. The best thing about these rope bridges from the Sherpas' point of view is that they offer a splendid opportunity of playing a joke on the man who is making the crossing. He is, of course, quite helpless, and a few well-aimed stones thrown into the water below will soak him to the skin. This pastime, it seemed, had never occurred to the Shimshalis, but they were so delighted with it that I fear it is now an established custom that may cause embarrassment to future travellers.

We were greeted on the farther side of the river by what must have been nearly the entire male and infant population of Shimshal. When I had been unstrapped from the bridge. I was immediately taken in charge by an elderly man, who could speak Hindustani fast and fluently. He was evidently an ex-servant of Europeans and had fallen on bad times. We learnt afterwards that he had been banished to Shimshal for some crime or series of crimes. It appeared that he relied for his living upon the charity of the natives. From the moment I landed, he started talking and continued without a pause for the next two hours. He talked so fast that we could understand little of what he said. Fortunately he did not attempt to ask any questions, and we were able to survive the verbal torrent without hurting his feelings. When we reached the village, he conducted us to a grand house which had been appointed for our use, and showed us our apartments with a flourish, while the Lambadar, our true host, stood somewhat mournfully in the background. It was a magnificent place, richly ornamented with carpets and brass. At first we thought we were being shown over a temple, but this notion was expelled when our garrulous friend showed us an alcove where we were to take our baths. We did not disillusion him by mentioning that we had been many months without a bath and did not propose to have one now. A number of ancient matchlock muskets, swords and stringed instruments decorated the walls. The Sherpas at once made themselves at home, strumming on the guitars and playing soldiers with the muskets. It caused them endless amusement to drill each other and march about as if on sentry-go. I suppose that they had seen this going on in Darjeeling, and regarded it as one of the more entertaining of the pointless activities of the British Raj!

As many people as possible squeezed into the place and squatted round, watching us gorge ourselves immoderately with all the good things that were brought. Apples, apricots, apricot kernels, cake and fried potatoes. Our arrival must have been a considerable hindrance to the work of the village. At length we were left in peace, and spent a happy afternoon lounging and over-eating under the novelty of a roof.

In the evening we were taken by the Lambadar and the ex-butler for a tour of the village and its orchards and fields. The world was very lovely, with the gold of the ripe corn and the early autumn colours of the thorn trees framing the deep green of the apple and apricot orchards and the slender Lombardy poplars. The air was filled with the peace and mellow beauty which autumn brings to these high mountain valleys. The people were busy with their various harvest jobs, reaping, threshing and stacking. We were surprised to see the dashing Abdulla engaged on one of these domestic tasks. He was solemnly driving a line of yaks slowly round and round on a bed of corn, a primitive method of threshing. Abdulla as the industrious husbandman, was hard to reconcile with our last memory of him galloping madly down the valley. We were introduced to Abdulla's ancient father, and we spent a long time chatting to other cronies of the village. There we found the ex-butler most useful, for he was able to translate the old men's stories of former times, and their answers to our questions about their country. The Lambadar pressed us to further overindulgence in his orchards.

In all our dealings with the Shimshalis, we met with kindness, courtesy and good humour. In this we were agreeably surprised, as we had not been led to expect these qualities. The community of Shimshal is remarkable for its isolation and independence of support from the outside world. Very few of the Shimshalis go out of their valley. From any direction their country is difficult of access, but they have sufficient arable land and grazing to support a much larger population than exists at the present day. They grow barley, wheat and peas, the flour of which, with cheese, butter and curd is their staple food. They have no tea, sugar or tobacco, and they do not grow many vegetables. They are a strong and healthy race; far superior in this respect to the people of Askole. We were surprised to find a complete absence of goitre among them. They weave all that is necessary to clothe themselves. They pay tribute and taxes in kind to the Mir of Hunza, who exercises jurisdiction over them. The control of the Mir, however, is somewhat laxly enforced. Of the founding of Shimshal, Colonel Schomberg writes in his interesting book *Unknown Karakoram*:

> 'Eleven generations ago (perhaps 300 years) a certain Mamu Singh, a Yeshkun or peasant of the Shinaka race from the valley of Chaprot in the Gilgit district, came with his wife and settled in this valley. His wife always disliked her husband, but she loathed him when he brought her from the comparative comfort of Chaprot to live in this cold and isolated place. She never

called him anything else but Shum, which means dog in the Shina tongue – for the subservience of Eastern women is largely a Western fiction – and the village was called Shimshal. When I asked what Shal meant the elders said briefly 'God knows'. In our maps the place is called Shingshal, and the people never refer to their village or themselves except as Shimshal or Shimshalis – so I suppose that, not for the first time, the Western traveller has been too ingenious and too learned. I have often asked them about this point, and never once have I found them agree with the pronunciation of the European pundits and map-mongers. Shum had one son called Shir, who in turn had three sons, Bakhti, Wali and Boki. Both Shir and his sons married Wakhi women from Gulmit, Ghulkin, and the neighbouring villages in the Guhyal district of Hunza. The men were positive that there was no Balti and no Hunza strain in them, but I am quite certain that they are wrong, and that there is a very large admixture of Balti blood.'

They are a happy community leading an ideal existence in magnificent surroundings. The country is sufficiently difficult, and conditions sufficiently severe, to foster in the people that hardihood without which it seems to me impossible for mankind to be content.

20   How an Expedition Ends

We returned over the fields lit by the glow of an ominous sunset. We found, when we got back, that two Hunza men had arrived with orders from the Mir to escort us down. It transpired that the bit of paper, bearing our names which we had given to Dildorbik's party at Chikar on the occasion of our first meeting, had been carried by an express runner to the Mir's palace, who then communicated the news to the Political Agent in Gilgit, who fortunately recognised our names and asked that we should be given every assistance. So these two men had been sent up to take charge of the two sahibs. When they saw us they stood for a long time in solemn silence with an expression of utter disgust on their faces. In spite of their huge drooping moustaches, which intensified their appearance of gloom, they reminded me irresistibly of Tweedledum and Tweedledee. It was easy to see what was going on in their minds. There had been some dreadful mistake. They had been ordered by the omniscient Sircar (government) not only to serve two of the illustrious heaven-born, but to be their guides and protectors. In these remote parts the glamour of the White Man's prestige is still undimmed. At their home they had exaggerated the importance of their mission, and all the way up they had basked in the happy expectation of reflected glory. Now they were faced with stark disillusionment. Here were two ragamuffins who surely could never have had anything to do with sahibdom. There was, quite obviously, nothing 'white' about them. Their clothes were dirty and ragged, their unwashed faces could hardly be seen through a tangle of unkempt hair and matted beard. But orders were orders, and there was nothing for it but to carry out the unsavoury task.

That night the Lambadar entertained us to a musical evening. Some surprisingly good talent was revealed with the fiddle, guitar and flute. There was also some clever dancing. The show was kept going until very late. A huge wood fire blazed in the centre of the room. The house was packed to capacity and the air was stifling. I was lying on a bed which had been produced from somewhere, and again disgraced myself by falling asleep during the performance.

The sunset's foreboding was accurate, and we awoke to a dismal morning. I was still in my sleeping bag when the Lambadar came to pay a call, escorted by a large number of villagers, who could not proceed with their harvest jobs because of the rain. It was a serious thing for them, and an atmosphere of general depression prevailed. After breakfast, I presided – merely as a figurehead

– over a vast council which had gathered together in order to decide what we should pay for the many presents we had received, and what tips should be given to the various people who had, in some way involved themselves in our visit. It appeared, for instance, that the rope bridge had been moved from its old place when news of our impending visit had come through. This apparently useless job had employed sixteen men for two days. Then there were the men who claimed to have brought the news of our arrival, first from Chikar to Shuijerab, then from Shuijerab to Shimshal. Also there were the brothers of those who had relayed – unasked – the tidings to Hunza, and the farmers who had supplied the food for last night's party, most of which, incidentally, had been consumed by the villagers. Many other payments were decided upon by the Committee but in general hubbub I was too bewildered to decide upon the justice of the claims. Taking advantage of a lull in the uproar, caused, I suppose, by a temporary lapse of imagination, I managed to exercise a chairman's authority and bring the proceedings to a close, before our moneybags were quite emptied. Soon after ten o'clock, we set out in the rain, accompanied by the entire population. They left the convoy in small groups, and as each party detached itself, we halted for a round of handshakes, and expressions of friendliness. These grew longer and more emotional as the gathering became smaller, and those taking their leave were more closely connected with our visit. At last only Abdulla remained. He was about to bid us a sad farewell, when we heard the sound of much shouting, and a figure appeared, running towards us from the village. This turned out to be Mohi Bacha, who must have overslept himself and had failed to put in an appearance at our departure. He seemed to be quite beside himself with grief. He was wearing a pair of snow-goggles, in order, I like to think, to hide his tears. At length words failed him, and we went on alone down the dismal, windswept valley. Tweedledum and Tweedledee preferred not to be seen in our company and had taken a path some way to the left of our route; but as the valley narrowed and we walked as fast as they did, they were forced to put up with our repulsive presence. I made repeated efforts to break down the barrier of their aloofness, and at last succeeded in forcing a smile out of one of them. After this our friendship gradually ripened. The way led us across the Mulunguti glacier. On this, our technique of glissading down steep ice slopes so impressed our escort, that by the time we reached the other side they were willing to believe that perhaps our beggarly appearance maligned our true worth, and we became on terms of rib-poking familiarity.

After leaving Shimshal we had plunged once more into a desolation of conglomerate cliffs, which made us realise more strongly the extraordinary isolation of the community we had just left. But every now and then we came upon patches of jungle clinging unexpectedly to the ravines or spread out along the gravel flats of the river. These thickets were now ablaze with autumn colours, and were unbelievably beautiful. The latter part of the day's march was along the gravel flats. In one place the river ran against the cliffs on one side, and we had to wade for a short stretch. But we were lucky in being able to do so, for as an alternative we would have had to perform a long and difficult climb, probably in the dark. By nightfall we reached an isolated hut known as Lashkar. Judging by the number of prayer-flags hung round the hut, we supposed that the place must have some religious significance. Certainly there seemed to be no other reason for the building to be there, as the site was bleak and uncomfortable, and appeared to be in danger of bombardment from falling stones. However, at the invitation of our guides, we made use of the hut, which was equipped with a fireplace and brass cooking pots.

Angtharkay has always had an instinctive dislike for anyone on any expedition who is neither sahib nor porter. In his view, only three grades of humans should be included in a party. Firstly, there is the sahib, who is there to be satisfied. Secondly, there is the Sherpa, without whom no expedition could achieve its pointless objective; and lastly, there is the local porter, a greatly inferior being, whom, unfortunately, it is necessary to employ when the party has more luggage than can be carried by the sahibs and Sherpas. Anyone who does not fulfil one or other of these roles is superfluous. Moreover, he is generally there to usurp the most dignified function of the Sherpa: namely, to look after the comfort and well-being of the sahib. From the outset Angtharkay resented the presence of Tweedledum and Tweedledee, and had made several efforts to persuade me not to have them. He could not understand that it would not be polite to refuse their assistance. During supper, Angtharkay, resenting Tweedledum's concern for our comfort, was seized by a fit of jealousy, and told the Hunza men that we were quite capable of finding our own way down the valley, and that it was quite unnecessary for them to be there. Poor Tweedledum was deeply hurt. With tears in his eyes he rose to his feet, packed up his few belongings, and ordering his companion to follow, stalked out into the night intending, I imagine, never to see us again. With a great deal of difficulty I managed to get him back and partly to repair his wounded feelings explained that without his help, not only would we fail to get down the valley, but even if we did, we would inevitably fall a prey to the wolves of civilisation.

The recent rain had caused a danger of falling stones, and the next morning we had to make a long detour to avoid a bad place, where there was a continuous cannonade. After this the river entered more fearsome gorge-country. The path took us 4,000 feet up the valley side over surprisingly difficult ground. The man who first found and colonised Shimshal must have had amazing determination. But as we toiled up the interminable zigzags of the path, my admiration for him was not unmixed with sympathy for his wife's loathing of him. At length we reached the crest of a sharp ridge from which we looked down on to the Monhill glacier, which rises in a group of 24,000 and

25,000-foot mountains, culminating in the magnificent peak of Dasto Ghil (25,868 feet). We made our way down to the main valley again, crossing the Monhill gorge by a ridiculously flimsy bridge spanning an alarming drop. The main river had then to be crossed by a similar bridge, which bounced and swayed horribly above the booming turmoil of the water. Across this was a wilderness of water-polished boulders lying at the bottom of the huge desolate valley. The place was known as Karun-i-Ben, and marked the spot where the river entered another gorge. Like the one above Shimshal, the natives consider this gorge to be impassable except in mid-winter, when it is possible to make a way up the river bed itself. In the winter of 1892, during one of his remarkable exploratory journeys in these parts, Sir George Cockeril made his way up this route, but I am unaware that any other European has traversed the gorge.

It was very tantalising. Only five miles separated us from the flesh-pots of the Hunza valley, but in order to reach them, we would have to climb 8,000 feet up a steep, waterless slope to the Karun Pir pass, which would lead us out of the Shimshal valley to the north. The idea of doing the climb in a single day did not appeal to us much, particularly as the men were still carrying heavy loads. But to camp half-way up without fuel or water was an even less attractive notion.

Angtharkay suggested an acceptable compromise; to do half the climb by moonlight and finish it off in the morning.

Karun-i-Ben is about 8,800 feet high. This was the lowest we had been since leaving the valley of the Indus in May. It was now three o'clock in the afternoon; the sun glared down from a cloudless sky; the stifling heat danced over the rocks and crags till they were too hot to touch. The heat was reflected into the stagnant air of the gorge, making the temperature and our tempers soar uncomfortably. We collected the few plants that somehow contrived to grow among the rocks, and were able with this fuel to cook our usual meal of bread and tea. We drank great quantities of tea in preparation for the thirsty hours to come. The place we were in was very like the delightful illustration of the 'dismal and desolate valley' up which the Beaver and the Butcher ventured in their search for the Snark.

My stomach was now suffering from the inevitable result of continuous fruit-eating, and I did not view the prospect of severe physical effort with relish. But I succeeded in performing a remarkably quick and complete cure by a remedy which does not seem to have occurred to the medical profession – eating a lot more fruit.

At six, an hour before dark, we packed up and plunged into the tangle of conglomerate gullies at the start of the climb. The cliffs formed by the remains of the ancient river terraces were a stupendous size, extending, in this part of the valley, as much as 3,000 feet above the present level of the river. It was a very beautiful evening. As we made our way through these ghostly relics of a former geological age, the clouds rolled away from the mountains of the Dasto Ghil range. While we climbed we were able to watch their glaciers flush in the snow of the setting sun. Later, when the glow had died, they sparkled like gigantic diamond drops in the moonlight. Inspired, no doubt, by the glories of our surroundings, Tweedles Dum and Dee began to rhapsodise about the opulence of their own country which we were about to visit. On reaching the first village in the Hunza valley (Morkhun), which was Tweedledum's home town, we should, they assured us, lack nothing. Every kind of fruit and vegetable known to agriculture grew there in profusion; all the spices and sweetmeats of the East were to be bought at the shops; an abundant supply of eggs, chickens, butter, milk and honey was to be had for the asking; the houses were built and furnished with princely luxury. This eulogy at first annoyed us; it shattered the enchantment of the moonlight. We were climbing in a dreamlike world, lost in its magic, and we had no thought of anything so mundane as bodily comfort. A climb in the early part of a moonlit night is an ethereal experience, for some reason very different from the ordinary departures of early morning. But even the most entranced mood sinks to earth when one is hungry and tired, and as aching thighs and empty stomachs took a larger share of our attention, the chant of the Tweedles in praise of the luxuries of the promised land assumed the importance of an enticing menu.

When we had climbed 4,000 feet we reached a sheep-fold built under the lee of a huge boulder. We slept in this until shortly before dawn, when we resumed the climb. The morning was disappointing. The perfect weather of the night before had promised a dawn view of the great sweep of country which our bivouac must command, but by daybreak the sky was overcast. Huge piled clouds, charged with rain, hid the great peaks of the Hispar watershed. Long tongues of mist rose from the valleys. Far away to the south loomed a gigantic mountain mass, wreathed with a wide swathe of cloud, its lower slopes lit by pale sunlight. At first we imagined that this was Nanga Parbat. But I think we must have been mistaken, and more probably it was Rakaposhi. As we approached the pass, the Tweedles became more and more excited, and chided us and the porters for our leisurely pace. Before reaching the crest we halted for about an hour in order to let the stragglers of the party catch up. This was more than Tweedledee could stand. He suggested that he should go ahead to the grazing village of Boibar, in order to warn the villagers and prepare the fatted calf. There had been great competition between the two Hunza men to carry the rifle. Tweedledee, who had been playing with the bolt during the halt, insisted upon taking the rifle ahead with him now – presumably in order to create a sensation in Boibar. Tweedledum agreed to this on the understanding that he should be allowed to carry it into his own village on the following day. We gave Tweedledee twenty minutes start and then followed him over the pass. The slopes on the other side were covered in deep snow. Down this we exhibited a turn of speed which amazed Tweedledum, who nearly broke his neck trying to keep up with us. I was following in the deep sunk tracks of Tweedledee when I happened to see a silvery object sticking up out of the snow. I picked it up and found that it was the rifle bolt. I put it in my pocket and said nothing about it.

Below the level of the snow we found ourselves in an entrancing grassy glen. Its sides were covered with juniper trees, and its smooth meadows were a strange contrast to the rugged barrenness of the other side of the pass. We lay for a long time by a spring of clear water before running on down through the richly coloured glades. On the way we met poor Tweedledee, rushing up the hill in a frantic state of mind. He had made his triumphal entry in Boibar only to find that the rifle was without its bolt! After his first torrent of frenzied chatter I managed to ask what was wrong. The poor man was in a desperate state, quite ready, I think, to cut his throat, if the Sherpas did not do it for him. Things were becoming serious when I casually took the bolt from my pocket and started playing with it, as if I had not understood what was the cause of the trouble. Tweedledum and the Sherpas laughed riotously. But Tweedledee, with a look of injured dignity, took the bolt from me and hurried down the hill again.

The village of Boibar was drowsily lazing through a still autumn afternoon, and our arrival awoke only a mild interest. Its setting was typically Alpine; unlike the vast scale of most Himalayan valleys, it had the charm of littleness. The gently sloping meadows were dotted with toy trees, and curved upwards to a miniature peak at the head of the valley. This mountain stood as high above the village as the Matterhorn above Zermatt, but after the stupendous scale of the mountains of the main range this new world seemed comfortingly small.

The next morning we were aroused by the Tweedles long before dawn, and hurried our departure in excited anticipation. Two hours hard going would take us down to the main valley, where we would feast on the promised luxuries of Tweedledum's saga. We started breakfastless. No leathery chapattis or unsweetened tea must be allowed to dull the keen edge of our appetite. As we ran down the valley we hardly noticed the clear blue and gold of the early morning, nor the aromatic scent of the junipers tingling in the frosty air. Our expectant stomachs governed our emotions, and as we raced along we thought only of scrambled eggs, roast potatoes and butter, fat juicy chickens, green vegetables, roast mutton, and fruit, and sweetened tea.

When we emerged from a deep gorge we found ourselves in the main valley, with the promised village just ahead. Our excitement was curbed by a faint apprehension, the village looked too ordinary to produce the succulent dishes of our dreams. It was. Tweedledum conducted us to a squalid stable, and sat us down on a couple of bug-ridden blankets, and left us to wait with gloomy misgivings. He returned half an hour later, empty-handed, and told us that we had only to say the word and anything we desired would be brought to us. Realizing from his expression that something was amiss, we precluded our demands with a modest request for milk. But he reluctantly confessed that there were no cows in the village. Eggs then? All the hens had died. Mutton? But the sheep were still in the higher pastures. Vegetables? Sugar? Our host pretended not to hear. Despairingly we asked him what he could produce. His gloomy countenance brightened as he repeated his boast: 'Anything you want.'

I diffidently suggested potatoes. 'Potatoes; but of course, as many as we liked.'

After another long delay these were brought and boiled. We washed them down with our own unsweetened milk-less tea, to an accompaniment of Tweedledum's fruitlessly hospitable offers. We made no further requests, but assured our host that we had all that we required. When our sparse meal was finished, in our embarrassment we paid far too much for it. We said goodbye to Tweedledum, who, looking like a balloon pricked by a pin, sadly intimated that his period of usefulness had come to an end. Poor Tweedledum! He had not wittingly deceived us. His behaviour was typically oriental. He saw things not as they were, but as he wished they were. His promises had not been deliberate lies, but the result of a desire to tell us the things we most wanted to hear.

The journey back to Srinagar took nearly three weeks. It was the most varied and the most interesting which I have made through the populated districts of the Himalaya. One by one the approaching landmarks of civilization absorbed us, and we lounged through the marches with an increasing sense of relaxation and wellbeing. The road was rough, which generally helps us to foster good fellowship among those who use it, and we seldom met a traveller without learning his intimate history and the reason for his journey. An astonishing variety of people use this road, which is the main route from India to Kashgar and Russian Turkestan. Spender and I were generally taken for poor Russians. No one would believe that we were English, and, later, we found it simpler to say that we were Shimshalis. The size of the party would fluctuate from day to day as we joined up with other caravans or left them behind.

As we went, the villages had more and more good things to offer us, and by the time we reached Hunza our visions of abundance were realized at last. Here, as guests of the Mir, we stayed for a day and indulged in a feast of fruit. We reclined on beds, like Roman Emperors, round a table six feet long by four feet wide, which was piled to a depth of two feet with peaches, apricots, pears, apples, melons, grapes and walnuts. In the intervals of fruit-eating we were shown something of this strange and beautiful place, with its miles of intensively cultivated terraces, and its ancient forts and palaces.

Below Hunza, a great landslide had occurred a few days before. This dammed the river, which, when the dam burst, swept away the road and caused much havoc, somewhat impeding our journey to Gilgit.

Gilgit marked an important stage in our return. We were delightfully entertained there by Major and Mrs Cropper. From them we heard a summary of events of the outside world during the past five months. The bus strike they had forgotten; Spain was still sunk in its inferno of civil war, with no hope of the end in sight; piracy in the Mediterranean was complicating European affairs; the Sino-Japanese war was a new horror. The world seemed an even blacker and madder place than when we had left it. We thought regretfully of the tranquil, beautiful seclusion of Shimshal.

It was here that we learned of the terrible tragedy which had overtaken our friends on Nanga Parbat in June.

From Gilgit our way led to the valley of the Indus, which we followed for some miles of its desert course, past the glistening flanks of Nanga Parbat. The Burzil pass, bleak and treeless, led us into the entrancing valley of Gurais. Here autumn's colours of orange and scarlet and gold burnt like little tongues of flame against the sombre green of the pines. There were tumbling streams, so lovely after the muddy glacier torrents of the high mountains, with here and there still, deep pools, brilliantly reflecting small bushes with pointed crimson leaves. Once more our path leads upwards, and one evening, at the end of a long day's march of twenty-five miles, we stood on the crest of the last pass. From above the pines, we looked down upon the whole vale of Kashmir, spread like a map below. Overhead the sky was flecked with coral sunset clouds. We stayed for a moment. Then we ran down the hill as the red-gold sunset faded from the snows of Haramuk, leaving them ghostly white in the blue dusk. Light ebbed from the sky, and the pines were black against the stars.

The next day we were welcomed back to Srinagar, and realized the full meaning of true hospitality, which gives comfort and rest and makes no demands. Kashmir was a delicious interlude in which to harvest a store of memories and arrange them in perspective for later delight.

Distance has no need to lend enchantment, although it seems to lessen the difficulties and soften the hardships; for the supreme value of the expedition centred in an experience of real freedom rounded off with the peace and content of an arduous job of work completed and enjoyed.

'The Ogre' (Baintha Brakk) from the Western side of Snow Lake.

Shipton and Tilman's indefatigable Sherpa partners – Angtharkay (left) and Sen Tensing ('Foreign Sportsman').

The pass (Sokha La) in the West Biafo Wall that Tilman used to reach the controversial 'Cornice' (Sokha) Glacier. Photo: Dan Morrison

The head of the Braldu Glacier looking south-west to the peaks along the Snow Lake watershed.

A camp on Crevasse Glacier.

A huge ice arch on Braldu Glacier.

Michael Spender in rags after three months in the field.images

A panoramic view across Snow Lake to the south and west from Khurdpin Pass.

Peter Mott surveying from above Snow Lake.

A crevasse on the edge of Snow Lake below Khurdopin Pass.

A view east from the camp on Hispar Pass showing the Sim Gang Glacier section of Snow Lake with the icy walls of the Ogre on the right and Bobisghir on the left.

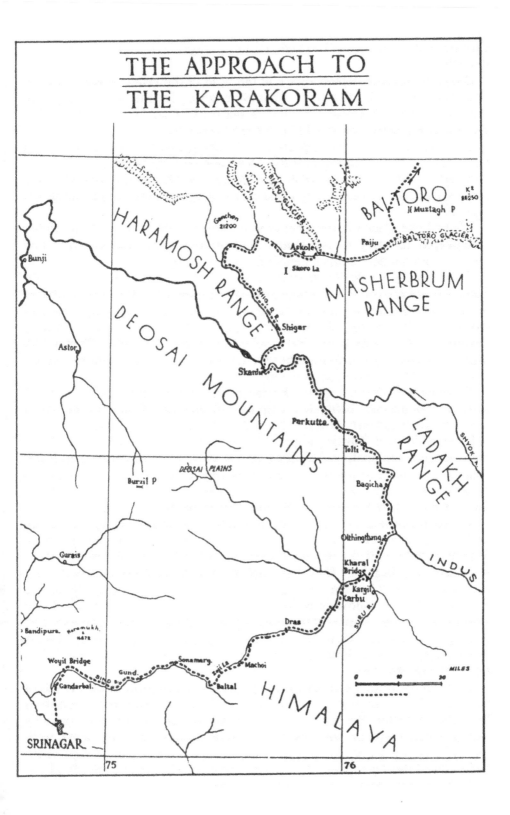

THE APPROACH TO
THE KARAKORAM

BALTORO

K² 28250

Muztagh P

Ganchen 21200

BIAFO GLACIER

Askole

Paiju

BALTORO GLACIER

HARAMOSH RANGE

Bunji

Saltoro La

Shigo R.

MASHERBRUM RANGE

DEOSAI MOUNTAINS

Shigar

Astor

Skardu

Parkutta

Telti

LADAKH RANGE

SHYOK R.

Burzil P

DEOSAI PLAINS

Bagicha

Olthingthang

Gurais

Kharal Bridge

INDUS

Kargil
Karbu

SUSU R.

Bandipura

Haramukh 16872

Dras

Woyil Bridge

Gund.

Sonamarg

Zoji La

Machoi

Baltal

SIND R.

Gandarbal.

MILES

0   10   20

HIMALAYA

SRINAGAR

75

76

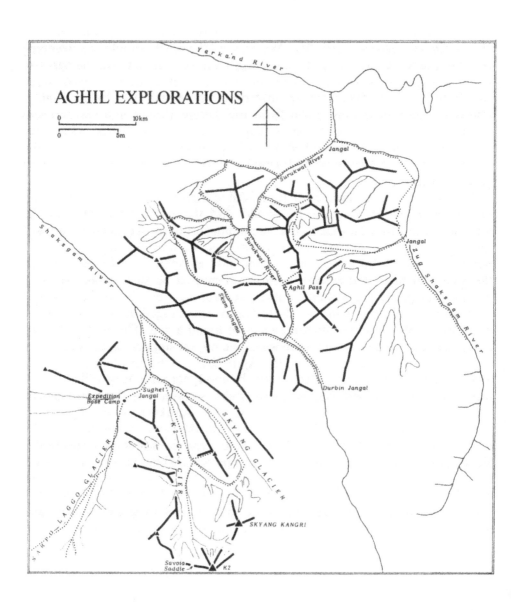

AGHIL EXPLORATIONS

0 _____ 10km
0 _____ 5m

Yarkand River

Jangal

Surukwat River

Shaksgam River

Surukwat River

Skem Lungma

Aghil Pass

Jangal

Zug Shaksgam River

Durbin Jangal

Expedition Base Camp

Sughet Jangal

K2 GLACIER

SKYANG GLACIER

SARPO-LAGGO GLACIER

SKYANG KANGRI

Savoia Saddle

K2

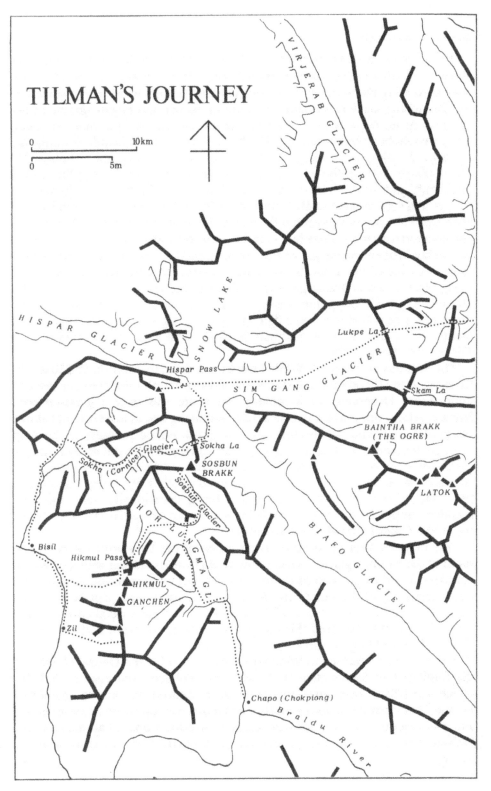

TILMAN'S JOURNEY

0   10km

0   5m

VIRJERAB GLACIER

SNOW LAKE

HISPAR GLACIER

Lukpe La

Hispar Pass

SIM GANG GLACIER

Skam La

BAINTHA BRAKK
(THE OGRE)

Sokha (Cornice) Glacier

Sokha La

SOSBUN
BRAKK

LATOK

Sosbun Glacier

H O H L U N G M A G U

Bisil

Hikmul Pass

BIAFO GLACIER

HIKMUL

GANCHEN

Zil

Chapo (Chokpiong)

Braldu River

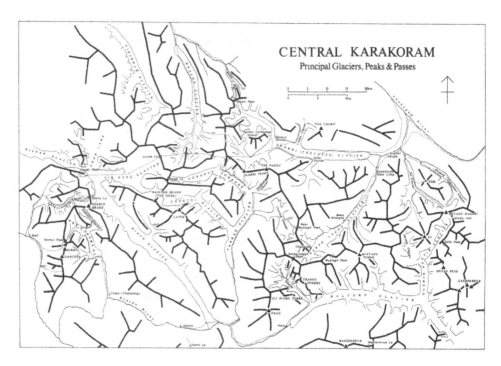

CENTRAL KARAKORAM
Principal Glaciers, Peaks & Passes

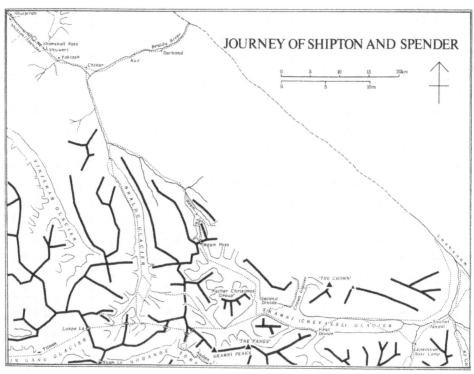

JOURNEY OF SHIPTON AND SPENDER

Printed in the USA
CPSIA information can be obtained
at www.ICGtesting.com
JSHW012016140824
68134JS00025B/2449

9 781912 560073